*Italy: A Short History* is a concise but comprehensive account of Italian history from the Ice Age to the present day. It is intended for both students of Italian history and culture and the general reader, whether tourist, businessperson or traveller, with an interest in Italian affairs. Harry Hearder places the main political developments in Italian history in their economic and social context and shows how these are related to the great moments of artistic and cultural endeavour. Amongst key events, he analyses the growth and decline of the Roman Empire, the remarkable cultural achievements of the Renaissance, Italian unification and the contradictions of the fascist dictatorship of Mussolini. Jonathan Morris brings the work up to the present day with an authoritative but colourful history of the corruption scandals that brought down the post-war Italian political system in the 1990s and the new political forces that have emerged in its place.

The late Harry Hearder was Professor Emeritus at the University of Wales. His many publications on European and Italian history include *Europe in the Nineteenth Century* (Longman, second edition, 1988) and *Italy in the Age of the Risorgimento* (Longman, 1983).

Jonathan Morris is Reader in Modern European History at University College, London. His publications include *The Political Economy of Shopkeeping in Milan 1886–1922* (Cambridge University Press, 1993). He is editor of the journal of *Contemporary European History*.

# *ITALY*

## *A SHORT HISTORY*

### HARRY HEARDER

*Professor Emeritus, University of Wales*

CAMBRIDGE
UNIVERSITY PRESS

PUBLISHED BY THE PRESS SYNDICATE OF THE UNIVERSITY OF CAMBRIDGE
The Pitt Building, Trumpington Street, Cambridge, United Kingdom

CAMBRIDGE UNIVERSITY PRESS
The Edinburgh Building, Cambridge CB2 2RU, UK
40 West 20th Street, New York, NY 10011–4211, USA
477 Williamstown Road, Port Melbourne, VIC 3207, Australia
Ruiz de Alarcón 13, 28014 Madrid, Spain
Dock House, The Waterfront, Cape Town 8001, South Africa

http://www.cambridge.org

First published 1990
Reprinted eight times
Second edition 2001
Reprinted 2002, 2003, 2004

Printed in the United Kingdom at the University Press, Cambridge

*British Library Cataloguing in Publication data*
Hearder, Harry
Italy: a short history
I. Italy, history
I. Title
954

*Library of Congress Cataloguing in Publication data*
Hearder, Harry
Italy: a short history/Harry Hearder with Jonathan Morris.
p.    cm.
Includes bibliographical references.
ISBN 0 521 80613 5. – ISBN 0 521 00072 6 (pbk.)
I. Italy – History. I. Title.
DG467.H43 1991
945 – dc20 89–13991 CIP

ISBN 0 521 80613 5 hardback
ISBN 0 521 00072 6 paperback

*FOR JULIA*

# Contents

# Contents

# Contents

# Illustrations

## Plates

## Maps

# Preface

In 1963 the Cambridge University Press published a book entitled *A Short History of Italy*, edited by Dr D. P. Waley and myself. We featured as 'editors', because the book had been originally written, though not published, by C. M. Ady and A. J. Whyte, during the Second World War. Dr Waley and I made the changes which seemed to us to have become necessary with the passing of time. The book was appreciatively received – especially by departments of Italian – and has been reprinted several times. The present book is in no sense a revision of *A Short History of Italy*. The only thing it has in common with the earlier book is that it is of roughly the same length and format. The Cambridge University Press asked me to write what can perhaps be best described as an 'heir' to *A Short History of Italy*, but it was to be the work of one author instead of the several who had contributed to the earlier publication, and it was to be an entirely new book.

For one person to write a history as long and rich as Italy's has clearly been a daunting proposition, even if the task has been an immensely enjoyable one. The selection of material, argument and narrative is bound to have been an idiosyncratic one, and I cannot hold anyone else responsible for it. I would like, however, very warmly to thank Professor John Percival for reading Chapter 1, Sections 3 and 4, and Professor Daniel Waley for reading Chapter 3, Sections 2, 3 and 4, and for their invaluable corrections and suggestions. Dr Peter Edbury, Mr

Tony Glazer and Professor Peter Walcot also gave me extremely useful hints on books to read to fill some of the gaps in my knowledge and understanding. Dr Rosemary Morris, a Cambridge University Press copy editor, gave invaluable suggestions for improvements in style and presentation.

If my interpretation is idiosyncratic in some respects, it is traditional in others. I realize, for example, that I have not given a great deal of space to the late sixteenth and seventeenth centuries, and that several scholars who have recently declared the Baroque and Spanish periods neglected would charge me with prolonging a traditional imbalance. I respect their opinions, but do not share them. It seems to me that Italy played a more important role in the political, economic and cultural history of the world under the Roman Republic and Empire, and during the Late Middle Ages and Renaissance, than she was to do in the subsequent two centuries. Traditional interpretations are not always mistaken.

My first view of Italy was of the Bay of Naples in March 1944, on a glorious sunny day, which gave no warning of the world of devastation and hunger which lay beyond the coastline. For a year from the May offensive at Cassino until the end of the war I was myself a humble, but I hope reliable, primary source for Italian history: the reader may detect one or two statements based only on my memory. Needless to say, I would not trust my own memory if there were any documentary evidence which contradicted it. The German army corps in Italy surrendered on my twenty-first birthday – a kind thought, for which I was very grateful.

I have tried to give a positive view of Italian history. British historians often seem to write of Italy in a slightly condescending, patronizing – if not positively disparaging – tone, and in so doing merely betray their own insularity. To all my Italian friends over the years – far too many to list – I owe an immense debt, and the biggest debt of all I owe to the one I married. The book is dedicated to our daughter, whose love of Italy is as great as my own.

*November, 1989*                                                    H.H.

Chapter 1

# ITALY IN THE CLASSICAL WORLD

## 1 Prehistoric Italy

No other country in Europe can claim the continuity of civilization achieved in Italy. Greece had her moment of cultural and intellectual brilliance, but the history of Italy has shown a sustained development, falling occasionally into comparative backwardness, but always returning to peaks of civilized excellence. It is this sense of continuity that most strikes the foreigner, an impression that people have for long ages lived, worked and built in this narrow peninsula.

There has, in truth, been continuous human life since the Ice Age. An early species of man, *homo erectus*, was in Italy some half a million years ago, and our own species, *homo sapiens*, was present some quarter of a million years ago. Palaeolithic, or Old Stone Age, man lived in Italy in the last stage of the Ice Age, a stage more severe than earlier ones. The temperature of Italy at that time is thought to have been about nine degrees centigrade colder, in winter and in summer, than it is today. In winter there was snow over most of Italy for many months. The country was radically different in another sense. As the oceans had frozen, the Mediterranean had partly dried up. The seas of the world were at least 130 metres lower than they are now, which meant that Italy was an appreciably larger country, with the coastline being twenty or thirty kilometres farther out than it is now. The Po plain must have extended

1

across what is now the Adriatic to Yugoslavia. These conditions prevailed about 16,000 years ago when Palaeolithic man was leaving his traces in caves and graves. The caves have left nothing to match the paintings of the Palaeolithic period at Lascaux in France or Altamira in Spain, but they have yielded up a wealth of stone tools and weapons, growing in sophistication as the millennia passed.

About 14,000 years ago the ice receded for the last time, and the generations of Mesolithic, or Middle Stone Age, man could adjust over the centuries to the new conditions which would enable the more accomplished Neolithic, or New Stone Age, man to emerge. Both Palaeolithic and Mesolithic men had been nomadic hunters, but with the Middle Stone Age the larger animals, for some reason, disappeared, and had to be replaced as nourishment by small animals, even rodents, or by fish when they were available. Mesolithic man settled in the wider areas which had not been inhabitable until the Ice Age receded, but in most respects the Middle Stone Age, which lasted until about 5000 BC was not marked by great developments.

A major social revolution occurred in the New Stone Age. Man ceased to be exclusively a hunter, and started to farm, to grow his own food. The next phase – some two and a half millennia later – was marked by the use of the first metal – copper – to replace stone in the making of tools and weapons. The Chalcolithic, or Copper, Age lasted for about half a millennium, and then, around 2000 BC, a more effective metal – bronze – gave its name to a new age in which mankind moved closer towards history.

Developments in the Bronze Age were sufficiently complex to justify sub-divisions into Early, Middle, Recent and Final. Here it will be enough to consider the last two of these ages and their transition into the Iron Age, the whole period, from about 1300 to 700 BC , taking us to the dawn of Italian history.

In these six centuries there was a growth of population which left more evidence of human existence than in the whole previous span of human life on earth. For some reason there was a comparatively sudden demographic growth at about 1300 BC, which was then sustained from the Bronze Age into the Iron Age. In Italy the process was an accelerating one. More remains from the eighth century BC have been discovered than from the ninth. Yet remains in caves, as opposed to man-made shelters, declined from the later Bronze Age to the early Iron Age, showing that human society was not only increasing numerically, but changing its customs, perhaps its economy or religion, and certainly improving its living standards. In the course of the Bronze Age there had also been variations of population change. In the Recent and final Bronze Ages, while the overall population of Italy was increasing, villages in the Po Valley were diminishing in number. They may have disappeared because of some human-inspired disaster, since the village sites themselves give evidence of burnings or destruction. Perhaps some incoherent war which was an ancestor of all the wars which have been fought in the Po Valley since the Middle Ages was fought in the thirteenth century BC. Seen in this full chronological context the few centuries of comparative peace which Augustan Rome was to bring to the area must be considered a blessed freak of history.

In this same period the peoples of Italy were increasingly cultivating the fields in addition to pasturing livestock. They were even beginning to breed their own stock. They were ceasing altogether to be nomadic hunters, and becoming farmers. Agricultural advance can be assumed from the fact of a growing population, but there is also direct evidence, because primitive axes, chisels and saws of the period have been found. Evidently the forests were being felled. The bronze implements must also have been used for making wooden objects, which have themselves perished, but which would have been more likely to be used for agriculture than for hunting or tribal warfare, for which bronze weapons would have been more effective. Society was becoming more peaceful, less plagued by fear and hatred. And these societies of the Bronze and Early Iron Age were moving away from areas suitable for pasturing, to areas more suitable for arable farming.

In human terms an even more interesting development was taking place: small patriarchal units were broadening into larger communities, communities containing several families. The settlements were not only getting larger; they were also existing for longer periods – sometimes for several centuries. In particular there have been excavations of cemeteries which had been in use for long periods – periods of marked population growth. Individual communities which would have contained less than a hundred people in the Middle Bronze Age were beginning to have three-figure populations in the Recent Bronze Age. But there was one exception to the rule that settlements were tiny in earlier periods: in the Tavoliere district of Apulia a number of large villages from Neolithic times have been discovered. But on the whole nothing approaching a 'village' – a fortified community rather than a simple extended family – had existed until the second millennium BC. The large settlements of the Recent and Final Bronze Ages sometimes have recognizable centres with smaller settlements dependent upon them. In other words they were the seats of rudimentary political power, and from the objects they contained they were evidently 'industrial centres', in the sense that artefacts were made there for the wider community, and specialized artisans would presumably live there. In Sicily examples of such settlements with populations running into four figures have been excavated.

The growth in population and social organization is illustrated most clearly by the cemeteries and urnfields. In the patriarchal clan burial grounds of the Early and Middle Bronze Age a few important males were given dominant positions, often central positions in a tumulus, with lesser figures surrounding them. In the Recent and Final Bronze Ages much larger groups of people, numbering hundreds or even thousands, were buried in single cemeteries. Whether these large settlements had anything approaching a fixed political organization, anything approaching a set of laws, is a matter of conjecture, but the very fact that many of them existed for long periods would seem to suggest that certain customs, even some kind of stable authority, were recognized. It would certainly be a mistake to assume that without a written language there could be no law. Yet there appear to have been no classes or hierarchies, or at least, no distinctions of rank or class were recognized in burial customs. Only with the eighth century BC, during the Early Iron Age, does a recognizable 'upper class' – probably a warrior class – become at all common.

With the Iron Age, during the first millennium BC, came the use not only of iron, but of glass and pottery, and pottery was finally fashioned on a wheel. In South-Central Italy the potter's wheel was used far earlier than elsewhere. The new products must have been exchanged for agricultural products, and metal used as capital and currency. The wealth of a family or village would presumably then be determined by its capital of either herds or metal, and as the Final Bronze Age merged into the Iron Age the hoards of metal became bigger, and metal evidently acquired greater importance as wealth. The metal hoards consisted of unworked metal, metal objects, and even deliberately broken metal objects, which were evidently kept in the hoards as capital wealth to be exchanged when needed.

Nothing has yet been said of cultural influences from outside Italy, a theme which must be more fully discussed in the next section. The Aegean civilization which influenced Italy in the Final Bronze and Iron Ages was that of Mycenae. The Minoan civilization, which must in several respects have been a strangely extrovert and liberated one, had flourished in Crete from about 3000 to 1100 BC, but about 1450 BC Crete had fallen under the control of the Mycenaeans from the Peloponnese. The Minoan script has never been deciphered, but the

Mycenaean script is an early version of Greek. This early race of Greeks were some of the first maritime traders in history, going East to Cyprus and Anatolia, and West to Italy.

Mycenaean influence in Italy was already considerable in the Recent Bronze Age, before the fall of Mycenaean civilization in the twelfth century. Subsequently the Etruscans, who are to be a main theme of the next section, were to mix Mycenaean influences with those of the indigenous Iron Age culture of Villanova, a rich settlement near the site of the future city of Bologna. Local pottery, made on the wheel and painted, was to replace that imported from Mycenae.

The Iron Age stretched from prehistory into history, in the sense that some people in Italy were literate at the end of it. There is much to be said for the use of the term 'protohistory', coined by archaeologists, and meaning an intermediate period between history and prehistory. In Italy the first millennium BC might be termed a period of 'protohistory'. Within it Villanovan society was an advanced prehistoric one. With Etruscan civilization Italian history has started.

### 2 The Greeks, the Etruscans and the arrival of the Romans

The Mycenaeans had traded with the peoples of Italy, and had influenced their art and their technology, but they had not settled. The first Greek settlement was made by the people of Euboea, the island to the east of Athens, and they chose a beautiful spot: Pithecusa (in Greek Pithekoussai) on the island of Ischia in the Bay of Naples. This was as early as the first decades of the eighth century BC, perhaps only a century or so after the Trojan War, and almost certainly before Homer's story had been recorded. The main function of Pithecusa was to be a trading post, and it must have developed into a cosmopolitan centre, since objects from Crete, Rhodes and even Syria and Egypt have been found there. In these early days the Greeks were going to Southern Italy to buy metal, especially iron, ore. From Pithecusa the Euboeans founded further colonies, first immediately opposite, on the mainland of Cumae, and then in Sicily. The modern towns of Catania and Messina in Eastern Sicily, and on the mainland, Reggio Calabria, date from these first Greek colonies. The people of Corinth were also trading in these regions in ceramics as early as the seventh century, and it was the Corinthians who founded Syracuse, easily the largest Greek city in Sicily or Italy. In 415 BC, when Sophocles and Euripides were still alive, the Athenians, in a wave of imperialist enthusiasm, and to grab some of the rich mineral wealth of Syracuse, sent an expedition to Sicily, but were defeated by the Syracusans. The rulers of Syracuse, until then despots, granted reforms in their government after this triumph. Their civilization developed in spite of frequent wars, and was to play a considerable role in bringing Hellenic culture to Rome. Of the Greek settlements on the mainland, or Magna Graecia as they were collectively called, the most impressive surviving reminders are the temples at Paestum, to the south of Salerno. Of the three temples at Paestum two are almost intact, and constitute as perfect an example of Doric architecture as anything in Greece itself. The temple traditionally regarded as being dedicated to Neptune has thirty-six massive columns. Dating from the fifth century, they are roughly contemporary with the Parthenon at Athens.

From Sparta and other Greek states other colonies were founded, and just as the colonists came from independent city-states, so they founded independent city-states in Sicily and Italy. What became Magna Graecia was thus not a single state, but a group of independent states, sharing a common language and culture, but no single imperial capital. Sometimes they were allied with each other in war, but sometimes at war with each other. The simple, stark difference between Greek and Roman imperialism was that the former lacked the single power base which the latter was so pre-eminently to possess.

The Greeks of Magna Graecia were an urban people, and

their towns were not only to be models for the Romans, but had already been so for the Etruscans in their first urban centres. The relationship between the Greeks and the Etruscans was basically one of peace, based on trade. There is evidence that the Greeks integrated socially with the indigenous peoples in Southern Italy and in Etruscan towns like Caere (the modern Cerveteri).

There is fairly clear evidence to indicate where the Greeks of Magna Graecia came from. About the Etruscans there has been less agreement, because of the absence of written records. Before the Second World War, historians were inclined to imagine great migrations of people coming to Italy from the Eastern Mediterranean or beyond the Alps, and to assume that Etruscan civilization was the result of such a migration. More recently, mainly owing to research and speculation by archaeologists, it has been assumed that indigenous development in Italy itself played a bigger role. That the Etruscans were influenced by trade, and eventually settlements, in Magna Graecia is undeniable, but that they were themselves the product of some important migration is no longer assumed. In this sense they have as good a claim to being the 'first Italians' as have some of their Latin contemporaries.

Since Etruscan civilization lasted for seven centuries, many of the generalizations made about it may be misleading. Remains which can be defined as Etruscan date back into the Iron Age, to about 800 BC, and are centred in the area between Rome and Florence, the area which the Romans were to call Etruria. The modern name 'Tuscany' – Italian 'Toscana' – comes, of course, from the Latin name 'Etrusci', sometimes shortened to 'Tusci'. Their wealth, and so their civilization, was based on the rich deposits of metals in the area – especially of iron ore, but also of copper, lead and tin. They share with the Greeks the distinction of being the first city-builders in Italy. Their civilization was, like that of the Greeks, based on several cities, rather than one imperial capital. At the peak of Etruscan civilization there were twelve cities, linked in a Confederation, but with each city retaining autonomy and a cultural identity. Several of these have survived throughout history: Arezzo, Cortona, Chiusi, Perugia, Tarquinia, Cerveteri. Caere (Cerveteri) is thought to have had a population of 25,000. An Etruscan city which was not to survive has been excavated comparatively recently. Even its original name is not known, but it was on the site of a village today called Marzabotto, not far south of Bologna – or, in more contemporary terms, Villanova. The place was evidently abandoned after being sacked by the Gauls about 400 BC. The Etruscans were to found the considerable city of Veii only a few miles north of Rome about 600 BC, and were eventually to establish a king in Rome itself.

No Etruscan literature has survived, either in concrete form or in oral tradition. But if sophistication of art and architecture, and the existence of a literate class, constitute civilization, then the Etruscans were a truly civilized people. Their art indicates that there was a leisured class, who spent much time at banquets, watching the gladiators, and hunting – no doubt for pleasure, rather than for survival. The women wore rich ornaments, with which they were buried in their impressive tombs. Remarkable imagination and a taste for the fantastic are also displayed by the immensely elongated figures from the fourth century found at Perugia and Volterra, diabolical masks found at Orvieto, and the wonderful bronze Chimera from Arezzo. The name of an individual artist, Vulca, who worked at Veii, has been identified. He has left a terracotta Apollo and other figures, and can perhaps claim the distinction of being the most ancient master in the long history of Italian art.

Maybe the highest single achievement of Etruscan art in existence is a two-figure piece of sculpture in terracotta found at Cerveteri, and now in the Villa Giulia in Rome. It was the lid of a sarcophagus, and dates from about 500 BC. It is of a man and woman reclining on a cushion, the man with an elegant

Plate 1. Lid of an Etruscan sarcophagus from Tarquinia

beard and the woman with a neat cap. Both have gentle, wise expressions, the expressions of civilized people. His arm rests on her shoulder in a gesture as strikingly modern as anything in Greek or Roman art.

The architecture which has survived from Etruscan Italy is no less striking than the sculpture and pottery, and rather more classical and Western in character. Perhaps it is sufficient here to mention the city gate at Perugia, under which traffic still passes, and the gate at Volterra which was part of a circuit of walls built to enclose a bigger city than the present one. The Etruscans were engineers as well as architects. They drained the land, and built good roads, anticipating the Romans, and they were also a sea-faring people, trading happily with Carthage. Their metallurgical industry was extremely productive. In particular, on Elba iron was extracted and smelted for some 400 years from the seventh century onwards.

The Etruscan language has still not been fully deciphered, partly because its roots are not wholly Indo-European, as those of Latin are, even though the Etruscans used a Greek alphabet. Short inscriptions can now be understood easily enough, but the few surviving longer passages have not yielded up their meaning. Even if they did, they would not constitute a literature. The Etruscans had, however, a religion, which was based on a belief in the fates; and, like the Romans after them, they discovered what the gods were planning by studying the flights of birds and the entrails of animals.

Long before Etruscan civilization had reached its peak, a Latin people was living on the seven hills of Rome. Two powerful myths were to be born concerning the foundation of Rome. One was that a Trojan, Aeneas, escaping from conquered Troy, after many adventures reached Italy, and founded the city of Lavinium in Latium. The myth was the basis of the *Aeneid*, the greatest single work of Latin literature, written by Virgil in the last years before his death in 19 BC. The more popular story of the foundation of Rome was told by one of the greatest of European historians. Livy (Titus Livius) lived from 59 BC to 17 AD, and wrote his monumental history of Rome over the last forty years of his life. Some of the episodes in his narrative were simply taken from earlier Greek stories, and Livy himself did not believe that they were literally true. His story of Romulus and Remus was known already to the

Romans, and Livy could refer to them initially as 'the twins'. The story was that a Vestal Virgin gave birth to the twin boys, who were saved from drowning by a she-wolf who suckled them, but Livy adds the sceptical note that 'some think' the real saviour of the babies was 'a common whore called Wolf by the shepherds'. Romulus subsequently killed Remus, and founded Rome, the traditional date being 753 BC, a date not inconsistent with archaeological finds.

Both Etruscan and Latin inscriptions dating from the late seventh, or early sixth, century have been found in Rome. According to the literary sources Etruscans ruled Rome for over a century. An Etruscan king, Tarquin, is said to have been on the throne in the early sixth century, and another Tarquin to have been the last, when, in 510 BC, the Romans secured control and founded the Republic. However close to accuracy these facts may, or may not, be, there seems little doubt that Rome was developed into a city in the sixth century. The Forum was drained and paved. The Sacra Via, a paved road, part of which has survived, was laid. On the Capitol, which was to become the historic seat of Roman government, a large temple to Jupiter was built in the Etruscan period; a few remnants of masonry remain, but the building was destroyed by fire in 83 BC. The most striking and best-known remnant of Etruscan Rome is the bronze Wolf of the Capitol, a magnificent piece of sculpture, which today is completed by the figures of Romulus and Remus by the Renaissance artist, Antonio Pollaiuolo, who was a worthy successor to the unknown Etruscan genius.

While Rome was undeniably ruled by Etruscans for a period, she never became part of the Etruscan Confederation. She remained less important, and less purely Etruscan, than the neighbouring city of Veii. According to the Roman tradition the last Etruscan king, Tarquinius Superbus, was expelled from Rome in 509 BC, but it was less a question of the Etruscans being expelled by the Romans than of a constitutional revolution against a king who happened to be an

Etruscan, by a Latin aristocracy. The leader of the revolution, according to Livy and his sources, was a Roman called Brutus, and his revolt against the tyrant Tarquin was to be cited as a sound precedent for the action of a more famous Brutus against Julius Caesar.

With the foundation of the Roman Republic came for the first time in Italy a dim realization of a basic principle of political philosophy – that the people were sovereign. The concept was to be lost with the decline of Rome and the coming of the Middle Ages, and not to be properly rediscovered until the ideas of the French Revolution crossed the Alps in the 1790s. In Rome it was expressed by the phrase 'Senatus Populusque Romanus', the Senate and Roman People, the initials of which, SPQR, are still stamped on public property in Rome. The Senate in practice was often in confrontation with the people, but disputes rarely led to bloodshed. The confrontation never, of course, allowed the people real power, but in the first century or so of the life of the Roman Republic resulted in a ruling coalition of the older upper class from the days of the kings with a new, rich, republican class. The headship of the executive government was provided by two Consuls, whose qualifications for office were that they had been in both of two junior posts – *quaestors* and *praetors.* Twenty *quaestors* were elected annually, and on election became members of the Senate. In practice, the system kept power in the hands of a limited ruling class, but did not fail to produce able and highly trained men. The more democratic element in the constitution of the Roman Republic consisted in the election of ten Tribunes. They could start legislation, and veto bills. The Tribunes themselves were often rich nobles, but they provided an important countervailing force against the Senate, and were supposed to represent the plebeians.

In the fourth century Rome was to assert her authority in Italy by successful wars, but only after passing through dangerous crises. In 396 the conquest of Veii seemed to have

13

Map 1. The expansion of Rome in Italy

sealed her success, but a decade or so later a Celtic people, the Gauls, sacked Rome itself. The Gauls halted Roman expansion in its tracks, but only for some thirty years. In the mid-fourth century, when Aristotle was studying under Plato in Athens, Rome was involved in wars with the Samnites, a mountain people, referred to by Roman writers as tough, tenacious fighters. Although primitive compared with the Etruscans, and mainly surviving on pasturing, the Samnites also grew some corn, vines and olives, built impressive defences, and much later, in the second century BC, had at least one small theatre of a Hellenistic type at Pietrabbondante in the Abruzzi. Rome was to fight three wars against the Samnites, subduing them only in the first years of the third century.

Colonization of the peninsula continued, and a pattern emerged: the Romans seem to have deliberately avoided conquering entire tribes, but rather defeated them piecemeal, by occupying their lands. They combined imperialism with democracy by giving the newly conquered land to Romans who possessed no land. The new landowners, or *coloni* as they were called, were allowed to develop their own centres, with their own market places, or *fora*, and their own species of police force, or *aediles*. The Roman authorities had not trusted the lower classes to serve in the army, but the *coloni*, acquiring responsibility with land, were allowed to serve in the legions, thus providing larger armed groups for further conquests.

The political and cultural unification of Italy was to be the result of Roman colonization. In the fourth century BC about forty different languages were spoken in Italy, and there were several written languages. Apart from Greek in the South and the unique non-Indo-European language of the Etruscans, these languages can all, however, be broadly termed 'Italic', provided that it is realized that they were distinct, if related, languages, not dialects of a single language. In addition to Latin, two were spoken over a sufficiently wide area to deserve mention. They were Umbrian, and – the more important of the two – Oscan. Inscriptions in this forgotten language crop up all over the South – Campania, Apulia and Calabria – and on coins of the fourth and third centuries BC. Among the graffiti on the walls of Pompeii in AD 79 were some in Oscan. The Umbrians were a separate, comparatively civilized people, who left a religious tract in their language – the Iguvine Tables. Dating from about 200 BC, the Iguvine Tables have been said by one recent authority to 'contain the largest body of religious ritual to survive from pre-Christian Europe.'[1]

Apart from Greek, which was spoken in Naples and the South until the sixth century AD, all these languages gave way to Latin in the course of two or three centuries. The triumph of Latin, at first throughout Italy, and then as the language of the literate classes of Europe, is one of the great success stories of world history. Ultimately, it was to influence more languages, languages spoken over greater areas of the globe, than any other language has ever done.

## 3 *The Roman Republic, c. 509* BC–AD *313*

The Roman empire was not the creation of the Roman Empire, but of the Roman Republic. Under the Republic Rome developed from being one force among many in the Italian peninsula, in the first place, to being in control of the whole territory of what we now know as Italy; in the second place, to being the dominant power in the Mediterranean; and in the third place, to controlling and dominating most of the known world. And the whole process took only three or four centuries.

Italy south of the line crossing the peninsula westwards from Rimini was conquered by Rome by 266 BC. The inclusion of the North, and so the unification of the territory now inhabited by Italians, was not to be complete until after the founding of the Empire by Augustus, but by 266 BC the Latin peoples and the various other people in the peninsula south of this line were under Roman control.

By that date the city of Rome herself had a population of perhaps 150,000, and so was still much smaller than Syracuse, which is calculated to have had a population of some 500,000, while Taranto may have had 200,000 inhabitants. The largest urban centres were thus still the Greek ones, but a century

---

[1] E. T. Salmon, *The Making of Roman Italy* (London, 1982), p. 29.

later Rome also had a population of half a million. It is interesting to remember that this was about the size of Paris in 1850. Apart from London, no other European city in the mid-nineteenth century was so large. Yet Rome was to grow much larger under the Empire.

Rome's long wars with Carthage, the Punic Wars, started in 264 BC, and in less than a century Rome was to be the major power in the Mediterranean. But the first two Punic Wars were the toughest she was ever to fight. In contrast the Hellenistic world, to which Rome owed most of her culture, collapsed with surprising ease and suddenness before the disciplined might of the young Republic, and the military and diplomatic ability of her rulers. It was the Carthaginian empire which gave Rome her most severe trial. Originally one of several Phoenician trading posts, Carthage had used her favourable position at the narrowest point of the Mediterranean, opposite Sicily, to build up an empire which stretched to Morocco, and included Western Sicily, Corsica and Sardinia, and eventually part of Spain. By 264 BC the city of Carthage was much larger than Rome, and probably only a little smaller than Syracuse. Little is known of her culture; if she had a literature it has not survived; the Roman destruction of Carthaginian civilization was to be a total one. But of the Punic Wars themselves a long and not entirely unreliable account was given by the Greek historian, Polybius, who lived from about 200 to 118 BC. For Polybius the First Punic War, which had lasted from 264 to 241 BC, was the longest one in history, and the three Punic Wars taken together extended over a period of forty-two years. They might be compared with the World Wars of the twentieth century so far as their significance for the history of civilization is concerned.

In the First Punic War Rome turned herself into a naval power. According to Polybius the Romans had no idea even of how to construct a large war-ship until a Carthaginian ship was grounded and taken by the Romans, who were then able to construct a replica. Yet Rome won what was primarily a naval war, although both sides suffered appalling losses of life. Even more important was the Second Punic War, which lasted from 218 to 202 BC. The Third Punic War, which did not follow until half a century later, lasted for only three years, from 149 to 146 BC, and ended with the annihilation of Carthage.

The First Punic War was fought over the control of Sicily and the great city of Syracuse, and, more generally, for the domination of the Mediterranean. Between the first two wars Carthage extended her empire to Spain, and it was with Spanish mercenaries and Spanish wealth that Hannibal launched his famous offensive against Rome, over the Alps, in 218 BC. The novel use of elephants, and Hannibal's imaginative generalship, won striking victories against the Romans, and established Carthaginian control over much of Italy for some fourteen years. The Roman Republic was saved from destruction initially by Quintus Fabius, called Cunctator, or 'the Delayer', because of his refusal to risk Roman forces in open battle, in the belief that Hannibal could not maintain an army of 40,000 men indefinitely so far from their base. These 'Fabian' or scorched-earth policies, however, led to the devastation of much of Italy, and incalculable economic consequences. If they saved Rome herself from occupation and defeat, more aggressive tactics were needed in the later stage of the war, and these were supplied by two dynamic generals, Mercurius in Italy, and Scipio, who finally defeated Hannibal in Africa and gained the title 'Africanus'.

For the future of Italy the behaviour of the various Italian peoples during the war was important. Several of them, including the Samnites, supported Hannibal when he appeared likely to defeat the Romans, but the Latins, the Sabines, the Umbrians and others remained loyal to Rome. The intervention of Philip V of Macedon on the side of the Carthaginians had no permanent significance. Roman victories in the war against Hannibal limited Carthage to North Africa, and peace seemed secure. It was only in 149 BC that Cato persuaded the Romans to provoke Carthage into a third war, and this time to raze the city to the ground. Marcus Porcius Cato had held public office half a century before. A grim figure, enemy of Hellenic culture, he was, in 149, as an old man of eighty, still a considerable influence in Rome. The destruction of Carthage was perhaps the most brutal act in Italian history. Those Carthaginians who were not killed in the siege and the fighting – about 50,000 of them – were enslaved, and the intrusion of so large a number of slaves into Roman society was to be an important economic factor in the collapse of the Republic.

The defeat of Carthage meant that Rome had inherited an extensive empire while she was still a republic – the whole of Sicily, Corsica and Sardinia, and a foothold in Spain. Her Spanish colony was to prove a considerable burden for many decades. More important for the history of Italy was the Roman conquest of the Po Valley, previously part of Gaul – Cisalpine Gaul. Although started after the Second Punic War, the conquest was not complete for half a century. It is of course only retrospectively that the Roman acquisition of North Italy can be seen as a completion of Italian unification. At the time it was seen as an extension of communications towards Spain, and as necessary for defence against the Gauls, who had launched an offensive against Rome between the First and Second Punic Wars, obligingly choosing a moment of peace between Rome and Carthage. But they had reached as far south as Talamone, near today's border between Tuscany and Lazio. After the defeat of the Gauls at Talamone in 225 BC the Romans had moved into the northern plain, forming colonies at Piacenza and Cremona. The victories of Hannibal temporarily cancelled out this Roman advance into Cisalpine Gaul, but after his defeat the Gauls were driven not only out of the Po Valley, but from the Ligurian coastline and the Alps. Soon after the beginning of the first century BC the Romans were in control of North Italy, and could found new cities, drain the low-lying country, and build roads, of which the Via Emilia was the forerunner of the northern stretch of the *Autostrada del Sole*.

Before the Third Punic War, in 171 BC, danger had come to Rome from the Greek world. Perseus, the son of Philip V of Macedon, had built up a fresh army, and confronted Rome in a three-year war. This time the Romans, having defeated the Macedonians, destroyed the monarchy which had once been Alexander the Great's, and turned it into four republics. They had conquered a rich and civilized country, and their commanders brought back immense wealth to Rome.

The society which the wealth of the Carthaginian and Hellenic worlds was enriching in Rome was in many respects a model for the European society of the future. It was based on the family, living in its own comparatively small circle. The Roman families with which Latin literature has made us familiar were, of course, those of the upper classes, and included domestic servants, who were either slaves or freed slaves. Legally the *paterfamilias* was the absolute authority in the household. Women had no legal identity apart from their husbands or fathers, or – if none existed – other male relative. And yet in practice Roman women seem to have been allowed greater independence than the women of most modern societies. They had control of their own property when they reached the age of twenty-five, and seem to have been in greater control of their own social lives than are the wives of many rich, important men in the twentieth-century Western world. Divorce was easier and more common than in most countries today.

But the major difference in the society of Roman Italy from that of modern times was the existence of the institution of slavery. In the last years of the Republic there were probably at least two million slaves in Italy, constituting 35 per cent of the population.[2] No evaluation of Roman society can ignore this aspect of it. Both the slaves and their offspring were entirely the property of their masters. While slaves were to benefit, along with free men, from the long period of peace inaugurated by Augustus, they were excluded from the free distribution of corn, and had to depend for nourishment – and for life itself – on their masters. Many masters were without doubt kind to their slaves, and manumissions (the granting of freedom) were very common. Even Cato, so severe with his slaves in most respects, allowed them each a bottle of wine a day. But material conditions, however good, can never make up for total servitude. In modern times it has seemed a paradox that a people as civilized as the Romans in their literature and their architecture could regard as natural and inevitable so evil an institution as slavery. An understanding of the Roman attitude to slavery can perhaps be best gained by an analogy with the institution of employment in the modern world. In twentieth-century Italy it would seem eccentric to regard the existence of 'employers' and 'employees' as unnatural and evil. In ancient Rome everyone – including the slaves themselves – felt the same way about slavery. Nor did the coming of Christianity change matters, since there is no condemnation of the institution in the Gospels or the writings of Saint Paul.

Roman religion, superficially so unlike the Christianity of later Catholic Italy, had many points in common with it. The many gods and goddesses of pagan Rome, each with his or her function of mercy or support to perform, were not so far removed from the saints of Christian Italy, and Latin writers often refer to Jupiter in much the same terms as Christians refer to their God. He is the ruler of the universe for whom rituals must be performed. If the Romans were not expected to love their Jupiter in the same way as Christians are expected to love their God, they certainly counted on Jupiter – and to a

---

[2] M. I. Finley, *Ancient Slavery and Modern Ideology* (London, 1980), p. 80.

lesser extent other gods – to further their cause as a state and a people. And the Romans, like the Christians, blamed themselves, rather than their gods, for great natural disasters which the twentieth-century legal mind would define as 'acts of God'. Rome had a high priest, the *Pontifex Maximus*, who was also an important state functionary, and was elected to office. Among the largest buildings in Rome were the temples, as the largest buildings in medieval Italy were to be the cathedrals.

If the Romans built great temples, they also built secular monuments on a grand scale, as they did their systems of roads and aqueducts. In material terms the unification of Italy was given substance by the building of the great roads, as it was to be again, in the nineteenth century AD, by the building of the railways. The Via Appia had been begun as early as 312 BC, when Rome had been linked to Capua, and the road was extended to Brindisi in 244 BC. Running in incredibly straight lines across the country, the Roman roads were paved and of a standard width. The Via Flaminia was built over the Apennines northwards to Fano in 220 BC, and subsequently extended to Rimini. The Via Aurelia was built up the west coast, eventually to Genoa. Still in full use as the ss.1, it has been slightly relieved of congestion since the Second World War by the building of the motorways.

Until 146 BC the history of the Roman Republic was one of intermittent warfare, but civil peace. The constitution, with its government of two Consuls (who were also usually commanders in the field) and its Senate representing the ruling class, worked smoothly and efficiently. In contrast the later history of Rome was to be one of international peace, but civil disturbances often leading to civil war and chaos.

In the fifty years preceding the final defeat of Carthage about a quarter of a million slaves are believed to have been brought back to Italy from the wars. Thousands of others were born or bought. The enormous influx of slave labour meant great wealth for some, the growth of large estates, and the drastic reduction of the number of small freeholdings. It constituted an agrarian revolution bringing with it social disruption and human misery. In 133 BC a Tribune, or representative of the people in the Roman constitution, Tiberius Gracchus, introduced a Bill which enforced existing regulations, but regulations for some time ignored. Public land acquired by the state, for example after wars, had been leased to private individuals, but the amount held by any one individual had been strictly limited by laws. The laws had not been upheld, and many people possessed far more land than they were legally entitled to do. But in trying to enforce the laws Gracchus was radically upsetting the distribution of land. His bill passed at first, and a considerable redistribution of land took place, but the bill started a complex constitutional crisis. Gracchus, who was rightly convinced of the wisdom and justice of his cause, used radical, and not always legal, methods. His murder, probably as the result of a conspiracy by a group of the Senators, ended the long period of civil peace in Rome. His brother, Gaius Gracchus, determined to continue the work of Tiberius, and to avenge his murder, and to do so by more revolutionary methods. Elected Tribune in 122 BC, he attempted to make the constitution a more genuinely democratic one by insisting that the People were sovereign through their Assembly, the *concilium plebis*, which elected the Tribunes. But he brought to his aid the *equites*, or Knights, who had originally been a military caste, but were, by the time of the Gracchi, a rich middle class with a corner in tax-farming. Gaius Gracchus bribed the *equites* with very lucrative tax contracts in Asia, and other valuable concessions. But the coalition Gaius built up against the Senate did not remain loyal to him. When it abandoned him, the Senate had him, like his brother, murdered.

The Gracchi had not depended on an army loyal to them

personally. After them power in Rome fell into the hands of men who had achieved brilliant success as military commanders: Gaius Marius, consul six times between 107 and 100 BC, and Cornelius Sulla, who took the title of *dictator* in 83 BC, after suppressing a rising against Rome of her allies in what is – misleadingly to modern eyes – known as the Social War (from the Latin *socii,* for 'allies'). The Social War was the last attempt of the other peoples of the peninsula to press their aims on Rome, though chief of these aims was the securing of Roman citizenship. They formed a Confederation, which they called 'Italia' – a use which is interesting as a historical curiosity, but had little permanent significance, because of the speed and thoroughness of Sulla's suppression of the movement.

A genuinely social war of a terrible nature, and with terrible consequences, was fought from 73 to 71 BC. A slave called Spartacus escaped from a school of gladiators at Capua, and built up a force of runaway slaves on Mount Vesuvius. Initially he defeated forces sent against him from Rome, and built up an army of 70,000. More armies led by the Consuls themselves were defeated before the rising was suppressed. Spartacus himself was killed, and an appalling retribution was imposed on his followers. Some six thousand of them were crucified, lining the Appian Way from Capua to Rome. Spartacus had not, of course, been challenging the institution of slavery itself, but had rather been trying to secure freedom for his followers, and protesting against the inhumanity of the gladiatorial games.

In the final drama of the fall of the Republic, there were four principal protagonists: Pompey, Julius Caesar, Mark Antony and Octavian. Here it must suffice to summarize their roles.

Gnaius Pompeius, who assumed the title 'the Great', made a reputation – not wholly deserved – in the war against Spartacus. With Crassus, who was perhaps the richest man in Rome, he was elected Consul in 70 BC, but only because of the presence of his army, which intimidated the Senate. After brilliant military, colonizing and administrative achievements in Asia, he formed an unconstitutional Triumvirate with Caesar and Crassus in 60 BC, and after the break-up of the Triumvirate became sole Consul, and in effect dictator, in 52.

Julius Caesar, one of the most brilliant, ambitious and unprincipled men in Italian history, had used his membership of the Triumvirate, and his consulship in 59, to secure command of the legions in Gaul. He used his conquest of Gaul for personal glorification. Even from his own account it is clear that his two expeditions to Britain brought no results, but his skilful command of the army in Gaul secured its intense loyalty to himself. The Senate demanded that he should return to Rome only after disbanding his army. He defied their ruling, and returned in 49 BC. Pompey had been reconciled with the Senate, and now appeared as their defender, but a defender without an adequate army. To secure such an army, and accompanied by most of the Senate, he left for Greece, only to be followed, and defeated, by Caesar. Pompey was murdered in Egypt in 48. Caesar returned to Rome in triumph and was made Consul and dictator. The few years during which Caesar ruled Rome were ones of feverish activity. He continued the land reforms started by the Gracchi, but halved the number of Romans to whom free corn was given. He increased, thereby weakening, the Senate. But his most permanent measure was the introduction of the calendar which was to be used by the European world for so many centuries. There is little doubt that he intended to rule for life, and perhaps to restore the ancient monarchy of the Tarquins, but in 44 he was assassinated by a group of idealists and dissatisfied subordinates, led by Marcus Brutus.

Caesar's death created a momentary power vacuum, which was filled by Marcus Antonius. A supporter of Caesar, Antony was Consul for the year 44. He was the strongest figure in a Triumvirate which seized control, and included Gaius Octavius, an eighteen-year-old boy who had been adopted by Caesar as his son and heir. Mark Antony's first act was one which has not endeared him to posterity: the loyal constitutionalist, philosopher and supporter of the Senate, Cicero, was murdered as one of a large group of proscribed men. Antony's period of power was marked by a military victory over Brutus and the republicans, an alliance with Cleopatra in Egypt, and finally defeat at the hands of Octavian in the naval battle of Actium in 31 BC. The climax of Mark Antony's life, his love affair with Cleopatra, and their suicides, were related in the vivid narrative of the Greek historian, Plutarch, and reinforced a millennium and a half later by William Shakespeare.

Gaius Octavius had impressed his contemporaries less than the other three figures who had played major roles in these years. That he was to rule the world empire of Rome for forty-five years was due partly to everyone's longing for peace after the internal and external strife of the preceding years. Posterity has always found it hard to define where his ability lay, but that he was an immensely skilful operator can hardly be doubted. The full picture given of his personality by Suetonius, who lived from about 70 to 140 AD, is full of contradictions and ambiguities, and suggests a mixture of kindness and brutality, arrogance and moderation, ruthlessness and compassion. Yet Augustus, as the Senate entitled him, brought to the world an exceptionally long period of peace and civilization.

## 4 *The Roman Empire*, AD *313–c. 400*

If the Romans excelled in engineering, architecture, and the administrative and military arts, it was in their literature that they came closest to the spirit of modern Italy. And this is not surprising since the great Latin writers were Italians rather than Romans. Of the two early humorous dramatists, Plautus (c. 254–184 BC was born in Umbria. The other, Terence (c. 195–159 BC) was neither Roman nor Italian, but probably born in Carthage, and enslaved, but subsequently freed, by the

Romans. Cicero, although educated in Rome and Athens, had been born, in 106 BC, at Arpino in Central Italy. It was Cicero who brought Latin prose to its most mature and majestic stage. He was regarded in his day primarily as an orator who could plead a case in the Senate with great power and persuasiveness, but his eight hundred surviving letters have passages of human warmth and intimacy which would not read strangely in letters written in the twentieth century. Of the two most significant poets of the Roman Republic, Catullus (c. 84–c. 54 BC) also came from an outlying region. Born at Verona in Cisalpine Gaul, he did not go to Rome until he was an adult. Of the other, Lucretius (c. 94–55 BC), little is known, except what can be deduced from the text of his poetry. His masterpiece is the *De Rerum Natura*, one of the finest defences of materialism ever written, and yet a deeply moving and basically optimistic poem.

If Virgil's epic, the *Aeneid*, expresses most completely the spirit of imperial Rome, his *Georgics* give a recognizable picture of the Italy which is still there, and has been known for centuries:

> a country fulfilled with heavy corn and
> Campanian wine, possessed by olives and prosperous herds...
> Number our noble cities and all the works of our hands,
> The towns piled up on toppling cliffs, the antique walls
> And the rivers that glide below them.[3]

Virgil came from Mantua, and the two great lyric poets of the Augustan age, Horace (65–8 BC) and Ovid (43 BC–c. AD 17), came respectively from Apulia, and Sulmona in the Abruzzi. The subsequent influence on European literature of both Horace and Ovid has been as great outside as within Italy herself.

Augustus was to reign for forty-five years, and the Empire which he created was to survive for several centuries. Yet

---

[3] Cecil Day Lewis's translation (Oxford, 1940), pp. 39–40.

initially he secured power in the vacuum left by the ruins of other men's ambitions. It is difficult to see how he could have ended the period of civil wars without ensuring that sole command of the armies remained in his hands. Command of provincial armies had encouraged a series of men to make a bid for power in Rome, and was to do so again before the end of the first century AD. But Augustus could not simply declare himself to be a permanent dictator. His solution was to create what he called a 'Principate' for himself, but he created it by a slow succession of steps rather than by any dramatic proclamation of a new regime. He simply held the office of Consul annually from 31 to 27 BC. In 28 BC he and his son-in-law, Agrippa, were both Consuls: the support of the able and self-effacing Agrippa was to be an immensely important buttress of the young Empire.

Throughout his reign Augustus was careful to leave the Senate with the outward trappings of power and influence, but very little of the reality. His was, in Gibbon's words 'an absolute monarchy disguised by the forms of a common-wealth'.[*] But it was a benevolent despotism, and unlike most despots Augustus was a man of peace. In 29 BC the doors of the temple of Janus were closed, symbolizing the end of an era of warfare. More than half of his sixty legions were disbanded, and attempts to expand the Empire were halted. Peace was thus secured not only in Italy, but throughout the regions of Europe, Africa and Asia which the Republic had conquered and which the Empire was to Romanize. And in Rome herself there was growing prosperity and architectural wealth. Augustus had, according to his well-known claim, found Rome a city of bricks and left her a city of marble.

He was succeeded by his stepson, Tiberius (AD 14–37). The most significant event for the future of Italy during the reign of Tiberius took place in Palestina, one of the more eastern provinces of the Empire. A religious teacher, Jesus of Nazareth,

[*] Edward Gibbon, *The History of the Decline and Fall of the Roman Empire* (London, 1983), vol. I, p. 85.

was suspected of leading a Jewish nationalist movement, and executed by the Roman authorities. His novel ethical doctrine – that all human beings should love each other – was never to be put into practice, but was to be an underlying influence in the culture of medieval Europe, although twisted into perverted forms, and used by the medieval Papacy in the establishment of its dominant role in Italian history.

Tiberius lacked the ability and dedication of Augustus, yet the Empire survived his reign unharmed, as it did even the four years of his successor, Gaius, better known as Caligula (AD 37–41), who was almost certainly deranged. On the murder of Caligula in AD 41 there was a moment when the Republic might have been restored. The Consuls summoned a meeting of the Senate and for a day or two the old republican authorities were in control. However, the Praetorian Guard (the imperial bodyguard) decided to proclaim Caligula's uncle, Claudius, Emperor, believing that this man of fifty-one, with his several physical handicaps, would be their puppet. But Claudius was to show ability as a military commander during the invasion of Britian, and was to be, after Augustus, the most effective of the Julio-Claudian dynasty, the dynasty which had opened with Augustus and was to close with Nero.

Claudius introduced something approaching ministerial government, by creating four departments – for law, finance, records and justice – and nominated an educated freedman (in a sense a permanent under-secretary) to supervise each of them. Claudius also built an artificial harbour at Ostia, at the mouth of the Tiber, and new aqueducts which were supported on the massive Porta Maggiore, which is still intact. Ostia Antica, excavated with the professionalism and care of modern archaeologists, today gives a vivid impression of a civilization which lived for so long in peace and prosperity, with its modern sanitation, shops, club houses and Turkish and sauna baths.

The rest of Italy, outside Rome, was scarcely aware of the

momentary crisis which followed the assassination of Domitian in AD 96. Apart from the troubles of the Year of the Four Emperors (AD 69), which followed the death of Nero, Italy enjoyed internal, as well as international, peace for 220 years. Domestic stability was the result of several factors. The emperors not only chose their successors, but gave them a considerable amount of power while they themselves still lived, so that the transition on the death of an emperor was usually smooth. Then, the armies remained loyal to the emperors, or, to put it in more general terms, men with military commands and weapons respected the civil authority – always a necessity for the survival of advanced forms of civilization.

Nero (AD 54–68) has survived in the popular memory for the burning of Rome and his persecution of the Christians. That he became increasingly unbalanced, though never to the same extent as Caligula, was illustrated by his obsession with his genius as a theatrical and musical performer. Nor can any interpretation of his place in history expunge the fact that he had his mother and wife murdered, many senators massacred, while the killing of the elderly Seneca, his former tutor and adviser, remains an inexplicably gratuitous crime. On the positive side, much rebuilding took place under Nero after the fire, and the persecution of the Christians, whom Suetonius described as 'a mischievous sect', probably did not seem an enormity to most Romans at the time. Religious toleration was normally one of the virtues of the Romans, who allowed conquered peoples to retain their local religions, provided they also respected the traditional and official Roman religion. The Christians seemed unique in their conviction that they had a monopoly of religious truth, a conviction which made them trouble-makers in a tolerant society. After the terror which he conducted in his last years against the senators, they finally conspired successfully against him, and forced him to commit suicide in AD 68. But power did not pass to the Senate. The legions in Spain declared Galba, who was about seventy years old, emperor, creating the ominous precedent that an emperor could be proclaimed by forces far from Rome. The precedent was followed in the 'Year of the Four Emperors' by the proclamation by the legions on the Rhine of Vitellius. Otho, the most worthless of the four, had Vitellius murdered by the Praetorian Guard, only to be killed himself in a brief return to civil war. He was succeeded by Vespasian, who had been shrewd enough to cut Rome off from her food supply in Egypt.

With Vespasian (AD 69–79) Italy returned to the domestic peace with which she had been familiar for several decades. The first of the Flavian dynasty, Vespasian returned to the practice of holding a consulship himself, and preparing for a successor by making his son, Titus, the other Consul. The son of a humble civil servant from the provinces, Vespasian was more of an Italian than a Roman, and brought with him to Rome new Senators with a similar background. After the extravagances of Nero, it was what Rome needed. Yet this careful, seasoned soldier carried out some of the most ambitious building projects even Rome was to experience. His large forum has disappeared, but the vast Colosseum, with its grim memories of the slaughter of men, women and animals, is today the most striking monument of classical Rome.

Before becoming emperor himself, Titus (AD 78–81) had suppressed a major rising of the Jews and captured Jerusalem in AD 70. Although emperor for less than three years, he earned immense popularity, and after his death an arch was built in his honour, an arch which, with its fine sculpture, is still in a good state of repair today. The Flavian dynasty ended with the assassination of Titus' brother Domitian, who had been emperor from AD 81 to 96. The attempt to keep a kinship link between successive emperors was then abandoned, and a policy of inheritance by adoption – in effect, by nomination by the emperor – was followed with some success. Trajan (AD 98–117) came from an Italian family which had settled in Spain. It can

Plate 2. The triumphal arch of Trajan at Ancona, built in AD 115

well be argued that under Trajan, and his successor, Hadrian (117–138), the Roman Empire was at its peak. If Rome had already had a population of half a million in 100 BC, by the time of Trajan it is calculated that her population had reached one and a half million. No other city in the history of the world was to be as large as this again until the nineteenth century, when it was finally equalled by London, and Rome herself was not to reach that figure again until the twentieth century. In the early second century AD she was thus a great cosmopolitan city of gleaming marble, with many Greek-speaking people and immigrants from all over the empire, especially from the other eastern provinces.

Hadrian was an active and constructive emperor, bringing in legal and military reforms, and touring all parts of the Empire. Two of the most famous landmarks in Rome – the Pantheon and the Castel Sant'Angelo – were in their origins his products, in the sense not only that he commissioned them, but that he himself designed them, with the help of Apollonius, the great Roman architect who had also worked under Trajan.

That Roman civilization had prospered in spite of the reigns of Caligula and Nero suggests that the characters of the emperors were of little significance. But the ability and wisdom of Hadrian's two successors, Antoninus Pius (138–61) and Marcus Aurelius (169–80), must have contributed to the continuation of civilization late into the second century AD. 'Pius' was a name bestowed on Antoninus, and forms a link with Virgil's use of this untranslatable adjective (which meant 'virtuous' or 'God-fearing', as well as 'pious' in the modern sense) and its adoption by medieval popes. The Latin language was to provide continuity from the classical world into the Middle Ages.

Marcus Aurelius came as close to Plato's concept of the philosopher-king as any other ruler in history. A dedicated Stoic, and a man of peace, he yet had to conduct defensive wars on a considerable scale on the Danube frontier. As an illustration of his vision it is perhaps enough to record that he sent an expedition to China in 166, not for conquest, but for trade. But there are no literary sources for the period of Hadrian and Marcus to compare with the writings of Tacitus and Suetonius for the earlier period. Marcus Aurelius's own *Meditations* inevitably give a favourable impression of his reign, but there is reason to believe that something approaching the spirit of the Republic must have returned. At least there was evidently mutual understanding and a sharing of power between emperor and Senate.

Marcus died in 180 in a terrible epidemic which spread from a war in the East, and which perhaps more than any other single cause started the decline of Rome. If literary sources become much thinner in the second century than in the first, in the third century they became fragmentary, and what there was to record became increasingly confused. Between AD 235 and the accession of Diocletian in AD 284 there were twenty-two emperors, not all with equally valid claims, and there were many other claimants of a yet more dubious kind. Meanwhile pressure from the Teutonic tribes increased on the Rhine and Danube frontiers, and the Goths invaded the Balkan provinces of the Empire. In the world of ideas there were also invasions. Some of the great emperors – Augustus, Claudius, Vespasian, Titus – had been recognized as gods after their deaths, but the concept of worshipping a living emperor was considered an oriental, non-Roman one, which Mark Antony would have introduced, had he defeated Octavian. Under the Emperor Decius (249–51) emperor-worship was made obligatory, but emperor-worship in its turn was undermined by the ideological invasion of mystical religions from the East. In the third century both Mithraism and Christianity were spreading. Marcus Aurelius, in the late second century, had regarded Christian fanaticism as a danger, and had, uncharacteristically, persecuted the Christians, but the future was on their side.

Italy was gripped by a certain malaise in the third century, a presentiment of greater disasters to come. Architecture became less civic and more military. Gallienus (253–68) built a defensive system from the Veneto across to Milan, a system only recently observed by archaeologists. Aurelian (270–5) built a massive circle of walls, nineteen kilometres long, around Rome. The city had reached her largest extent, and for almost all the rest of her history – until the twentieth century – was to remain within these walls. Indeed, even in the nineteenth century there were still large tracts of open country within the Aurelian walls.

The accession of Diocletian (284–305), who was perhaps born a slave in a peasant family in Illyria (today in Yugoslavia), was to bring a temporary return to the reassurance of happier days. With his wise, if harsh, rule, the cities and countryside of Italy acquired greater prosperity. He rationalized the administration of the Empire by appointing two rulers for the eastern part and two for the western part, the senior of the two to be known as Augustus, and the junior as Caesar. Diocletian himself took the title of Augustus in the Eastern Empire, ruling from Nicodemia in Turkey. He visited Rome only in 303, then decided that Roman society was too debased to support any longer the court of the Western Empire, which he moved to Ravenna, while the administrative offices of the Empire were moved to Milan. From this moment Milan was to be an important Italian city, but Diocletian left one monument in Rome – his baths, still an impressive ruin near today's Stazione Termini. In 305 he abdicated, and withdrew to his vast palace whose remains today dramatically enclose the centre of the Yugoslav town of Split. The succession was a bitterly disputed one, and it was only in 324 that Constantine emerged as the *de facto* as well as the *de jure* ruler in Rome.

The two steps of universal significance taken by Constantine (306–37) were the recognition of Christianity as a legitimate religion, and the founding of a new capital of the empire at Constantinople. The second step raised the possibility that Italy would cease to be centre of the civilized world, but in the event Rome was to play her second role in history as the heart of the medieval Church.

In the Empire of Diocletian many were being converted to Christianity, though mainly among the poor in the towns. Diocletian himself saw the dramatic growth of this strange monotheism as a social and political threat. In 303 he encouraged an appalling massacre of Christians, an act which for many centuries was to overshadow his achievements in the eyes of posterity. Only ten years later did Constantine's Edict of Milan grant the Christians toleration, and almost immediately, with the emperor's patronage, an impressive building programme of cathedrals and churches started in Italy. In a few years the enormous basilicas of St John Lateran and St Peter were built in Rome. Christian bishops were allowed to give Roman citizenship to slaves, and to conduct their own law courts. A new hierarchy and a new kind of authority had come to Italy.

Although the Christian authorities did not condemn slavery as an evil institution, Christian writers joined with several pagan writers in pointing out that slaves and the free shared a common humanity. In the first century only Seneca, in his *Epistulae Morales*, had movingly argued that slaves should be treated with consideration and kindness, in the knowledge that only coincidence of birth or warfare had decided who should be slave and who should be free. In the third century writers who interpreted and codified Roman Law displayed a greater respect for the humanity of slaves than had been shown in the earlier age, which, in other respects, had been more civilized. Partly this was because the number of slaves per head of population declined with the lack of victorious wars, and slaves became more valuable. Free tenants were replacing slaves in the third century.

The two halves of the Roman Empire remained linked for

half a century after the reigns of Diocletian and Constantine. Only in 395, with the death of Theodosius, who had success- fully fought bitter campaigns against Goths and Franks, did the complete break occur. At that time a dominant figure in Italy, and a friend of Theodosius, was the Bishop of Milan, Ambrose, later to be sanctified, one of the four Fathers of the Church. Initially consular prefect of Upper Italy, he was elected bishop in 374, and was to combine widespread political and spiritual authority for no fewer than twenty-three years.

Theodosius and Ambrose were struggling in a world which was disintegrating. In the fourth century there was a dramatic fall in population, caused by famine, plague and war. Civiliz- ation was receding.

Chapter 2

# THE EARLY MIDDLE AGES

*1 Barbarian invasions and Byzantine Italy, c. 400–c. 600*

Theodosius had commanded the army himself, but his successors in the fifth century allowed military authority to slip from their hands. Thus Honorius (395–423) appointed a man who was by race a Vandal, Stilicho, as commander, or *magister militum*. Stilicho drove the Visigoths, under Alaric, out of Greece, and continued his victories into Northern and Central Italy, but in an attempt to regain control of the armies, Honorius had Stilicho murdered in 408. The immediate future for Italy lay with the Visigoths, the westward branch of the Goths, a Teutonic tribe which had probably been dislodged from Southern Russia by nomadic peoples in the 370s. The Visigoths thus reached Italy at the beginning of the fifth century, under their leader, Alaric.

Alaric I, like Stilicho, was in a sense a product of the Empire. He had been appointed by Theodosius as leader of initially loyal Gothic auxiliaries. But in 395 he had invaded Northern Greece, and in 400 or 401 made an unsuccessful attack on Northern Italy. In 401 he besieged Milan, and in 410 sacked Rome. In spite of the waves of horror which swept the Empire at the news of the sacking of Rome, the city recovered in some twenty years, with renewed building activity. Meanwhile other barbarians were approaching Italy from another direction. The Vandals arrived in Africa in 429, having crossed Gaul and Spain with remarkable speed. Their control of North Africa deprived Rome of her previous source of corn, which now had to be produced in Sicily. Economically Sicily gained from the barbarian invasions, in that when the Goths came to control Italy they left Sicily to her own resources, while depriving much of mainland Italy – especially the North and centre – of land on which Gothic troops and veterans were settled.

The Goths thus settled in Italy, and must have brought much new blood to Italians of the North, though far less than the Lombards were to bring. Southerners can almost certainly claim to be closer in kin to the Romans than the Northerners can, even when due consideration is given to the Greek element in the South. The Italians, like the other peoples of the West, had many years in which to accustom themselves to the Teutonic invaders, who acquired the trappings of civilization as they settled within the borders of the Empire. But in 370 a quite different people, the Huns, who were Mongols and nomadic came westwards from Russia. In 434 a leader of the Huns emerged in the person of Attila, who collected a large army, containing Vandals, Ostrogoths and Franks as well as Huns. Although he conquered huge areas of South-Eastern Europe, he failed to break through the fortifications of Constantinople. In 452 he was in Northern Italy, and after a three-month siege took the great city of Aquileia. Traditionally it was the invasion of the Huns which was said to have encouraged the people of Aquileia and Grado to found the city of Venice as a refuge. In fact Attila died in 453, and it was not until 466 that a group of Italians met at Grado, and formed what might arguably be considered the first government of independent Venice, though they were still, like other Italians, theoretically subjects of the emperor in Constantinople.

The early claims of the Papacy to temporal power can be traced to these middle years of the fifth century. Leo I, 'the Great' (440–61), was the first pope to play a significant role in

Italian history. In several respects he can be considered the founder of Catholicism. He rejected the claim of the Patriarch of Constantinople to be the head of the church, and Western Christianity at this time gained enormous prestige from two myths, both without foundation. The first was that Leo, by his spiritual authority, had persuaded Attila not to attack Rome. The second was a forged document, known as the Donation of Constantine, which professed to record Constantine's gift of the Western Empire to the Papacy. The most successful forgery in history, the Donation of Constantine was not to be exposed for a thousand years. Only after so long a history was its credibility destroyed by a brilliant Renaissance scholar, Lorenzo Valla, who will merit mention in a later chapter.

The Vandals had found a successful leader in Gaiseric, who ruled Sicily from North Africa in 440. He commanded a navy as well as an army, and his active career lasted for about half a century. He sacked Rome in 455, but the Vandal conquests were never very permanent. Only in 468 was Gaiseric in complete control even of Sicily, and then for only eight years. In spite of invasions by Goths, Huns and Vandals, the Roman Senate and emperor survived, if in name only, and as pale shadows from a remote past. Finally, in 476, the year traditionally taken as marking the end of the Roman Empire, the last emperor, Romulus Augustulus, was deposed by Odovacar (476–93) at the head of a mixed group of Teutonic invaders, serving nominally under the Empire. An Italian nationalist writer, Cesare Balbo, whose *Storia d'Italia* was published in 1856, saw the reign of Odovacar as the beginning of a 'war of Italian independence against the German peoples, which has lasted for 1,357 years, and is not finished'. Against this somewhat sweeping generalization, it could be argued that under the Goths, until about 530, Italy was closer to being a single independent state than she had been for many decades, and that from about 400 to 1000 more than half of Italy was

Plate 3. Medieval and later buildings on the site of the Roman arena at Lucca

under a single king, who was not, of course, an Italian, but an Ostrogoth, Lombard or Frank.

A much greater Gothic king than Odovacar was Theodoric (488–526), who murdered Odovacar with his own hands, after a war of five years. Theodoric's reign was one of peace and prosperity. He did not interfere with the culture, laws or religion of the Romans, but ruled his own Gothic people through their own laws. A strange segregation of the two

41

Map 2. Italy about 600 AD

peoples prevailed. Theodoric was an Arian Christian, belonging to the sect who argued that God the Father must have
existed before the Son, and to that extent the two could not be
identical. But Theodoric insisted on religious toleration by the
state, and did not interfere in a bitter schism which developed
among the Roman Christians. Regarded as a neutral in
religion, he was actually asked to choose a pope. He kept peace
in Rome in spite of the bitterness of the religious schism which
cloaked a class war between the poor and the senatorial class,
who clung tenaciously to their status and their wealth.

Gothic rule in Italy was ended during the reign of the Eastern Emperor Justinian in Constantinople (527–65), who embarked on the reconquest of Rome. His reputation owed perhaps less to his own qualities than to those of the empress, Theodora, and two generals, Belisarius and Narses. Belisarius reconquered the Vandal kingdom of Africa, and then proceeded to re-establish imperial authority in Rome. The long wars which he and Narses fought almost certainly brought considerable suffering to the Italians, in sharp contrast to the good times under Theodoric.

Justinian's true claim to fame was not so much in the reconquest of Italy – which, after all, could not be permanent – as in his codifying of the laws, which took the form of a *Codex*, published in 529, and the *Institutiones*, published in 533.

Under Theodoric Ravenna experienced an outburst of architectural achievement, and was subsequently to be the setting for great works of Byzantine art, in particular the mosaic portraits of Justinian and Theodora in the church of San Vitale. In Rome, too, it was a period of achievement in Byzantine art, of which perhaps the finest surviving examples are the mosaics in the church of Saints Cosmas and Damian.

But in the last decades of the sixth century conditions in Italy deteriorated. Barbarian invasions continued. Ravenna, Rome, Genoa and Naples preserved remnants of Roman institutions, but were often isolated and out of touch with each other. Many towns were abandoned. The *magister militum*, now called the Exarch, ruled in Ravenna, and elsewhere also military governers predominated over civilian ones.

## 2 Lombard Italy and the foundation of the Papal States, c. 600–800

At the turn of the sixth to the seventh centuries one figure of significance for the future emerged – the last of the four Fathers of the Church, Pope Gregory I, called the Great. Born about 540, he came from a rich family which could claim senatorial status in Rome. About 575 he gave away his wealth to the poor and entered a monastery. Drawn by the pope back into public life, he was sent as papal nuncio to Constantinople for several years, and in 590 was elected pope himself. His administration of the Church was thorough, and set the pattern which Catholic services and ritual were to follow throughout history. He sent Augustine to Britain to convert the English, not knowing that they had already encountered Christianity through missionaries from Ireland. Gregory was a humanitarian, who improved the conditions of the slaves, and provided free bread in Rome on the old Roman model. The repairing of aqueducts during his pontificate also showed respect for a lost, if pagan, civilization. At his death in 604, he left a body of writings to which subsequent Catholic dogma was to owe much.

When Gregory was still a young man the Lombard invasion of Italy had started. The Lombards arrived about 568, and heavy fighting ensued until 605. They appeared to the Italians to be quite as barbaric as the Goths or Vandals had been. As they moved south, evasive rather than defensive action was taken. Some of the hill-top towns of Central Italy date from this period, when settlements were moved up from the plain to escape from the Lombards. Farther south, in the duchies of Spoleto and Benevento, under their Lombard rulers records of bishops and their sees disappear. Comtemporary accounts at the turn of the century tell of wholesale disasters – floods, famine, the plague – but also of dragons, which make the accounts seem a little less reliable.

The Lombard invaders are estimated to have been only some 200,000, but they were numerous enough to put the clock of civilization yet further back in the regions which they occupied. What happened to the Romans or Italians in these regions is imperfectly known. There is a genuine 'Dark Age' in the very early history of Lombard Italy between the murder of

Alboin in 573 and the accession of Agilulf in 590. Historians in the past tended to accept Gregory the Great's impression of the Lombards as a totally barbaric and destructive people, who completely dispossessed the Italians of all land and property, but such a picture is not accepted quite so readily today, if only because Gregory was clearly a partisan witness. At least the Lombards signed treaties, and sometimes alliances, with the Byzantine Italians. And because they were few in number they probably quickly disappeared in the Italian melting pot. Metalwork and pottery found in Lombard burial sites suggest that there had rapidly been some kind of fusion of cultures.

The Lombard language did not long survive their arrival in Italy. Probably by 700 they had adopted something akin to Latin. Only a few words of Lombard origin exist in modern Italian. Perhaps the most common is *schifo*, which means a 'boat' (and has supplied the English word 'skiff'), or, more usually, 'disgust', as in 'Che schifo!', which might be rendered as 'What a disgusting affair!' *Malma*, a 'mire', or 'mud', is another. There is also evidence that the Lombards abandoned their social customs – long hair and striped linen clothes – and acquired those of the Romans. Another example of social integration comes from names: a single family in the early eighth century could contain both Roman and Lombard names, and in extreme cases could have names which combined the two languages, as in the case of a landowner in Lucca in 774 called 'Daviprand'.

The most tenacious feature of Roman civilization was Roman law. As with the case of the Goths, the Lombards brought their own laws, and ruled their own people according to those imported laws, but Roman law survived, especially with regard to property. Private property, either absolute or leased, was a basis of Roman law, and by the eighth and ninth centuries seems to have been adopted by the Lombards, replacing their more communal concept of land and property tenure. Another respect in which the Lombards adapted themselves to Italy was that they became city-dwellers, and their leaders made cities their capitals. No longer did they live in remote, fortified castles in the countryside. Even before the end of the sixth century Roman cities were being ruled by Lombard dukes, and a century later, during the reign of Cunipert (679–700), there is evidence of a civilian Lombard aristocracy living in Brescia, and a suggestion of such an aristocracy in Pavia and Vicenza also. By the eighth century the cities of Northern Italy were inhabited by a population which is no longer easily distinguishable as 'Lombard' or 'Roman'.

As the modern name 'Lombardy' suggests, the part of Italy most intensely settled by the Lombards was that around Milan, Pavia and Brescia, but also around Verona, and as far east as the Friuli. Slavery, of course, still existed, and many Romans were enslaved by the Lombards, though the Lombards brought many slaves with them. Legal status did not correspond precisely to social status, any more than it had done in the Roman empire, when slaves had sometimes been high-ranking bureaucrats. In Lombard Italy Romans still owned land, and many of them were absentee landlords living in the city – an Italian habit which was to die hard. So, while the Lombards almost certainly dominated society, they did not entirely enslave the indigenous population. The total enslavement of a population by a conqueror has occurred in black moments of history, but on the whole the Italians have escaped this fate. The claim made by the Chinese, that their conquerors have always ultimately themselves been conquered by the civilization they have possessed themselves of, might be made by the Italians. By the time the Franks arrived in the late eighth century, the Lombards had been integrated with the Italians to the extent that the newcomers were regarded as aliens by a united society.

The capital of Lombard Italy was Pavia, today a charming and quiet university town. For several centuries from the 620s

Pavia remained the most important city in what is now Lombardy, taking the role Milan had previously held, and was to hold again. The Ostrogoths had built a palace in Pavia, and the Lombards built many churches there, and even preserved – or perhaps renovated – public baths, a reminder of the days of Roman civilization. Pavia was evidently intended by the Lombards to rival Ravenna, if not Constantinople, as a great city. Under King Desiderius (757–74), Paul the Deacon, the most important historian of the period, was working there.

Italian nationalists in the nineteenth century did not entirely disown the Lombards. Cesare Balbo, writing in the 1850s, commented:

Many of their laws and customs remained for several centuries; much blood in the veins, many words in the language and dialects of almost the whole of Italy have survived. And from them has remained the name of a great, beautiful, good, rich Italian province, today subjected to the Austrian emperor and king.[1]

The Lombard conquest of Italy was never a complete one. Byzantine Italy survived in the Exarchate of Ravenna, and in Rome; nor were Venice, or Naples and the far South, occupied by the Lombards. The first Exarch of Ravenna had been appointed by the Byzantine Emperor Maurice (582–602). Once appointed, the Exarchs preserved virtual independence, and declared complete independence in 619, and again in 651. The organization of the Exarchate was more sophisticated than that of Lombard Italy. Regular taxes were imposed and troops were paid regularly, instead of being given land or the loot of war. Not until 751 was the Exarchate conquered by the Lombards, under Aistulf (749–56).

The basic difference between Byzantine Italy of the seventh century and the Italy of the late Roman Empire was that the ruling class had become a purely military one. Senators, traditionally a civilian upper class, left Northern and Central

---

[1] Cesare Balbo, *Sommario Della Storia d'Italia* (Florence, 1962), p. 113.

Italy. The last Italians still claiming to be 'senators' left records in Sicily, while some had moved from Italy to the heart of the Empire in Constantinople. Naples was an exception in the increasing militarization of Italy in the seventh century; civilians remained the dominant class. Only in the eighth century was the ruler of Naples a military man, with the title of duke, emerging as a figure with autocratic powers.

In 754 and 756 the Franks invaded Italy under their king, Pepin, and deprived the Lombards of much of their territory. Pepin's arrival provided the opportunity for what might be considered the foundation of the Papal States – that unique principality which was to survive until 1870. The Donation of Pepin, issued in 756, gave land which was nominally under the Eastern Empire to Pope Stephen II. Added to the Donation of Constantine, the Donation of Pepin virtually proclaimed the pope to be the heir of the Roman emperors.

In the second half of the eighth century the Lombard Kingdom of North and Central Italy fell to the Franks. To the south of the Kingdom a Lombard chief had established himself as an independent Duke of Spoleto. Initially his duchy was also conquered by the Franks, but the conquest was only nominal, Spoleto in practice retaining its independence.

Charlemagne, the greatest European ruler of the early Middle Ages, became King of the Franks in 1774, and visited Rome that year. He confirmed the Donation of Pepin, but in reality his presence in Rome illustrated Frankish domination of much of Italy. The popes in theory retained their state, which now included the former Exarchate of Ravenna, as well as Rome itself. In contrast with the Duchy of Spoleto, however, the Papal States were in practice controlled by the Carolingians – a situation strangely analogous with that to be created by Napoleon a millenium later. To the south the Duchy of Benevento, under a Lombard who had established his independence from the Lombard Kingdom before its collapse, preserved its independence also from the Franks. Duke Arichis

II had taken the title of *princeps* of Benevento in 758, and ruled until 787, issuing seventeen laws. He died while resisting an invasion by Charlemagne, who was acting with the blessing of Pope Hadrian I (772–95), while Arichis was trying to secure Byzantine support. His successor as Prince of Benevento, Grimoald III (787–86), accepted the suzerainty of Charlemagne, and was obliged to resist and defeat the Byzantine army which had duly arrived. Grimoald retained independence in practice, and continued to fight the Franks. Some of his coins have survived.

Charlemagne started the imperial practice of crowning his son 'King of Italy'. In 781 Pepin, a child of four, was given the title, and held it until his early death in 810, while making a vain attempt to subdue Venice. For the next quarter of a century Charlemagne was establishing his empire in Central and Western Europe. In 800 he returned to Rome to restore the pope, Leo III (795–816), who had been driven out by popular riot. On Christmas Day, 800, the pope crowned Charlemagne emperor in St Peter's. The Holy Roman Empire, with its claim to be heir of the Empire of Augustus, started its long history, but the paradox created by the fact that the Franks had encouraged the popes to have similar claims was to provide the central theme of Italian history throughout the Middle Ages. The struggle between pope and emperor, between Church and State, was to be present in one form or another into modern times.

### 3 The Empire and the Papacy, 800–1216

Then all the loyal Romans, seeing the great love and care which he showed for the Holy Church of Rome and for its vicar, inspired by God and by St Peter who holds the keys of the kingdom of heaven, cried out aloud with one voice: 'To Charles, most pious Augustus crowned by God, mighty and peacable emperor, long life and victory!' Before the holy tomb of St Peter the apostle it was said thrice over with the invocation of many saints, and by all the company he was established as emperor of the Romans. Whereupon the most holy priest and pontiff anointed Charles his most excellent son as his king with holy oil, on the very day of the nativity of Our Lord Jesus Christ.[2]

The author of the *Liber Pontificalis*, probably a near contemporary of the event, captured the spirit of the moment which marked a triumph for Western Christendom. Yet Charlemagne was not in any permanent sense to become the ruler of Italy; nor were the German emperors who were to succeed him. Clausewitz was impressed by the fact. In warning his readers against regarding a state as an individual who can be expected to act from rational motives, the philosopher of war commented:

Let us only think of the continual expeditions of the Emperors of Germany into Italy for five cenuries, without any substantial conquest of that country resulting from them, or even having been so much as in view.

The German emperors were not behaving as a solitary individual would behave. In their continual descents into Italy they were impelled by

a hundred important causes, which we can partially realize in idea, but the vital energy of which it is impossible for us to understand so vividly as those who were brought into actual conflict with them.[3]

Clausewitz was certainly right in suggesting that the causes for these latter-day barbarian invasions were more complex than the simple desire for loot and excitement which had motivated their ancestors in earlier centuries. They were attracted by the ghost of the Roman Empire. Rome still had some imponderable and mystical significance for them. But with arrival of conquerors from the North there appeared a paradox in Italian history. It seemed that only under a foreign

[2] H. R. Loyn and J. Percival, *The Reign of Charlemagne* (London, 1975), p. 26.
[3] Clausewitz, *On War*, edited by Anatol Rapoport (Harmondsworth, 1968), p. 379.

ruler was Italy likely to secure something approaching unity – as she had done under Theodoric, and was to do ephemerally under later German conquerors, while in the absence of foreign rulers Italy remained dangerously disunited. Yet the periods of disunity and independence from the foreigner were to correspond with the great periods of Italian civilization, the periods of the medieval city-states and of the Renaissance benevolent despotisms of the fifteenth century. When Giuseppe Mazzini in the nineteenth century argued that independence and republicanism were necessary for the flowering of Italian culture there was more than a grain of truth in what he said. The rest of Mazzini's dream – unity under a native Italian government – did not come remotely near achievement until his own day, except in the imagination of a Machiavelli.

After Charlemagne's death his empire broke up, and his heirs never succeeded in integrating Italy with the empire, though the Carolingian rulers of Italy retained the title of emperor. Charlemagne's heirs, who claimed to be kings of Italy, did not live there, until Louis II, who became emperor in 850 and settled in Italy for the twenty-five years of his reign.

When Louis II became emperor the Moslems were already in Sicily, having arrived in 827, ostensibly to support a revolt by a Sicilian, Euphemius, who had proclaimed himself emperor. After the murder of Euphemius, however, the Arabs did not depart. In 831 they took Palermo, which became their capital, with the name of al-Madinah. By 842 their conquest had reached Messina. Attempts from Constantinople to save Sicily from the Arabs failed, and the Byzantines' own capital of the island, Syracuse, which had been an important city since the original Greek settlements – before Constantinople or Rome had been imperial capitals – fell to the Arabs in 878.

There were many positive features to the Arab conquest of Sicily. On the most tangible level, cotton, sugar cane, orange and lemon plants were introduced. The bulk of the population probably did not suffer much from the very alien invasion. The

Arabs did not conscript the Sicilians into their armies as the Byzantine rulers had done, and under the Arabs taxes were lower. Sicily was to remain under the Arabs for two and a half centuries, but it was by no means an era of uninterrupted peace, since Arab groups fought among themselves, and in the early eleventh century the Byzantines invaded in an ultimately unsuccessful attempt to reconquer Sicily. But Palermo became not only an important trading post, but also the centre of a rich, cosmopolitan, civilization. Its population of something over 100,000 made it larger than any Christian city except Constantinople. Hundreds of mosques were built, and the elegant Arabic style of architecture was to survive as an influence after Sicily became once again a Christian country, under the Normans. There was no harsh persecution of Christians by their Moslem conquerors, who neverthless asserted their social predominance, and practised discrimination in a variety of small ways. Yet Moslems and Christians lived together in peace in a manner which underlines the futility of the crusading wars which were soon to begin.

If Sicily marked a high point of the Moslem tide, which was to threaten to swamp Europe, the rest of Italy remained Christian. The German emperors who claimed also to be kings of Italy in the ninth and tenth centuries were powerful men on the international level, but they had little control of life in Italy in the local level. This was true both of the Carolingian Louis II, and of his Saxon successors a century later – even of Otto I (936–976), called 'the Great', of whom Cesare Balbo said that his 'greatness was certainly one of the major calamities of Italy'.[*] Louis II, however, ruled as king of Italy through a recognizable bureaucracy, the *missi*, as the agents sent out to the provinces by Charlemagne and his successors were called. Loyal counts and bishops also ruled on the king's behalf. In the

---

[*] Balbo, *Sommario della Storia d'Italia*, p. 186.

course of the tenth century this control by the emperor, as king of Italy, was fading. The local agents of central government were disappearing, as was the sense of loyalty to the king felt by counts and bishops. The end of royal power in Italy was symbolized in Pavia in 1024, when the citizens burnt down the palace.

For a quarter of a century after the death of Louis II in 875 there was warfare in Italy, with local Italian rulers divided in their support of French or German claimants to the imperial title and kingship of Italy. Not surprisingly the Italian counts and bishops in the North-West, like Anspert, the Archbishop of Milan, supported the French claimant, Charles the Bald, and those in the North-East supported the German claimant, Louis. From 875 to 897 there were no fewer than five French claimants and four German claimants. These men, whose power lay north of the Alps, visited Italy rarely. An exception was the German, Charles the Fat, who was in Italy from 879 to 886, and several of them came to Rome for the honour of being crowned emperor by the pope: Charles the Fat in 881, Guido of Spoleto in 891, and Arnulf in 894. Charles the Fat was overthrown in 886, and Berengar of Friuli was elected king of Italy by his Italian supporters. Opposed to the German line under Berengar was the French line represented by Guido of Spoleto. Having defeated Berengar, Guido took the imperial title. His Italian-sounding family, the Guideschi, were really of Frankish extraction, but he was the first non-Carolingian to be crowned emperor. An ambitious man, Guido probably intended to establish himself as a second Charlemagne, but was prevented from doing so by his sudden death in 894.

A pattern was beginning to emerge in Italian history as rulers from beyond the Alps used Italy as a battleground, but through their rivalries created a power vacuum in which cities could acquire autonomy and grow in size as refugees entered from the countryside. And in the cities the dynamic life of the commune was beginning to develop as *de facto* republics emerged.

When Otto I invaded Italy in 951 his main preoccupation was to cement his power in Germany through his alliance with the Papacy. A late wave of barbarians, the Magyars, had descended upon North-Eastern Italy, and Otto's first task, successfully accomplished in 955, was to defeat them. Subsequently he reached Rome, and established his own claimant, Leo VIII, as pope in 963. Otto I, his son, Otto II, and his grandson, Otto III, ruled in Rome until 1002, establishing the tradition of a link between Germany and Italy through a papal coronation of the German emperor in Rome. Otto III clearly intended to restore a universal Roman empire, but he was driven out by the citizens of Rome in 1002, and died that year.

While the Franks had controlled much of Northern and Central Italy in the ninth and first half of the tenth centuries, the Byzantine South was split into independent republics, nominally recognizing the Eastern Empire. Naples was already an independent city-state in the ninth century, ruled by two or three families. For long periods a sole ruler was both bishop and temporal ruler ('duke' or 'consul'), which was the case with Stephen II from 754 to 800, and Athanasius II from 876 to 898. Ninth-century sources for Naples and the Byzantine South generally are a little less sparse than for the Frankish North. It is known, for example, that Naples produced linen and minted gold coins.

Amalfi, still today a gem of a town, had a unique history in the early Middle Ages. She had secured her independence from Naples in the 840s. The citizens of Amalfi allied themselves with raiding Arabs, and received considerable help from them. Soon Amalfi was one of the major trading republics in the Western Mediterranean. Amalfi, and the sister republics of Gaeta and Naples, had become cosmopolitan cities through maritime trade, as had Salerno while still a Lombard principality. They traded with the Eastern Mediterranean, and had

Jewish minorities. In the eleventh century Salerno was famous for its medical school. If the term 'university' is loosely defined, Salerno can thus claim to have the oldest university with a continuous existence in Europe, although by a slightly more stringent definition of the term, this claim must be allowed to the University of Bologna.

Only in the eleventh century were these independent maritime states of Southern Italy to decline, when the Normans arrived, and competition from the northern ports of Genoa and Pisa became too strong. In the second half of the ninth century the Arabs were attacking Southern Italy from Sicily. They secured Bari for some years, having initially been employed as mercenaries by one of the Lombard dukes of Spoleto against rival Lombard claimants.

Also arriving first as mercenaries in Southern Italy, in the early eleventh century, were visitors who were to stay longer: the Norman knights. They fought indiscriminately for the Lombards against the Byzantines, and for the Byzantines against the Arabs. Unlike the South Italians, the Normans were fanatically Christian, and would never ally themselves with Moslems. After 1030 they began to settle. The most successful of the Norman knights was Robert Guiscard, who graduated from being a landless adventurer to assuming the title of Duke of Puglia and Calabria, and defeated the army of Alexius Comnenus, the Byzantine Emperor, at Durazzo in 1081. Guiscard took his titles as a vassal of the pope, enabling the papacy to claim sovereignty over Southern Italy. In the years 1072–91 the Normans conquered Sicily, and in 1130 a nephew of Robert Guiscard was crowned Roger II, King of Sicily, his father, Roger I, having united Southern Italy and Sicily into a single kingdom.

The Normans displayed a strange mixture of hard-headed *Realpolitik* and religious piety. When Pope Leo IX resisted their aggressions in Southern Italy, they made war on him, and defeated him at Civitate in 1053. They then accepted the papal blessing devoutly, and released him. They were thus perfectly suited to be a spear-head of the powerful movement of papal reform conducted by Hildebrand (c. 1020–85), who was created Archdeacon of Rome and Cardinal by Leo IX, and became Pope Gregory VII in 1073. That Hildebrand began his campaign as an idealist determined to bring the world under the rule of a loving God cannot be doubted. But to accomplish this ambitious aim he believed that the pope and priesthood had to assert their authority – the pope by insisting upon his prerogative in the appointment of bishops, and the priests by observing rules of celibacy and thus sharply distinguishing themselves from the laity. The great medieval confrontation between pope and emperor known as the 'Investiture Contest' is thus rightly named so far as its origin – the dispute over the investing of bishops – is concerned, but it became a struggle for power between Church and state, a struggle which was to reappear in several guises into modern times.

Other issues were caught up in the Investiture Contest. In Milan something approaching a class struggle was developing between the aristocracy who resisted the reforms which Rome was trying to impose on their priests, and a popular movement in favour of clerical reform. A strong man had established his rule in Germany, the Emperor Henry IV. To assert his powers over the church he invested as Archbishop of Milan a man who had resisted reforms and was unacceptable to Gregory VII. In 1076 Henry declared Gregory deposed, and in reply the pope excommunicated the emperor. The Saxon nobility insisted on the performance of penance by Henry, who, according to the traditional story, waited in the clothes of a penitent for three days in the snow outside the castle of Canossa, near Reggio Emilia, where the pope was living under the protection of the Countess Matilda of Tuscany, his powerful Italian ally. Henry's penance was an insincere move on the chess-board of European politics. He subsequently invaded Italy, and in 1084 entered Rome, to have himself crowned emperor, by the antipope, Clement III. Gregory's supporters, the Normans, retaliated by sacking Rome in three terrible days of violence. It was only after Gregory's death that a new emperor, Henry V, conceded most of the papal claims on the investiture question.

The struggle between pope and emperor provided a rallying cry for parties in Italy, parties within the city-republics, whose growth and importance will be considered in Chapter 3. But in the second phase of the struggle, which was inaugurated by Frederick Barbarossa, the German emperor, something approaching an 'Italian' spirit was to be shown by the cities of Northern Italy. Italian nationalists of the nineteenth century were to see Frederick I, the 'Red-bearded', as a foreign intruder, and while it is misleading to read the standards of nineteenth-century nationalism into Italian developments of the twelfth century, it would be equally misleading to assume that the people of Milan felt as alien from those of Bologna or Venice as they did from those of Frederick's retinue. Frederick invaded Italy in 1154, two years after his election as emperor. One of the excuses for his expedition was his intention to suppress a republican rising in Rome, a rising in which Arnold of Brescia found a leading role. Arnold stands out as a unique figure in Italian history, although the sources give only occasional glimpses of his career. Born about 1100, he was a strange mixture of classical and medieval features, which give him almost the character of a Renaissance figure born out of his time. He led a popular reform movement in Brescia against the bishop, and was banished by the Lateran Council in 1139. In France he supported the teaching of his friend, Peter Abelard, teaching which appears today so rational and revolutionary, and was not surprisingly regarded as subversive by the papacy. In the confrontation between Peter Abelard and a fanatically orthodox Saint Bernard of Clairvaux, Arnold was identified as a danger to the church, and for some years lived in comparative obscurity in exile. In 1143, hearing of a popular insurrection in Rome, he returned to Italy. The curious Roman Republic which he found there was evidently intended to be a restoration of the original one, with a 'Senate', and a 'Parliamentum', or general meeting of the citizens, who could accept or reject proposals put to them by general acclamation. Yet it was created rather in imitation of the Northern communes than from any clear knowledge of the insitutions of the ancient Roman Republic. Arnold gave it greater coherence, and united the various forces – popular, merchant and noble – behind it. The Republic lived out its dramatic life for over a decade, Arnold himself being excommunicated by the pope, and on Barbarossa's arrival in 1155, arrested and hanged. Yet this remarkable and dynamic product of the commune of Brescia had been a devout Christian, with great respect for classical scholarship, but mainly preoccupied with the purification of religion.

In 1162 Frederick Barbarossa destroyed Milan, an act which led to the formation of the Lombard League of Italian states, a league supported by the pope and the republic of Venice. When Frederick entered Rome in 1166 the pope, Alexander III, took refuge in the Colosseum, which must have been still intact. The next year a larger league came into existence, to resist Barbarossa. In the words of Cesare Balbo:

On the immortal day of the 1st of December 1167... the Veronese and Lombard Leagues joined in a single league Venice, Verona, Padua, Treviso, Ferrara, Brescia, Bergamo, Cremona, Milan, Lodi, Piacenza, Parma, Modena and Bologna, fifteen cities whose names will remain, whatever happens, always sacred to Italy.[5]

In 1176 the armies of the Lombard League defeated the imperial forces at Legnano, considered by Balbo to be 'the most beautiful battle of our history'. By the peace of Constance in 1183 Frederick recognized the full autonomy of the cities of the Lombard League under his nominal suzerainty.

Frederick died in 1190. His successor, the Emperor Henry VI, conquered Sicily from the Normans – an episode of Italian

---

[5] Balbo, *Sommario della Storia d'Italia*, p. 184.

history which will be considered in Chapter 3. But when Henry died in 1197, his succession to the empire was disputed between his own house of Hohenstaufen, and the rival house of the Welfs, or Guelfs. The Hohenstaufen, in the person of Henry VI's widow, Constance, could not hold Sicily without the pope's assistance. One of the most brilliant and successful popes in history was elected as Innocent III in 1198, and immediately assumed control of Sicily as the guardian of the infant son of Henry and Constance – Frederick, who was one day to be emperor and to have achievements even more colourful than those of Barbarossa, or even of Innocent himself.

By supporting the Guelf cause Innocent secured recognition of papal authority over most of Italy south of the Po. When Otto, the Guelf, tried to refute Innocent's claims, the Pope proclaimed the young Frederick King of the Romans. At Innocent's death in 1216, when Frederick was still only twenty-two, the Papacy was at the peak of its power in the Middle Ages, perhaps in the whole of history.

## 4 Venice and her maritime empire, c. 600–c. 1300

Precisely when and by whom Venice was founded is not known, but it seems likely that the first founders were refugees from barbarian invasions – perhaps that of Alaric the Goth in the early fifth century, or perhaps that of Attila the Hun in the mid-fifth century, which is the more popular tradition. There is some evidence that in 551 Venetians transported troops by sea for Narses, Justinian's general who was reconquering Italy for the Empire. There is much stronger evidence that a large settlement in Venice took place in 568, this time by refugees from the Lombard invasion. These refugee settlers accepted the sovereignty of the Eastern Emperor, but in the eighth century they took part in a general revolt against the Emperor Leo III (717–41). Leo had ordered that all icons and holy images throughout the empire should be destroyed. Pope

Gregory II (715–31) rejected the order, and was supported by the peoples of Byzantine Italy, including the Venetians. It seems probable that resistance to Leo III's puritanical orders was the occasion of the election of the first *dux*, duke, or – in Venetian – *doge*, and that he was called Orso. If so, Orso's place in history is a significant one, since he was the first of 117 doges who were to reign in Venice until the fall of the Republic in 1797 – more than a millennium later. The first doge listed on the walls of the Hall of the Great Council in the Doge's Palace is a Paoluccio Anafesto, said to have been elected in 697, but there is no reliable evidence that he ever existed.

Before the ninth century the islands of Venice felt little sense of unity, even though they accepted the authority of a single doge. But in so far as they were federated into a single body, their centre was Malamocco. The original Malamocco has since been washed away, but the name has been preserved as that of a village on the Lido. When Pepin and the French attacked in 810 the Venetians found unity against a common enemy. The people of Malamocco evacuated their women and children to the Rialto island, and when the Franks had been defeated, the Venetians decided to make that island their capital. It has remained the heart of Venice ever since. In 811 the ageing Charlemagne reached an agreement with the Eastern Emperor, Nicephorus, by which Charlemagne was recognized as emperor in the West, but Nicephorus as suzerain over Venice. It was purely nominal suzerainty: Venice was now undeniably an independent power. The links she maintained with Constantinople were cultural and economic rather than political, but they were stronger than any links she had with Italy.

The leader under whom the Franks had been repulsed was a Doge Agnello, who supervised the move to the Rialto island and started the building of Venice on the site where she is today. It was a city built on wooden piles driven into the mud and sand, and the houses, too, were of wood. A first doge's palace, of which nothing now remains, was built on the present site, and like the churches, but unlike the houses, of stone.

About 828 a Venetian merchant ship arrived from Egypt with what was said to be the remains of St Mark. Agnello's son, Giustiniano, had succeeded him as doge. Giustiniano was shrewd anough to realize that the remains of one of the four apostles gave Venice religious prestige second only to that of Rome. The body was buried in the doge's chapel where the Church of St Mark was later to be built. The emblem of St Mark, the winged lion, was to be carried throughout the Eastern Mediterranean in the years ahead.

Venetian strength and wealth were founded on commerce, but in stealing commerce from the Eastern Empire, Venice had to avoid a fatal breach. One of her most successful commercial diplomats was Pietro Orseolo II, elected doge in 991. In the year after his accession Orseolo clinched a deal with the Emperor Basil II by which Constantinople agreed to the import of Venetian goods with tariffs much lower than those demanded of other traders, Italian or whatever. For this favour Orseolo agreed to provide ships for the transportation of Byzantine troops when the emperor required it. But his diplomacy did not end there. When Otto III arrived in Italy in 996 en route for Rome for his coronation, Orseolo was quick to reach an agreement with him, an agreement by which Venice secured trading rights on the Italian mainland. In the eleventh century Venetian ships were thus sailing in great numbers on Italian rivers, but also, more impressively, throughout the Mediterranean to the Black Sea.

A drawback which Venetian commerce had to overcome was piracy. Slav – more specifically Croat – pirates in the Adriatic, operating from points on the Dalmatian coast, had repulsed a Venetian expedition in 887, in a battle in which the Doge Pietro Candiano had been killed. In the tenth century the Venetians paid protection money to the pirates in order to sail in the Adriatic. Pietro Orseolo halted the payments, and in encounters with the Croat pirates took the island of Lissa. Non-Slav, Latin, peoples on the Dalmatian coast, nominally subjects of the Byzantine Empire, sought the protection of Venice against the Croats, and in the year 1000 Orseolo extended the Venetian possessions down the coast to Split, or Spalato as the Italians called it.

The third and surviving church of St Mark was begun about 1063 by the Doge Domenico Contarini, and took some thirty years to complete, being consecrated in 1094 under Doge Vitale Falier. With its five cupolas it is a superbly Byzantine building, one of the finest in the world, though the Gothic elements in the façade were evidently the work of Lombards and Florentines in the thirteenth century.

The year after the consecration of St Mark's Pope Urban II summoned Christendom to a more desperate venture, by preaching the First Crusade for the recapture of the Holy Lands from the Moslems. The First Crusade moved primarily from France and Germany. Part of it, the People's Crusade, inspired by Peter the Hermit, was a tragic disaster. Great numbers of impoverished and disorganized crusaders died before reaching Constantinople. The more official part of the First Crusade, led by French nobility, succeeded in re-taking Jerusalem, but afterwards indulged in the most appalling massacre. Only in an indirect sense was the crusade a part of Italian history: the Venetians controlled the sea route to the Holy Lands, and Italian ships transported some of the armies. The Second Crusade (1147–9), organized by the Emperor Conrad III and Louis VII of France, managed to murder some ten thousand Jews in the Rhine Valley, but was less successful against the infidel in the Holy Lands. The Kings of England and France went on the Third Crusade (1189–92), but once again it was not of central importance in Italian history. However, there is evidence that Italians as individuals had responded to Pope Urban's initial call in 1095. A later letter has survived from the pope to the citizens of Bologna, warning them not to leave for the Holy Lands without consulting their priests, and their wives. Of the Italian ports, Pisa and Genoa prepared fleets in response to Urban's call, although probably with economic gain rather than holy warfare in mind. Venice, on the other hand, was reluctant to antagonize the Moslems – whether Arabs or Seljuk Turks – if it were possible to avoid doing so. Only after the French had occupied Jerusalem in 1097 did a large Venetian fleet set sail. They got as far as Rhodes, where it is believed that they may have been requested by the Emperor Alexius I actually to abandon the project. Alexius had originally appealed to the West for a manageable supply of mercenaries. The vast, undisciplined hordes who had arrived to fight a holy war had alarmed him, and he may well have preferred to do without the additional hazard of a huge Venetian fleet. In the event the Venetians clashed not with the infidel, but with their commercial rivals, the Pisans. After a long and savage naval battle, the Venetians forced the Pisans to agree to withdraw entirely from the Eastern Mediterranean. Pisa did not keep the agreement, but was to remain a bitter rival of Venice for several centuries.

Between the First and Second Crusades, in 1124, the Venetians besieged and captured Tyre from the Arabs. The city became part of the Christian kingdom of Jerusalem, but a third of it was left in Venetian hands. Venice now had the nucleus of an overseas empire, and the taking of Tyre was a comparatively creditable operation with the Doge Domenico Michiel present in person to prevent the massacre and destruction which usually followed crusading victories. In the 1160s Venetian commerce in the Eastern Mediterranean began to suffer from competition from Genoa and Amalfi as well as from Pisa. The Genoese had a settlement in Constantinople itself, at Galata, across the Golden Horn from the old city. In 1171 a mysterious assault was made on the Genoese settlement for which the Venetians, probably unjustly, were blamed. The Emperor Manuel ordered that all Venetians in the city, who numbered some ten thousand, should be imprisoned and their property confiscated. The grave incident marked the end of the long alignment of Venice with the Eastern Empire. The tower in Galata survived the disaster, and a fourteenth-century rebuilt version is still today a striking feature on the dramatic landscape of Istanbul. It houses a night-club where tourists are entertained by belly-dancing, which would no doubt have pleased the Genoese merchants of the twelfth century.

In 1193 a blind man in his seventies, perhaps in his eighties, was elected doge: Enrico Dandolo. In 1201, with the full approval of the Great Council and a huge public gathering in St Mark's, Dandolo agreed to provide fifty galley-ships and a large army for a crusade. When the expedition, consisting mostly of French crusaders, assembled in Venice the following spring, it became apparent that the Venetians could not be paid the full amount which they had been promised for the services of their fleet. The debt to Venice provided Dandolo with a bargaining counter and the possibility of achieving his own aim against the Eastern Empire, rather than Christian aims against the infidel. A year later, in June of 1203, the fleet reached Constantinople. The Venetian sack and acquisition of Constantinople brought immense wealth and empire. Although Michael VIII Paleologus was to re-take Constantinople for the Greek Empire in 1261, the Fourth Crusade opened the way to great opportunities for Venice. Not only the Dalmatian coast down to Albania, but Corfu, Crete, many other Greek islands, and even part of the Greek mainland in the Morea, were to constitute the Venetian empire. At the time of the Fourth Crusade, Venice, with Florence, was already probably one of the two richest cities in Europe. In the course of the thirteenth century she grew yet richer. But Genoa, too, was growing in size and wealth at great speed. Her population had probably reached 50,000 by the year 1200, and was to double in the next century or so. Commercial rivalry between Venice and Genoa led to wars in the second half of the thirteenth century, wars in which the Venetian fleets were generally victorious.

The Venetian constitution had become more sophisiticated over the years. The powers of the doge had been modified in 1172/3 by the creation of the Great Council, or *Maggior Consiglio*, an assembly of 480 Venetians, who were to be responsible for electing ministers to serve under the doge. The doge himself had in the past been elected by a general assembly, or *arengo*, but with the growth of the city this had become increasingly impracticable. The Council was now to appoint eleven electors, who had the privilege of appointing a doge. In 1297 the Great Council was limited to a closed circle of the nobility, and an oligarchy – but one of the most efficient oligarchies in history – was created.

A chapter on the early history of Venice should end on a happy note, with mention of one of the great travellers of all time. Marco Polo was born in 1254. As a boy he accompanied his father to China, and was received by the Mongol Emperor Kublai Khan, who had established Peking, the capital of the defeated Chinese Empire, as the centre of his vast realms. The Polos returned on subsequent occasions, and the Khan employed Marco as his own envoy, sending him to Burma and Southern India, and for some years making him in effect an honoured prisoner at his court. Not until 1295 did Marco Polo return to Venice. He gave an oral account of his travels, which was written up, probably originally in French, though no version was to be published until 1824.

## Chapter 3

# THE HIGH MIDDLE AGES

### 1 Sicily under the Normans and Frederick II, 1130–1250

The Normans had come to Sicily as adventurers with few skills other than the military one. But by the time Roger II was crowned king of Sicily in 1130, they had shown themselves to be able administrators, and – what was perhaps more remarkable – they governed with considerable tolerance and flexibility. The kingdom included Calabria on the mainland, and Roger I (1031–1101) was able to draw on Byzantine experience in administration, through Greek officials. But the Normans constituted an undisputed, if small, ruling class. The Sicilian population they ruled was, of course, an extraordinary ethnic mixture, in which Greeks and Arabs predominated. From Norman charters it would seem that whereas the Normans brought their own laws for their Latin population, they allowed Greeks, Moslems and Jews to retain their own laws and to be judged by their own judges. The distinction between religious and secular law was, of course, an ill-defined one. Moslem countries have usually regarded the Koran as the basis of any legal system, and when the Normans referred to 'Jewish Law' they meant religious practices in the family and society. Greek and Arabic were used as official languages alongside Latin. Moslems were not violently persecuted by the government, but they were regarded as an inferior group, much as Christians had been under the Arabs, and both

Moslems and Jews were discriminated against in tax policy. There is evidence from place names that many Moslems emigrated from Sicily and settled elsewhere in the Mediterranean area. They were replaced not only by Norman or French settlers, but by Italians, notably from Liguria, or Lombardy.

The architectural and artistic achievements of the Norman period in Sicily were considerable. If the men from the North brought with them their beautiful, astringent, Romanesque architecture, they blended it with oriental themes. Thus the Church of San Giovanni degli Eremiti at Palermo combines Romanesque arches with cupolas, so that it might equally pass as a mosque or a Greek or Norman basilica. Mosaics, like the impressive work in the great Abbey of Monreale, are unmistakably Byzantine, yet have movement and vitality not always present in Byzantine art. Palermo also became a centre of scholarship where Greek, Arabic and Jewish intellectuals could debate, free from censorship.

Roger II spread Norman rule to Malta and Libya. But Norman decline in Sicily started with the accession of Roger's successor, William I (1154–66), whose hold on the Norman feudal nobility, and on the towns, weakened. William was unfortunate, too, in having to deal with the dynamic English pope, Nicholas Breakspear, or Adrian IV. The King of Sicily was obliged to accept the right of the priests to elect their own bishops, and to recognize papal overlordship of his territory in mainland Italy. Norman rule in Sicily was to end with the death of William I's son and successor, William II (1166–89), who left no legitimate male heir.

William II's aunt, Constance, had married a Hohenstaufen king, who became the Emperor Henry VI in 1190. Constance was the legitimate heir in 1189, but her accession was disputed by Norman barons, who supported an illegitimate nephew of William – Tancred – who would prevent Sicily from falling under German influence, and who was supported by the Pope

Clement III. Tancred was established as king, until his death in 1194, when the German emperor invaded and was crowned king of Sicily on Christmas Day. But for Henry Sicily was simply a suprisingly rich outer province of the Empire, a source of loot. For three years, until his death in 1197, he conducted a campaign of appalling terror and torture. His heir, Frederick, was a child of three, destined to become one of the most remarkable figures in Italian history. Constance was still alive in 1197, and became regent. Before her death, the following year, she made Pope Innocent III, who had just been elected, guardian of Frederick, but for the time being German nobles asserted what authority there was in a scene of desperate anarchy.

At the age of fourteen Frederick took over the full powers of kingship. In the thirteenth century young teenagers were expected, and prepared, to accept heavy responsibility. Four years later he went to Germany to establish his position there. in 1215 he became emperor, but in 1220 returned to Sicily. Although German emperor, and patron of the Teutonic Knights, Frederick II was a southerner, half Norman and determined to make Sicily his base. In a sense he was perhaps neither a German nor a Norman but an Italian, if by 'Italian' is meant someone who speaks and writes a language which is recognizably Italian rather than Latin.

But the popes, too, were mostly Italian, and the papacy was to resist Frederick's domination of Italy. Rivals to the Hohenstaufen in Germany had been the Welfs, and it was at this time that the papal party in Italy assumed the name of 'Guelfs'. The pro-imperial party became known as the 'Ghibellines', an Italian version of the Hohenstaufen rallying cry: 'Hie Weibling'. But Frederick did not immediately break with the Papacy. On his return from Germany in 1220 he was crowned by the Pope Honorius III, in Rome, uniting his imperial German title and his regal Sicilian one. But when he failed

immediately to keep his oath to organize a crusade, he was
excommunicated. Subsequently taking an army to the Holy
Lands, in defiance of his break with the Papacy, he made
himself king of Jerusalem.

Frederick's position in history depends not on his audacious
military adventures, his relations with the papacy, nor his wars
with Guelf forces in Italy, so much as on the civilization
centred on his court at Palermo. His administration was a
blend of Greek bureaucracy and Norman feudalism, but more
fully integrated into a united state than it had been under his
predecessors. He maintained and deepened the religious
toleration which gave freedom of worship to Moslems and
Jews. He issued a code based on the principles of Roman law.
His insatiable curiosity freed him from the theological strait-
jacket of his age, and encouraged him to patronize Arab,
Hebrew and pagan Greek thought. The chief scholars at his
court were not themselves Arabs, but were men, like Michael
the Scot, who studied Arab science at second hand – or even at
third hand, through Jewish translators. Frederick made a point
of patronizing translations from the Arabic. It is only at rare
moments in history that an individual ruler with the intellectual vitality of a Frederick II has the opportunity to
experience so many cultures – in his case, Latin, Provençal,
Norman, Greek, Arabic and Hebrew. But his major importance
in the Italian context is perhaps that he patronized the Italian
vernacular, the language which was being created out of Latin,
with Provençal influences, the language which was to have its
full blossoming in the poetry of Dante.

If, as seems likely, the love poem usually ascribed to
Frederick was really his, the argument that he was not only an
Italian, but one of the earliest Italian poets, is a strong one. The
rhyme – not an unsophisticated one – laments that so
oppressive is his desire that he can find no peace, and even
laughter or sport makes him feel guilty:

che non mi lassa in posa in nessun loco;
sì mi stringe el disio
che non posso aver pace,
e fami reo parere riso e gioco.[1]

Frederick's founding of the University of Naples in 1224 gives the city its claim to having the fourth oldest university in Italy, and the eighth in Europe, after Bologna, Paris, Oxford, Vicenza, Cambridge, Palencia and Padua, in that order. His varied interests and abilities would have given Frederick the reputation of a *uomo universale* (the universal man, who excelled in many fields) in the fifteenth or sixteenth century. In the thirteenth century he was regarded with a mixture of awe and terror as, in the phrase of Matthew Paris, the *stupor mundi*.

A near contemporary of Frederick was a man who lived in a very different world: St Francis of Assisi. The movement of friars was essentially a product of Italy. Unlike the much broader movement of monasticism, which had pre-dated Christianity, especially in India, the movement of mendicant friars was essentially Christian, and especially did the Franciscans stress God's love of man, rather than man's fear of God. The monastic movement has escaped attention in this history so far, mainly because its impact on Italian history was an oblique rather than a direct one. But it should be remembered that the Benedictine movement had originated in Italy. Born near Spoleto, about 480, St Benedict had established the great monastery of Monte Cassino, and the Benedictine movement had done much to save European scholarship from the devastations of the sixth century.

Of the friars' movements the first was the Dominican. St Dominic had been a wholly orthodox Catholic, and had buttressed the pontificate of the great Pope, Innocent III, by preaching total obedience. Born about 1170, St Dominic was a Spaniard, and his work against heresy was mainly carried out

1 George Kay, editor, *The Penguin Book of Italian Verse* (Harmondsworth, 1958), p. 19.

in France. But many Dominican houses were founded in Italy, where he died, at Bologna, in 1221. He is buried in the Church of St Dominic in Bologna and his tomb is honoured by two exquisite Renaissance angels, one by Michelangelo, perhaps the least known of his works of finished sculpture.

The Franciscan movement did not get involved in the brutalities of the Inquisition to the extent that the Dominican movement did. Francis took the teaching of Christ literally (as few, if any, had done before), and preached poverty and the corrupting influence of riches. He had been born, in 1181 or 1182, in Assisi, the son of a merchant. After a youth of self-indulgence, he suddenly realized, in his early twenties, the true value of life, gave his possessions to the poor, and started to preach fundamentalist Christian communism. Such teaching was dangerous to the Church, and especially dangerous to the Papacy, but it must also be said that it was impossible for the Franciscans to organize themselves, undertake scholarship and build churches without dealing in finance. Pope Gregory IX (1227–1241) was involved in the desperate struggle with Frederick II, a hard enough task without also having to combat total truth and absolute selflessness – two of the most dangerous and subversive weapons in the political arena. It is perhaps to Gregory's credit that he retained some of the positive features of the Franciscan movement, while taking the sting out of it by turning it into something more akin to monasticism and closer to the Dominican movement.

If Francis is rightly remembered as a saint rather than a political leader, he has some claim also to being considered a poet. A pleasing feature in the history of the Italian language is the contrast between the two points of its origin – the rich court of Frederick II and the humble simplicity of the Franciscan movement. The *Cantico delle Creature* ('Canticle of Created Things') of St Francis praises God for the sun, the moon, the stars, the wind, the air, the weather, water and fire, the earth which sustains and governs fruit and coloured flowers and grass, those who forgive because of God's love, those who suffer in peace, and finally for the death of the body. Since Francis sees all the elements of creation as his brothers and sisters, he comes near to pantheism, or to a wonderful synthesis of humanism, materialism and Christian faith. If thirteenth-century Italy had produced only this one poem its contribution to human understanding would not have been negligible. *The Cantico delle Creature* was a worthy forerunner of the more sophisticated poetry which was soon to flow out of Florence.

## 2 *The city-states and the republics*

In the twelfth century and throughout the thirteenth and fourteenth centuries a new kind of political institution emerged in Italy – the city-states or city-republics, whose political organization became known as the 'commune'. The characteristics of this institution were that it was essentially secular, its executive officers were elected, by varying methods, and it had *de facto* independence, although often – and initially, always – under the nominal overlordship of emperor, pope, king or duke. Communes in their more typical form existed in North and Central Italy, but they were not unknown in the South. Naples, for example, retained a commune with a good deal of autonomy under several differing sovereigns. Palermo and Sicilian cities established independent, republican communes after the popular rising known as the 'Sicilian Vespers'. This chapter must start by considering the history of the South, and the background to the Sicilian Vespers.

Hohenstaufen power in Italy collapsed not long after the death of Frederick II in 1250. Frederick had only one legitimate son to succeed: Conrad, who wanted to move the fulcrum of the Empire back to Germany, but anyhow died in 1254. In Italy, however, an illegitimate son of Frederick, Manfred, was to seize power and rule for sixteen years.

Initially it seemed that Manfred might succeed as brilliantly as Frederick had done. He was not immediately opposed by the pope, and a Ghibelline party supported him in Lombardy, and a republican party in Rome.

But the pope did not reconcile himself to Manfred's power in Italy for long, and eventually a French pope, Urban IV, formed an alliance with Charles, Count of Anjou and brother of the French king, (St) Louis IX. A man of some ability, and even more ambition, Charles marched an army down the length of Italy, and defeated Manfred at the battle of Benevento in 1266. It was to be one of the decisive battles in Italian history, marking the beginning of Angevin rule – and long-lasting French claims – in Southern Italy. One last imperial army was to attempt to restore the Hohenstaufen position in Italy when a sixteen-year-old grandson of Frederick II, Conradin, a boy of great charm and brilliance, invaded Italy, in 1268, but was defeated by Charles of Anjou at the battle of Tagliacozzo. The beheading of Conradin shocked Christian opinion and was long to be remembered against the Angevins. But its immediate significance in Italy was that French influence had replaced German influence. French armies were to come to Italy at intervals until 1859, always in alliance with at least some native powers in Italy. The influence of the Holy Roman Emperors, on the other hand, was never again to be a very serious threat to Italian independence, but was to transform itself into Austrian or Spanish influence.

Having established himself in Southern Italy, Charles of Anjou tried to halt the growing strength of the communes, which had retained much autonomy under the Byzantines, Normans and Hohenstaufen. The citizens of Naples were courageous enough to continue operating the institutions of their commune, but they were an exception. The imposition of royal authority, however, when Charles became king of Sicily, improved justice by punishing the corruption and brutality of local officials, and heavily suppressing the common crimes of murder, theft and brigandage. Charles imposed heavy taxes, especially on the richer landowners, who grew increasingly resentful. The normal activities of an efficient, and in some ways enlightened, dictator characterized his rule: he repaired roads, reformed the coinage, imposed standard weights and measures, improved the equipment of ports, and opened silver mines. But he remained a hated foreigner, although he finally settled on Naples as the seat of his government, and probably came to think of Naples as his home, as Frederick II had thought of Palermo.

By 1282 Charles had become one of the most powerful men in Europe, not only as 'king of Sicily', which meant Southern Italy as well as Sicily, not only because he had a grip on papal policy, but also because he dominated his nephew, Philip III of France. He had also taken the title of King of Jerusalem, and had led a notable expedition to Tunis. More significantly, he was about to lead an expedition to Constantinople to make himself emperor. Since the Byzantine Empire had never fully recovered from the terrible sack of Constantinople in 1203 at the hands of the Franks and Venetians, his success was far from improbable. But Charles had enemies to the West in the shape of the House of Aragon, where, after Conradin's defeat, Sicilian exiles had settled in Barcelona. Peter III, king of Aragon, had married Manfred's daughter, Constance, in 1262, and could therefore claim to be the rightful heir to the Hohenstaufen, a claim which was to begin the long-lasting Spanish presence in Italy.

The event known as the Sicilian Vespers may have been the result of a conspiracy formed by the Aragonese and Sicilian exiles in Spain, but it is treasured in Italian memory as a spontaneous, popular rising against the foreigner. On Easter Monday, 1282, a Sicilian woman on her way to church in Palermo was assaulted by a French soldier, who was killed by the crowd. The rising which followed in Palermo spread throughout Sicily, taking the form of a massacre of the French. The citizens of Palermo held a public gathering, and declared an independent republic, in the spirit of the communes of Central and Northern Italy. The other towns and villages in Sicily followed suit, each preserving its own independence but joining a league against the Angevins, a league which recognized the nominal sovereignty of the pope, though Pope Martin IV himself refused to recognize the Sicilian popular authorities.

Five months after the rising in Palermo Peter of Aragon arrived in Sicily, and was proclaimed king, largely at the instigation of the nobility, who had asserted their control. Sicily, now under a Spanish dynasty, was thus separated from the Neapolitan mainland, which was still under the Angevins.

While these developments were taking place in the South, the North and Centre of Italy were experiencing the growing importance of the commune, partly the result and partly the cause of changes in society. A new middle class in the cities contained a great number of lawyers, who were to take office in the communes. Their most revolutionary characteristic was their secularism. The rule by bishops had disappeared, and the communes produced their own secular administrators, educated in law and rhetoric. Justinian's code was a basic classic in their education, but their reading went back also to pagan antiquity, with the study of Cicero, while they themselves began contributing on a considerable scale to the legal traditions: they were forming one basis for the humanist culture of the fifteenth century. The centre which was producing them was the University of Bologna, the first great school of law in European history. It is a mistake, however, to regard these lawyers and judges as 'a rising middle class' in the familiar sense. Many of them were from landowning families, even noble families. But there was a humbler, yet still literate, class of clerks (in the modern sense of the term), the notaries, whose main function was to make written records of business or legal transactions, and these men were certainly not noble, nor were they clerical (in the medieval sense of the word). By the late thirteenth century there were many such officials – perhaps 2,000 in Bologna and 1,500 in Milan.[2] Independent artisans – smiths, tailors, bakers, millers – who might be defined as a lower middle class, also grew in numbers as the cities became more prosperous. In the early thirteenth century they were also growing in political influence. Modena's town council already in 1220 had many artisans and shop-keepers, including fishmongers and clothes-repairers or rag merchants (*strazaroli*, more humble than the *sarti*, or tailors), as well as the always numerous smiths.

If the variety of classes exerting political influence was growing in the twelfth and thirteenth centuries, the populations of the cities were also growing rapidly. The assessment made by historians of population in the Middle Ages is, of course, approximate, and such rough guides as the extent of the area included in the city walls are used. Some idea, however, can be formed. It is estimated that Padua grew from about 15,000 around 1175 to rather more than 35,000 around 1320. Florence may have had 50,000 already in 1200, and nearly 100,000 in 1300. But many towns developed sophisticated constitutions and independence with remarkably small populations – sometimes with less than 50,000 people. By 1300 it has been estimated that only twenty-three cities of North and Central Italy had a population of 20,000, yet these places enjoyed a rich cultural life.[3] About 1340, just before the plague started to reduce Italy's population, there were four cities with populations between 80,000 and 100,000. They were Florence, Venice, Milan and Genoa. They were followed by Bologna and Palermo with about 50,000. Rome, in the

[2] Daniel Waley, *The Italian City-Republics* (London, 1969, rev. edn 1988), p. 15.
[3] Ibid., pp. 21–2.

Plate 4. Centre of Florence from the air

middle of the period when the popes were in Avignon, had only about 20,000.[+]

The central officials of the commune were the 'consuls' – a word brought back into use in eleventh-century Italy from the faint memories of the Roman Empire. At some stage consuls came to be elected and to acquire executive power. The first time the term appears in the records of medieval Italy is in

[+] J. K. Hyde, *Society and Politics in Medieval Italy. The evolution of the civil life, 1000–1350* (London, 1973), Map 5.

1081–5 when consuls were in office in Pisa. In Siena consuls appear on the records for the first time in 1124.[5] In these early days in the history of the commune, consuls exercised their authority alongside bishops, but the power of the bishop was beginning to fade. A very early example of consuls holding considerable power is provided by Genoa, where, in 1162, consuls were elected not only with judicial authority, but were recognized by the emperor to have the right to make war or peace, or sign alliances. The number of consuls in office varied enormously, even within the same city. Milan had twenty-three consuls in 1130, but only four in 1138, and the more normal number was two – as had been the case during the Roman Republic and Empire.

There was also variety in the methods of choosing consuls. Sometimes names were put to a general assembly for approval or disapproval by acclamation, as at Pisa in 1162. Often the consuls had to have executive decisions approved by a council, either a large, popular one, or a smaller one, packed with the rich. Councils of varying size, and sometimes two or three in number, took the place of the popular assembly, or *arengo*, as cities grew larger and the practical difficulty of formulating policy in a huge gathering became too great. Only in smaller towns did the *arengo* still operate. The councils were often themselves large assemblies, like the Great Council in Venice, usually of several hundred, and sometimes three, or even four, thousand. Verona, with a council of 1,285 in 1154, was not exceptional, but in such cases there would be an inner council of about forty. Methods of election of councils were varied, sometimes involving a system of indirect election of electors, sometimes the drawing of lots. If the drawing of lots appears a somewhat irrational way of choosing delegates, it at least diminished the risk of corruption. Members of a council were anyhow meant simply to represent the citizens, and in theory

[5] Waley, *City-Republics*, pp. 32–5.

the office could be performed by any sane adult. Fear of corruption played an important role in the evolution of the communes. Consuls were in office for only very short periods – sometimes only a few months. Sometimes, too, as at Gubbio, they were obliged to live in complete isolation during their brief periods of office, to avoid any contacts which could result in bribery.

Another kind of official, the *podestà*, was originally imposed upon the commune by the emperor when asserting his authority. Frederick Barbarossa appointed a *podestà* for each city he defeated or dominated in 1162, and the Lombard League of 1167 directed much of its energies against these imperial appointees. For nearly half a century afterwards many communes retained the title *podestà*, but now for an officer appointed by themselves to keep peace between parties within the commune. The *podestà* was usually someone from outside the city, and was not often asked to serve for more than a year. For this brief period he was entrusted with considerable power, and was expected to bring with him a board of judges, and his own troops to keep order.

The alternative to a republican form of government was that of a lord or *signore* – a personal or family despotism. Powerful families had indeed done much to form the communes and to shape and dominate their institutions. But the distinction between the two forms of government was not always very clear-cut, since *signori* often retained republican institutions, and often ruled in a paternal or benevolent manner, with the full confidence or approval of the citizens. Nevertheless there is a contrast between Florence, which retained the reality of a republic until 1434, when it accepted the very mild despotism of the Medici, and Milan, where a strong authoritarian government emerged over a century earlier. In Milan the della Torre family represented the popular party, while the Visconti represented the Ghibelline nobility. Ottone Visconti was made Archbishop of Milan by the emperor in 1262. His nephew,

Matteo (1255–1322), was made imperial vicar (*vicario*) by the Emperor Henry VII, destroyed the power of the della Torre, and extended Milanese control over Pavia and Cremona. Giovanni, also archbishop from 1349, secured the much greater prizes of Genoa and Bologna. But it was Giangaleazzo Visconti (1351–1402) who turned Milan into the predominant power in Northern Italy. By warfare, marriage alliances, and successful diplomacy generally, Giangaleazzo converted Milan from an Italian city-state into a European power.

The Visconti have had a varied press. The war between the Florentine Republic and Giangaleazzo Visconti in 1402 was proclaimed by Florentines at the time as a war for liberty – *libertas* – against the tyranny of the Milanese despots. Since Florence produced more historians during the Renaissance than Milan the interpretation was accepted by later historians, and repeated in a scholarly, if slightly exaggerated, form by a distinguished historian in our own day.[6] On the other hand Italian nationalist historians of the late nineteenth century and Fascists of the twentieth century admired the Visconti for resisting the French and building a strong Italian state.

The history of Florence in the later Middle Ages contrasted sharply with that of Milan. After the battle of Benevento in 1266 the Florentines had expelled the Ghibellines. Guelf Florentines, middle-class members of the guilds or *arti*, took over the government of the city. But the old nobility resisted the change, and became a violent element in the life of the city. In the fourteenth century the Guelfs were split into the Blacks, representing bankers, merchants and artisans, and the Whites, representing the declining nobility. Pope Boniface VIII (1294–1303), whose impact on the history of the Papacy will be considered later, made more extravagant claims in temporal affairs than any pope had ever made before. The Fraticelli – the fundamentalist wing of the Franciscans – condemned his

[6] Hans Baron, *The Crisis of the Early Italian Renaissance* (Princeton, 1966).

worldliness, and in Florence the Whites turned against him. But the Blacks accepted an alliance with Boniface VIII and Charles of Valois, brother of King Philip IV. The Whites, among them Dante, were forced into exile.

Temporary disasters, like the failure of the Bardi and Peruzzi banks in the 1340s, and – far more terrible in human terms – the Black Death of 1347–8, did not permanently alter the fact of Florentine prosperity. It was based on finance, commerce, and the wool trade. The *Arte della Lana* (the wool guild) employed over five thousand workmen. But it was precisely the poorer workers in the woollen industry, the *ciompi* or wool-carders, who were to rise in revolt in 1378. The poorest workers were not citizens, and were thus denied the vote for any of the elections in the republic. For a moment they secured the support of the lesser guilds, and some of them were even elected to office. A *balia*, or special commission, including many working-class members, held power for six weeks, and arranged for the creation of the new guilds in which even the poorest in the woollen industry would be represented. The aims of many of the *ciompi* were not all that radical, but others wanted a new social order. However, a second rising was not pushed to its conclusion, no leaders emerged, and the majority of workers were too hungry to struggle for long. But as the first urban working-class rising in European history, the *ciompi* deserve to be remembered.

The cultural achievements of the late medieval ages and the Renaissance will be considered later. They were made equally under republican forms of government or despots. It is impossible to say which were the more productive patrons, though it could perhaps be argued that elected republican officers were more conservative in their tastes than despots like the Visconti, or the Medici. Because historians have concentrated so heavily on Florence and Venice the impression has developed that the fourteenth century was a largely republican one, with despots taking over in the early fifteenth century, as the Medici did in Florence. But the communes in other cities – and not only in Milan – were already, by the end of the thirteenth century, dominated by single families, or *signori*. An oligarchy composed of many families had often been replaced by a dynasty, whether with or without the assumption of titles. Although the *signori* would sometimes cloak their despotism with a bureaucracy, their individual tastes would emerge in the patronage of the arts as in the formulation of foreign policy.

However, the fourteenth-century world of the communes can be seen as a transition from the Middle Ages to the Renaissance. That the Holy Roman Empire in its medieval form would never again dominate Italy was illustrated by the Emperor Henry VII's Italian expedition of 1310–13. Henry, already Count of Luxemburg, had been elected King of the Romans in 1308. His aims in Italy were pure ones: he wanted to end the conflict between Guelfs and Ghibellines, Blacks and Whites, and bring justice and peace. Dante's dream of universal peace placed great hopes in Henry, and Pope Clement V agreed that he should be crowned emperor in Rome. Henry hoped that rival factions in the cities would make peace, issue amnesties, receive back exiles. When this laudable programme went less smoothly than he had expected he punished the offending cities with needless ferocity. But Henry reached Rome in 1312 and was crowned emperor – not, however, in St Peter's, which was in the hands of Angevin forces opposed to the coronation, but in St John Lateran. When the pope transferred his sympathies to the Angevins, and the cities – Florence foremost among them – resisted imperial policy, it looked doubtful if Henry's programme could succeed. The question was quickly decided by his death in Pisa in 1313. The contrast between Dante's aspirations for Henry VII's expedition and its achievements could not have been greater.

## 3 The decline of the Papacy and the Avignon period, 1216–1378

Both the Holy Roman Empire and the Papacy declined at the end of the Middle Ages. The medieval empire was later to be transformed into the Habsburg territorial empire, but as Holy Roman Emperors the Habsburgs were to have only vague claims of authority throughout Germany and Italy. They were sometimes to rule parts of Italy as dynastic princes, but the Empire was never again to have the mystical significance it had claimed in the earlier Middle Ages. The Papacy, on the other hand, was not only to regain its temporal strength in the fifteenth century, but also its spiritual strength with the Counter-Reformation in the second half of the sixteenth century.

For an institution to conduct campaigns of gross violence it must clearly have considerable material strength. On the other hand, for it to feel the need to embark on violent persecutions it must have an underlying sense of insecurity and moral weakness. The Papacy had not suffered from moral weakness in the time of Gregory VII, but if it was more powerful under Innocent III (1198–1216), it also started on the process of destroying other Christian communities which did not accept a strict orthodoxy. The term 'crusade' was now employed not only for war against the infidel, but also for campaigns against heresy. In 1209 Innocent III started on the destruction of the innocuous Albigensian communities in Southern France. The next pope, Honorius III (1216–27) passed a death sentence for heresy in 1220. But the term 'Inquisition' was not used until the 1230s and the pontificate of Gregory IX (1227–41). The medieval Inquisition, it has been argued, was less savage than the Spanish Inquisition of the Counter-Reformation, and the reputation of the thirteenth-century Papacy has suffered from confusion between the two. The argument is a specious one, rather like saying that the pogroms of the Jews in Czarist Russia can be forgiven because they were on a so much smaller scale than Hitler's holocaust. Nor are arguments centred on the 'standards of the times' convincing, since there were churchmen in the thirteenth century who believed that conversions were only valid if they were the result of argument rather than terror. Heretics were burnt alive in Milan, Verona and Pisa during the pontificate of Gregory IX. Guelf-dominated communes allowed inquisitors to conduct burnings at the stake in Orvieto in 1268 and 1269, and in Florence in 1282. Standards with regard to the treatment of heretics had declined since the mid-twelfth century, when the execution of one particularly subversive heretic – Arnold of Brescia – had been reported with some horror. It had then been argued that the pope could not have been responsible, but that Arnold's death should be on the conscience of the lay authorities in Rome.

If a decline in the Christian spirit of the Papacy can be traced after the pontificate of Innocent III, there was one exception. A semi-literate hermit from Naples was elected Pope Celestine V in 1294. Perhaps slightly deranged, Celestine certainly fulfilled the demands of the more extreme Franciscans in the rigorous asceticism of his life. But after five months he was persuaded to resign, an act of renunciation to which Dante is probably referring when he condemns the 'great refusal' (*il gran rifiuto*) of an unnamed shade he meets in hell. Celestine had two distinctions after his resignation: his successor, Boniface VIII, imprisoned him, and a later successor canonized him in 1313.

With Boniface VIII (1294–1303) the Papacy reached the peak of extravagance in its temporal claims. Boniface came from a noble Italian family, and his main preoccupation was probably to extend his family's influence and wealth. Trained in the law, he may have had few religious convictions, but he made the largest claims for the temporal supremacy of the Papacy which had ever been made, or ever would be made. He embodied them in the Bull *Unam Sanctam* of 1302, which claimed supremacy in worldly as in spiritual affairs. He was said to have declared: 'Papa sum. Caesar sum', which would have been no more than an abbreviated, and more graphical, version of the claims of *Unam Sanctam*. Dante also met Boniface in hell, but considerably lower down than the meeting with Celestine.

The culmination in the decline of the Papacy in the fourteenth century was marked by the move from Rome to Avignon. The French pope, Clement V (1305–14), formerly Bishop of Bordeaux, stayed in France on his election, and his successor, John XXII (1316–34), also a Frenchman, made Avignon the seat of the Papacy, as it was to remain until 1377. Six more popes were to live out their pontificates in Avignon, in the period which came to be called the 'Babylonian Captivity'.

Without the pope Rome became a pale shadow of itself. Goats and cows grazed on the Capitol and in the Forum. At certain times the population is estimated to have fallen to something like 17,000. Churches which had been surrounded by houses came to be isolated in open ground, and were fortified against brigands. Natural disasters added to Rome's misfortunes during the Avignon period: two earthquakes, in 1346 and 1349, and the plague in the years between. The popes did not give up their claim to be the temporal rulers of Rome, and tried to retain their authority through agents. One of the more successful was a Spanish priest, Gil Alvárez Albórnoz, Archbishop of Toledo. Clement VI (1342–52) made Albórnoz a cardinal and sent him to Italy, where he preserved a degree of papal control for a while. But the immediate rulers of much of Central and Northern Italy during the absence of the popes were the *signori,* or lords, who established despotic rule, especially in the cities of the Romagna. The Ordelaffi family established themselves at Forlì in 1315, the Manfredi at Faenza in 1320, and the Malatesta at Rimini in 1334. Powerful families of the *signori* like these survived attempts by Albórnoz to dominate the Papal States, and eventually the popes from

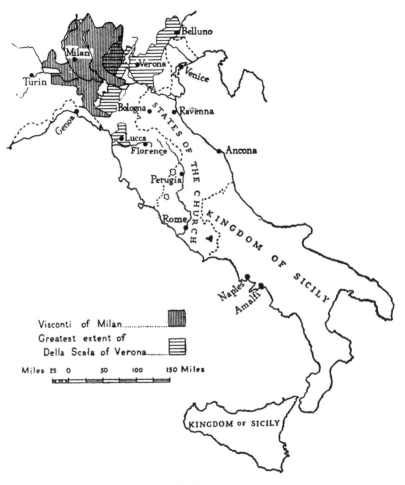

Map 3. Italy about 1340

Avignon recognized the *faits accomplis* and nominated the lords their vicars. The Este family at Ferrara had held power before the Avignon period, but in 1308 Clement V's authority had been recognized. In 1317 there was a popular rising in favour of the Este, who were to be among the most brilliant of Renaissance despots, and to survive as rulers in the Romagna into the nineteenth century.

The decline of the Papacy and the Avignon period

One of the arguments used by popes in the nineteenth century to justify their retention of temporal power over a Central Italian state was that when they abandoned it in the fourteenth century to go to France, they lost their independence and fell under the influence of the French monarchy. Paradoxically the stay in Avignon had really given the popes greater independence than they had enjoyed in Rome in the early years of the fourteenth century. Nevertheless the popes never regarded their stay in Avignon as a permanent arrangement. It was in Rome that St Peter had founded the Church and suffered martyrdom, and to abandon Rome for ever would have been a blasphemy. And although the seven popes of the Avignon period were all Frenchmen, they remained deeply involved in Italian politics, and – with the significant exception of Clement VI (1342–52) – rarely showed much respect for French or Angevin rulers.

In the history of Rome during the Avignon period one figure stands out with a certain quaint glamour. Cola di Rienzo briefly succeeded in restoring a republic in Rome, as Arnold of Brescia had done two centuries before. But whereas Arnold had been concerned primarily with the theological debates of early Christianity, Cola's idea of a republic was a more classical one. Born in Rome about 1313, the son of an innkeeper, Cola received enough legal training to become a notary. He read those Latin classics which had not been lost, or which were not still awaiting discovery, and he studied the remains of ancient Rome, and Roman inscriptions with their beautiful lettering. He was sent on two occasions to Avignon by the Roman authorities, to beg the pope, Clement VI, to return to Rome. He failed to achieve that end, but made a favourable impression on Clement who gave him an official title, though not that of 'consul' which he himself now assumed. His respect for the memories and remnants of the classical world was mixed with ecstatic Christian convictions, as that he was in touch with the Holy Spirit. On Whit Sunday, 1347, he rallied about a hundred mercenaries, deposed Rome's civic government, and declared himself and the pope's legate joint rulers of Rome. A few days later a popular gathering made him 'tribune' of the 'Holy Roman Republic'. He then appealed to all Italian governments to be represented in a parliament to consider how 'security and peace' could be obtained for *universa sacra Italia*. Before these extraordinary acts are dismissed as the fantasies of an over-heated imagination, it should be added that twenty-five Guelf communes sent representatives in reply to Cola's appeal. But the forces of orthodoxy united against him. Pope Clement realized that his earlier trust in Cola had been misguided, and his legate, with the help of the Roman nobility, drove Cola out of the city. After imprisonment at the hands of the emperor in Prague, Cola returned to Rome, where – ironically – the nobility succeeded in stirring up a popular rising against him, and in having him executed. It was a tribute to the man's unbalanced genius that Petrarch had hastened to Rome to support him, and it is undeniable that no one again was to speak of 'Italy' in exalted terms, and yet with a political programme to match those terms, until the nineteenth century.

Gregory XI returned from Avignon to Rome in January 1377, to find a ruined and half-deserted city. The papal church of St John Lateran, according to one account, had sheep and goats sheltering inside it. Papal headquarters were moved to the Vatican, which was better fortified, and included the formidable Castel Sant'Angelo. But Gregory lived for only just over a year after his return. On his death Urban VI was elected in Rome, but a few months later another conclave of cardinals at Fondi in Southern Lazio elected a rival pope, who took the name of Clement VII, and returned to Avignon. With the beginning of what was to be known as the Great Schism, when there were two claimants to the title of pope – or for a while, three – the Papacy and the Church reached a low ebb of their existence.

## 4 Cultural achievements in the age of Giotto, Dante and Petrarch

It sometimes happens in the history of art that a transitional period between two great schools or styles produces single works of immense worth. In the late thirteenth century in Italy a transition from medieval traditions – Byzantine or Gothic – to the first glimmerings of the Renaissance, a new spirit and new techniques, combined to produce one of the great phases in the development of the powers of human expression.

Although the most remarkable achievements were to be in painting and architecture, the first signs of the new spirit can perhaps be detected in sculpture. Nicola Pisano (c. 1225–84) has strong claims to being an ancestor of Renaissance sculpture. Little is known for certain of Nicola. By about 1250 he was living in Pisa, but it is believed that he came from Puglia, and may have worked initially under the patronage of Frederick II. His most important surviving works are the pulpits in the baptistery at Pisa and in the cathedral at Siena, and the fountain in Perugia. They show an understanding of Roman sculpture, combined with a new expressiveness.

But the artist who towered above all others in the age of Dante was Giotto, and the strongest influence on Giotto was the work and teaching of Cimabue (c. 1240–1302). Giovanni Cimabue was a Florentine, who worked in the church of St Francis at Assisi, and was later appointed superintendent of the execution of the mosaics in the cathedral at Pisa. Byzantine artists in Italy in the mid-thirteenth century had become heavily formalized in their work, and Cimabue's early works were inevitably executed under their influence. His later figures – Christs and Madonnas – have a solidity, and what can only be called a classicism, which were to enable Giotto to break into a freer and more natural world. But Cimabue was an inspired artist in his own right, and his reputation would perhaps be still greater if he had not been subordinated by the critics to the role of Giotto's tutor. As Dante said in *Purgatorio*, Canto XI, lines 94–6:

> Credette Cimabue nella pintura
> tener lo campo, e ora ha Giotto il grido
> si che la fama di colui é scura.

(Cimabue believed that he led the field in painting, but now it is Giotto's turn, so that the fame of the other is darkened.)

Giotto was born in 1267, near Florence, and is traditionally said to have started his life as a shepherd boy, before his discovery by Cimabue. A sculptor and architect as well as a painter, Giotto left one famous and exquisitely designed building: the *campanile* of the cathedral at Florence. But it was as a painter that he made his biggest impact. His near contemporaries already recognized that he was a quite exceptional innovator. In the years 1303–5 the son of a rich money-lender, Enrico Scrovegni, had an oratory built near his palace in Padua, inside what had been a Roman arena. The internal decoration of the chapel was entrusted to Giotto. To enter this modest little building is to undergo an artistic experience which probably cannot be surpassed, perhaps not equalled, by any available in Europe, whether it be that of entering the Sistine Chapel, or the Sainte Chapelle in Paris. Giotto's frescoes narrate the lives of Mary and Christ. What distinguishes them from the art which preceded Giotto is their sense of human drama, the immediacy of their psychological insight. Of the thirty-seven pictures two of the more remarkable are the scene of the dead Christ, where the surrounding figures express a deep poignancy of human grief, and the kiss of Judas, where the two heads – the serene and noble head of Christ, and the furtive and bestial head of Judas – are framed in a criss-cross of waving staffs and pikes, and the sweep of Judas' cloak. With such compositions Giotto made some of the rarer accomplishments of drama in art.

The architects of the period were also blending classical,

Plate 5. Detail from the fresco by Giotto in the Scrovegni Chapel, showing the Pact of Judas

Gothic and massively functional themes. The Palazzo Vecchio in Florence, designed by Arnolfo di Cambio (c. 1250–1301), is only one of the many superb communal palaces built in the thirteenth century.

In literature there was a beginning of an awareness of pagan traditions and thought. Between the mid-twelfth and the mid-thirteenth centuries there were translations into Latin from Greek and Arabic. Ibn Ruoshd, more often known as Averroës (1126–98), was an immensely influential Arabic philosopher, born in Cordova. Just as he had reconciled the Koran to the doctrines of Aristotle, so it was to a great extent through Averroës that Aristotle's philosophy was re-established in Italy. The work of Averroës was translated into Latin about 1250. His doctrine, that while man partook of a universal reason he did not have immortality as an individual, was inevitably condemned by the Papacy, though not until Leo X in the sixteenth century. The interpreter of Aristotle who was to find favour with the Church, and to influence the whole direction of Christian thought, was St Thomas Aquinas (1225–74). Educated at Monte Cassino by the Benedictines, and at the University of Bologna, Aquinas joined the Dominicans in 1243. His *Summa Theologica* was concerned to prove the existence of God, but to reconcile such a belief with Aristotle's respect for the validity of reason. Aquinas believed that true faith and sound reason were not in conflict, that the truth which Aristotle taught and the truth which Christ revealed did not contradict each other. It was a comfortable doctrine for the Church, and it had the beneficial effect that Italian Christianity never lost its grip on the real world, or its respect for good works. From 1252 to 1258 Aquinas was teaching his version of Aristotelianism – which he obtained from Latin translations – in the University of Paris, and was rescuing Aristotle from the taint of Averroism. Pope Alexander IV recalled him to Italy in 1258, and his doctrines have remained an orthodoxy to Italian Catholicism ever since. Dante's theology owed much to Aquinas, though exactly how much has been disputed.[7]

Dante Alighieri (1265–1321) towers over Italian literature as Shakespeare does over English literature, and as no single figure does over French, German or Russian literature. Dante was born in Florence, the son of a lawyer. His life was

[7] Bruno Nardi, *Dante e la Cultura Medievale* (Bari, 1942) argues that the influence of Aquinas has been exaggerated, and that Dante should be considered an original philosopher in his own right.

dominated by his meeting with Beatrice, who became for him an ideal, a symbol of perfection, and, in the *Divina Commedia*, the vision which guides him to heaven. In real life he married Gemma Donati, from whom he had seven children – six sons, and a daughter, inevitably called Beatrice. The Donati were a prominent Guelf family. Dante fought with the Florentine Guelfs at the battle of Campaldino in 1289, when the Ghibellines were defeated. In 1300 he became a prior – one of the six executive officers of the commune of Florence who held office for two months. A supporter of the White Guelfs, he was sentenced to exile in 1302 when the Black Guelfs came to power. He never returned to Florence. His movements during his long years of exile are not known precisely, but the last of them were spent in Ravenna, where he died and is buried. Until Dante there was no written vernacular language which would be understood by the literate throughout Italy. The first form of a written language is usually verse rather than prose. When Dante wrote in prose, he wrote in Latin, with the exception of the strange, original, autobiographical work, the *Vita Nuova*, which is a collection of verses linked by passages of Italian prose. His poetry virtually created the Italian language. In his unfinished Latin work, the *De Vulgari Eloquentia*, he traced the birth of the Italian vernacular from the Sicilian school to his own Tuscan school, and defended the vernacular as a suitable vehicle for serious poetry. His other important work in Latin, the *De Monarchia*, was superficially reactionary in that it looked for a return of imperial power in Italy, but profoundly radical in its vision of a world at peace under the twin complementary authorities of pope and emperor. The central point of his political philosophy, as of his theology, was contained in the simple statement in *Paradiso*, III, 85: 'E'n la sua volontade è le nostra pace' ('And in His will is our peace').

As a poet Dante emerged from the Florentine school, the *Dolce Stil Nuovo* (the 'Sweet New Style'), whose members were his friends. He, of course, used a far more powerful language than the one used by the other poets of the *Dolce Stil Nuovo*, but it had come from the same sources. An important source was the poetry of Occitan (Provençal) troubadours, who wrote in the twelfth and early thirteenth centuries. From lines at the end of *Purgatorio* it is evident that Dante understood and could write Occitan. The founder, and in a sense the leader, of the *Dolce Stil Nuovo* was Guido Guinizelli (1230–76), who, with a contemporary who lived until 1300, Guido Calvalcanti, wrote sonnets of a more sophisticated and elegant form than anything accomplished by their predecessors. But none of these writings can be considered adequate forerunners of the great poetic explosion that is the *Divina Commedia*. Not since the works of the Greek and Latin classics – perhaps not even then – had such powerful imagery been used to convey so rich a variety of human emotions. Dante's nightmare of the consequences of human greed, pride, weakness and the yet greater sins, and his dream of universal peace and divine love, marked the peak of European civilization in the Middle Ages.

Also exiled from Florence in 1302, with Dante, was a lawyer whose son was to have a place in the history of Italian literature second only to that of Dante himself. But Francesco Petrarca (1304–1374) was to enjoy a quite different kind of reputation from that of Dante. The immense contemporary reputation of Petrarch was based on his Latin writings, in particular his epic poem, *Africa*, and his collection of biographies, *De Viris Illustribus*. Petrarch was taken to Papal Avignon by his father in 1312. He went to Bologna to attend the university, but returned to Avignon in 1326. It was in Avignon that he became famous as a classical scholar, but his fame spread to Italy. He travelled in France and Germany collecting classical manuscripts, and found unknown works of Cicero. In 1341 he was crowned poet laureate by the senate in Rome. His fame today, however, is of course not as a classical scholar, but as a great lyric poet. The wonderful Italian sonnets which constitute the *Canzoniere* depend partly for their beauty on the tension created by Petrarch's Christian – medieval – piety, and his sensuality, which seems to owe more to the classical world and to anticipate the Renaissance. His love for Laura became, paradoxically, almost more sensual in his poetry after her death. He was to have a permanent influence on Italian poetry, an influence as strong in the twentieth century as ever before.

A close contemporary of Petrarch was Giovanni Boccaccio (1313–75). Probably also a Tuscan, Boccaccio came, however, from a rather different background than that of either Petrarch or Dante. He was the illegitimate son of a merchant, and he himself started on a commercial career, but abandoned it to live at court in Naples. Not entirely a dilettante, however, he took posts as a diplomat, travelled to Rome, Avignon and Brandenburg, and indulged in serious scholarship as a friend of Petrarch. Unlike Petrarch, he knew Greek. But his main gift to posterity was the collection of a hundred short stories known as the Decameron. Boccaccio wrote the Decameron probably between 1348 and 1353. It tells of seven women and three men who have been obliged to find a retreat in a villa in the Tuscan countryside to escape the plague which was killing so many people in Florence. In the course of ten days they take it in turn to tell each other stories. The results are the first European short stories, written with a robust sense of humour, but an exquisite balance and timing. In the most literal sense they were 'escape' fiction, and the terrible world from which they were providing an escape is the theme of Section 1 of the next chapter.

## Chapter 4

# THE RENAISSANCE

## 1 The Black Death and the economic recovery of the fifteenth century

In the age of Dante and Giotto, during the thirteenth century and at least the first two decades of the fourteenth century, Italy had experienced economic growth, in the sense that agricultural production and commercial activity had increased. There is some doubt as to continued growth in the period 1320–40, but if there were reverses, they were not great ones, although the population may have started to decline. In contrast the economic disasters of the middle of the fourteenth century were very real, and brought human suffering on a massive scale. There were four major famines between 1339 and 1375, which would not have been more disastrous than those of the previous century, had they not been accompanied by many wars. Large mercenary armies spread destruction. Perhaps the most impressive of these *condottieri* was the 'Great Company' founded in 1342, and led by an ex-friar, Moriale d'Albano. Later, others in the 1360s and 1370s were led by Ambrogio Visconti and the Englishman, Sir John Hawkwood, whose painting, by Paolo Uccello, is on the wall of the cathedral in Florence. But famines and wars were minor affairs compared with the horror of the Black Death of 1348, which struck when the resistance of Italians had already been lowered. One manifestation of economic decline had been the bankruptcies of great Florentine banking houses – the Peruzzi in 1343, the Acciaiuoli in 1345, the Bardi in 1346. In 1345 there were freak floods in the Po Valley. 1346 was a year of famine. But the plague was much more than just a culmination of these disasters.

The term 'Black Death' was applied in the seventeenth century retrospectively to the pestilence of 1348. In the fourteenth century it was simply referred to as 'the plague', in Italian 'la peste', a term which was used indiscriminately to signify infectious diseases. There are references to 'the plague' – not only to the Black Death of 1348, but to outbreaks of what were probably quite different epidemics – on into the mid-fifteenth century. But by the 1430s the rich in Florence, anyhow, had discovered that they could sharply reduce the chance of infection by imposing rigid quarantine measures, shutting up infected people. The effect of these measures was to make the rich almost immune, at the expense of the poor, and to ensure that outbreaks were less well reported.

The Black Death struck Europe with amazing speed and ferocity. Only in 1346 were there rumours of a terrible epidemic said to be devastating India, the Middle East and the Crimea. It was probably from the Crimea that Genoese merchants brought it to Western Europe. It reached Italy – or more precisely, Messina – in October, 1347, brought, according to a near-contemporary source, a Franciscan friar, by twelve Genoese ships. Soon hundreds of people were dying every day in Messina, while the survivors fled from the city, to spread the plague far and wide. Catania was the next city to be devastated. It spread in Italy at first from port to port: from the Sicilian ports to Genoa, Pisa and Venice, as most epidemics had done, and were to do, although the pneumonic plague was exceptional in the speed with which it soon spread inland, presumably because it was acutely infectious, and could spread from one infected person to another, without the intermediary of the rat and flea – the original sources of the disease.

The plague reached Genoa and Pisa by January 1348. It raged in Venice from February to August, and in the inland cities of Tuscany from March to September. Florence was perhaps worse hit than any other Italian city, and has left the most eloquent account of it in Boccaccio's introduction to the *Decameron*. According to Boccaccio over a hundred thousand Florentines died, though he adds that before the calamity no one would have imagined that the population of Florence was that high – nor, indeed, was it. Siena illustrates one sad victim of the plague in her unfinished cathedral. Beautiful as it is, even in its incomplete form, it would surely have been magnificent if the plague had not halted its building – apparently for ever. The pestilence reached the Romagna and Umbria in April. In Northern Italy it reached Milan and Parma several weeks later than Florence, and these two cities suffered less than other places.

There was no medical science worthy of the name which could handle the crisis. 'Doctors' considered it a scourge of God, or the result of unusual constellations. We now know, of course, that it was spread by fleas on the bodies of black rats, and that it came in two varieties – the 'bubonic' and 'pneumonic' plague. The bubonic version had the characteristic symptom of black boils, or buboes, under the armpits and in the groin, and usually, but not always, killed in a few days. The pneumonic version could kill in a few hours, without any visible symptoms, or it could lead to the coughing of blood and death in some four days: it was always fatal. The number of people who died in Italy during the plague is uncertain, and has been the subject of some debate. Contemporary, or near-contemporary, accounts spoke of some 70 per cent of the population of Venice, 68 per cent of that of Genoa, and something between the two figures for Italy as a whole. Historians and demographers today usually assume that these figures are grossly exaggerated, and prefer to cite a figure of one third of the population. Perhaps there has been a tendency to place too little credence in the contemporary figures: whenever specific groups, in which each individual can be identified, are known (as with priests in a given see) the figure is usually nearer a half than a third. And when more detailed studies of cities in 1348 have been made, as with Orvieto and Siena, it emerges that, indeed, one half of the population would seem to have perished.

The administrative structure of Italian cities stood up incredibly well to the disaster. Alongside the inevitable superstitious and panic reactions, sensible regulations were introduced. Wages were frozen, for example, doctors' salaries doubled – presumably to keep them at work – emigration was controlled, more severe penalties were introduced for crime, and arrangements made for the disposal of the corpses. Elections of officers in the commune continued normally. The Council of Seven in Orvieto were elected in June, 1348. By the end of July two were dead, and by the end of August four more were dead. The one who survived had been struck down by the plague, but recovered.[1]

Less severe plagues recurred at other dates in the fourteenth century. In Orvieto there are records of plague breaking out again in 1363, 1374 and 1383. As elsewhere in Europe, it became endemic until the eighteenth century. The contemporary records, however, are rarely conclusive evidence that the outbreak in question is really the plague, rather than smallpox or any of several famine diseases. But in Milan some form of pestilence is recorded in 1361, 1373 and 1382, in Florence in 1363, 1374 and 1383, and in Bologna in 1361–2, 1374 and 1382.

The economic disasters of the mid- and late fourteenth century inevitably slowed down the brilliant progress Italian civilization had displayed in the twelfth, thirteenth and early fourteenth centuries. Petrarch and Boccaccio survived the

[1] Philip Ziegler, *The Black Death* (London, 1970).

Black Death, but no literary figures of their stature were to
emerge in Italy for many decades. There was a corresponding
halt in artistic development. The revolution that Giotto had
presaged was not completed until the Renaissance of the early
fifteenth century. A smaller number of artists and architects
were bound to produce less significant work in the second half
of the fourteenth century. However, so strong a tradition had
been established that much fine painting, sculpture and
architecture was still being produced in the later fourteenth
century, and it is only in contrast with the astonishing
achievements of the late thirteenth and fifteenth centuries that
an artistic lull can be traced. The exact dates of births and
deaths of artists in the fourteenth century are rarely known.
They were born and died 'circa' this, and 'circa' that. One such
was Ambrogio Lorenzetti, who painted the wonderful murals
in the Palazzo Pubblico in Siena entitled 'The Effects of Good
Government' and 'The Effects of Bad Government'. The latter
has unfortunately not been preserved in a state in which it can
be appreciated, but 'The Effects of Good Government' pro-
vides a vital and sophisticated panorama of Italian life just
before the disaster. Lorenzetti is traditionally said to have died
'circa 1348'. He was not alone.

If the disasters of the mid-fourteenth century had brought a
lull, the economic recovery of the fifteenth century brought the
brilliance of the early Renaissance. Italy had for long enjoyed a
primacy in economic affairs. Tuscan cities had prosperous
merchant banks in the thirteenth century. The Florentine
houses of Bardi and Peruzzi in the first twenty years of the
fourteenth century had no equal for the scale of their business
operations in the whole of Europe. The golden unit of currency
taking the name of Florence – the florin – was used for
international exchange all over the continent wherever barter
had been replaced by coinage. A piece of silver coinage called a
'florin' was still in use in Britain in the middle of the twentieth
century. Before the Black Death the Florentines were minting

some 400,000 gold florins a year. It had first been minted in 1252, and in the same year the Genoese had produced a gold coin, the *genovino*. The Venetian golden ducat had appeared in 1284.

After the terrible depression of the second half of the fourteenth century, the fifteenth century combined financial sophistication with renewed economic growth. Capital investment in land and trade encouraged greater productivity. In the North huge schemes of drainage and irrigation were undertaken. Canals were dug; marshlands were turned into ricefields. The mulberry was introduced on a vast scale, and the silk industry developed, to some extent replacing the woollen industry, which was beginning to decline in the face of foreign, especially English, competition. In Tuscany many hillsides which had been waste-land were cultivated. Formerly deserted countryside became alive with people. These were characteristics, however, of Northern and North-Central Italy. Around Rome and Naples reverse processes were sometimes occurring. The contrast between North and South, which was to become so familiar a feature of modern Italy, was appearing.

Economic expansion required investment, and it was in the widespread adoption of credit finance that fifteenth-century Italy was so innovative. Usury had been defined as a sin in the Middle Ages. Dante says in the *Inferno* that 'usury offends the divine goodness' ('usura offende la divina bontade'): it is an unnatural way of earning a livelihood.[2] Clement V condemned it in a bull of 1312. But in practice the charging of interest in moderation had come to be regarded as a legitimate compensation for the risk of lending or investing. Usury came to mean not simply the making of money from money – or capitalism – but the charging of excessive interest. Banks clearly could not exist unless they could charge for their services, and one service was the conversion of one kind of coinage into another

---

[2] *Inferno*, Canto xi, lines 95–6.

– gold into silver, or one currency into another. The Medici
bank in Florence specialized in exchange banking. When loans
were made by physically transferring coinage or bullion, on
what Fernand Braudel has called an 'unending flow of mule
trains', from one coast of Italy to another, or even from one end
of Europe to another, it was clear that a great risk was
involved, and the lender or investor deserved some interest.
The development of credit finance may have brought with it a
new kind of risk, but it immensely facilitated the operation.
The cheque was first used in Pisa in the fourteenth century,
and was in common use, especially in Genoa, by the middle of
the fifteenth century. Insurance was another aspect of modern
finance which developed in fifteenth-century Italy. The Florentines led the way, under-writing two thirds of Venetian
maritime trade by 1400, while the Genoese and the Venetians
themselves had taken over much marine insurance by 1450.
The methods of modern capitalism were spreading in Renaissance Italy.

But the days of Italian economic primacy in Europe were
numbered. In 1492 the American continent was visited by a
European (it could hardly be said to have been 'discovered',
since there were already people living there), and in 1499 a ship
sailed around the southern tip of Africa to India. The
Mediterranean would one day lose its importance in a larger
world. The second of these two events was the achievement of
a Portuguese, Vasco da Gama, and the Portuguese led the way
in the voyages of discovery. But the first of the two events was
the work of an Italian, and one of the most remarkable men in
history. Cristoforo Colombo, known to his Spanish employers
as Cristóbal Colón, was born in Genoa in 1451. Attempts by
the Spanish and Portuguese to deny his Italian origins are no
longer accepted. He was the son of a humble worker in the
woollen industry, and at fourteen went to sea, to lead a sailor's
life of adventure and danger, very much as Giuseppe Garibaldi
was to do from that part of the world three and a half centuries

later. Before Colombo was thirty, or had any position in the world, he conceived the amazingly imaginative idea of sailing westwards to reach India, and possibly find a shorter route than the slow land route across the Middle East. His attempts to secure the patronage of John II of Portugal, Henry VII of England (not the most generous of men) and the Duke of Medina failed, but after hesitations Ferdinand of Aragon and Isabella of Castille accepted his proposals in 1492. Before the year was out, he had 'discovered America', or, more precisely, landed in what – rightly respecting his blunder – have ever since been called the 'West Indies'.

Posterity has shown less respect for Columbus in naming the new continent after another Italian, Amerigo Vespucci. Born in Florence in the same year as Colombo, Vespucci at least sighted and explored the coastline of South America – where Venezuela is today – in 1499. More impressive claims concerning him have proved to be false, but he succeeded – by whatever means – in giving the new continent an Italian name.

## 2 Humanism and the impact of printing

In sailing across the Atlantic and finding a new world an Italian had in one sense inaugurated 'modern times', and deprived the Mediterranean of its central position in the world. But much earlier in the fifteenth century Italy could claim to have given birth to 'modern times' in several other senses, and especially in scholarship. In the Middle Ages scholarship had been largely a monopoly of the Church. In the fourteenth century there were already appearing in Italy scholars who were laymen – lawyers, doctors, secretaries to political leaders. These men were concerned with the rediscovery of classical learning – the learning of Greece and Rome – and came to be called 'humanists', in that they were preoccupied with human culture, society and values, rather than with theology. They anticipated Alexander Pope's dictum on the 'proper study of mankind'. The term 'humanist' did not, of course, mean that they had rejected Christianity, except in a very few cases, but it did mean that the focus of their attention had moved away from the theocentric world of the Middle Ages.

In the late fourteenth and early fifteenth centuries humanist scholars were sometimes elected to high office and became political leaders themselves. Two of the scholar-statesmen who pioneered the civic humanism of the Renaissance were Coluccio Salutati (1331–1406) and Leonardo Bruni (1369–1444). Salutati grew up in Bologna, where he studied the law. He was Chancellor of Florence for no fewer than thirty-one years, from 1375 to 1406, in an age when offices usually changed hands with great rapidity. As chancellor he played the role of a modern administrator, conducting day-to-day correspondence, and exerting a full political responsibility. One of the world's great letter writers, Salutati could mix abstract philosphical reasoning with friendly comment on everyday life. During the three-year war between Florence and the Papacy, he showed himself to be a brilliant propagandist and rhetorician, depicting the struggle as a war for republican freedom. But his political idealism was perfectly merged with his love of the classics. Although he never acquired a very full knowledge of Greek himself – if rather more than Petrarch did – he established a chair of Greek in the University of Florence, which had been founded only in 1349.

Salutati broke with the Middle Ages in several senses. He admired the activities of this world – politics and prosperity – and saw marriage in a far more positive light than the medieval devotees of St Paul had ever done. In the *De Fato et Fortuna*, written in 1396–7, Salutati argued that although God had laid down an irreversible programme for the universe, man is yet responsible for his acts of good or evil, and that although this seems illogical it must be true. The human will and human morality were therefore not controlled by God, but were man's responsibility. Salutati came to believe that an active public life, which could benefit others, was more praiseworthy than a monastic life, which could benefit only the individual monk. It was a belief that lay at the base of Italian humanism.

Leonardo Bruni, belonging to a later generation than Salutati, but much influenced by him, also had an active and distinguished political career. Papal Secretary from 1405 to 1415, he was made Chancellor of Florence in 1427. He wrote a history of Florence in a Latin as close to that of Cicero as he could manage. He translated Aristotle, and those fragments of Plato that had not been lost, into Latin. He believed that the discoveries which were being made of the ancient classical world would bring a return to civilization after the darkness of the Middle Ages. Although he wrote lives of Petrarch and Dante in Italian, he believed that Ciceronian Latin – as cosmopolitan as medieval Latin, but far more subtle, elegant and expressive – should be the written language of the new age. He was a convinced republican both in his writing and in his life. While Dante had put Brutus at the bottom of Hell, hanging from the mouth of Satan and being eternally devoured by him, because Brutus had killed Caesar, Bruni believed that Brutus had been a hero who had risked his life to save the republic. Bruni was convinced that an independent Florence, and the democratic communes, had been on the side of progress against the imperial traditions of the Ghibellines, and, in his own day, against the Visconti of Milan. The struggle from 1390 to 1402 between a free Florence and the despotism of Giangaleazzo Visconti was to set a problem for Italian nationalists of the future. The Florentines believed, with some reason, that they were fighting for freedom, the freedom of the independent Italian communes, but many Italians believed that the Visconti were fighting for Italian unity under a highly cultured native prince. Not for the first nor the last time the causes of freedom and independence seemed to be at odds with the cause of national unity.

Salutati had inaugurated, and Bruni and others had developed, an attitude to life which no longer set great store by the medieval values of piety, humility and poverty. The accumulation of wealth, and the employment of credit finance, were no longer viewed with suspicion. The medieval condemnation of usury was modified. But the new attitude did not amount to a rejection of Christianity, only to a rejection of the medieval version of Christianity. The rediscovery of the ancient world was bound to bring pagan elements into Renaissance thought and culture, but they were nearly always to co-exist with Christian faith. The civilization of fifteenth-century Italy was secular rather than pagan. People still went to church. Rich merchants and bankers may have preferred paintings of pagan themes or profane portraits, but they still left generous bequests to religious houses.

Knowledge of Greek literature and philosophy had been largely lost in medieval Italy. Aristotle's reputation as 'the Philosopher' had been owed to Latin translations and comments by Roman writers. There was once a traditional belief that the fall of Constantinople to the Turks in 1453 led directly to an exodus of the first Greek scholars to Italy. The truth is more complicated, as truth has a habit of being. Long before 1453 Greek scholars had come to Italy, one of the first being Emmanuel Chrysoloras (1350–1415), who, already before his arrival in Venice, had given lessons in classical Greek to the Italian, Guarino da Verona (1374–1466), in Constantinople. Before the end of the fourteenth century Chrysoloras was teaching Greek in Florence, and counting Leonardo Bruni among his students. Other Greek scholars came to attend the Council of Florence in 1439. One aspect of the Renaissance was the rediscovery of Plato. The *Timaeus* – not the most important of Plato's many works – had survived in the Middle Ages, but the *Republic* had been lost. Dante displayed an understanding of Aristotle, but gave in the *Convivio* a very garbled version of the thought of Plato, a version wholly dependent on Cicero. Marsilio Ficino's major work as translator of Plato came in the later fifteenth century, and will be considered below, but already in the early years of the century Bruni had translated several of Plato's works, and already considered Plato the greatest of philosophers. Plato's concern with the individual human soul endeared him to the writers of the Italian Renaissance.

The early phase of the Renaissance in Italy, however, was a Latin rather than a Greek one, not surprisingly since the ruins of ancient Rome were omnipresent. Archaeological activity in Rome had a profound influence on Renaissance architecture. Pomponio Leto (1428–98) founded a 'Roman Academy' for the pursuit of archaeological interests, but fell foul of Pope Paul II when his pagan beliefs led him to conspire against the Papacy. A greater danger to the Papacy was the work of Lorenzo Valla (1407–57), an earlier humanist who, in his way, was equally sceptical of medieval values. The 'Donation of Constantine', the forged document from the fifth century, which purported to make a gift of the Western Empire from Constantine to the pope, has been mentioned in Chapter 2.1. Its legal validity had been rejected by several writers, including Dante, but its authenticity as a document had not been doubted. Valla was the first scholar to realize that it was a forgery, written at least a century after Constantine's death. In a brilliant treatise Valla used historical argument and literary textual criticism to show that the claims of the papacy were based on a long-lived fraud. The 'Donation' was expressed in a debased Latin which was incompatible with the claim that it had been written at the time of Constantine. So far as historical argument went, Valla pointed out that there were no other records of reactions to the Donation. How did the pope respond? What steps did he take to accommodate the gift? What governors did he appoint to administer newly acquired provinces? With a surprisingly modern flash of humour, Valla adds:

> 'We know nothing of these things', you will say.
> I see. So they took place at night and no one saw.

What Valla had done was no less than to claim that historical and literary scholarship were autonomous disciplines, which could exist on their own without reference to tradition or authority. He, like other humanist scholars, was anticipating the outlook of the modern world. All the same, the anonymous monk, whose forgery had been undetected for a thousand years, deserves his own niche in history.

In the second half of the fifteenth century interest shifted from Latin and Cicero to Greek and Plato. Florence under the two great Medici – Cosimo and Lorenzo – will be considered in the next chapter, but mention must here be made of Marsilo Ficino (1433–99) and the Platonic Academy which he founded in Florence, under the patronage of Lorenzo de' Medici. Unlike the earlier humanists Ficino was not only a Christian, but a devout one, and he was concerned to reconcile Plato with Christianity. His massive achievement in translating Plato into Latin gave Western Europe its first full knowledge of Platonic philosophy.

A greater genius than Ficino was his young friend Pico della Mirandola (1463–94), who had only brief contacts with the Platonic Academy, but was an accomplished Platonist. Pico was not a humanist in the narrow sense of being a classical grammarian, but in a deeper sense his work marked the highest point in Renaissance humanist philosophy. His scholarship included a knowledge of Greek, Latin, Hebrew, Arabic and Thomistic Christian philosophy. He believed that a grain of truth could be extracted from every system of thought or creed, but the result of the extractions in his case was an immense respect for the place of man in the universe. He composed 900 theses, and invited all comers to debate them with him in Rome in 1486. Pope Innocent VIII, less broad-minded than other Renaissance popes, detected heresy in a few of the theses, and would not allow the debates to proceed, but his successor, Alexander VI, absolved Pico of heresy. Yet

Pico's theses were more radical, if less significant for European history, than Luther's ninety-five theses, composed thirty-one years later. Pico's famous 'Oration', later called 'Oration on the Dignity of Man', contained an understanding of the nature of mankind which the nineteenth-century historian, Jacob Burckhardt, called 'one of the noblest of that great age'.[3] In the 'Oration' Pico makes God say to Adam:

I have set you in the midst of the world that you may the more easily see all that is therein. I created you a being neither heavenly nor earthly, neither mortal nor immortal only, that you may be free to shape and overcome yourself... To you alone is given a growth and a development depending on your own free will. You bear in you the germs of a universal life.

The achievement of Pico, who died at the age of thirty-one, might have been considered simply an eclectic one, if it had not been for his grand respect for human values.

Humanism in its later phase received a large boost from the invention of printing, which, although coming from Northern Europe, was developed on a commercial scale in Italy, and specifically in Venice. It was in the last quarter of the fifteenth century that Venice made its great contribution. John Gutenberg's printing industry with movable type had started in the Rhineland only about 1450. By 1470 two other German craftsmen had gone to Venice with the skills and tools of printing. One of them, John of Speyer, set up business there, but operated very slowly, printing only 100 copies of Cicero's letters in four months. Still, this compared favourably with the speed of copying by hand, which was a laborious business, though inevitably a major industry before the invention of printing. When Cosimo de' Medici in the earlier fifteenth century wanted to found a library at the Badia, now the home of the European University, he employed the Florentine

---

[3] *The Civilization of the Renaissance in Italy* (1860; Phaidon edn, London, 1944), p. 215.

scholar Vespasiano, who, with forty-five assistants, took twenty-two months to produce 200 volumes of manuscript. They were beautiful objects, and printed books were to meet much resistance on aesthetic grounds. John of Speyer's second edition of Cicero's letters increased his speed six-fold. Soon a lively trade in printed books was being conducted from Venice, exports going all over Europe, and eastwards as far as Poland. The paper industry of the little town of Fabriano in the Apennines had always supplied Venice: its trade now boomed. Until the end of the fifteenth century Venice was printing a huge proportion of the books in the world: to be precise, in the three years 1495–7, 447 publications came from Venice out of only 1,821 from everywhere. Second to Venice, Paris produced only 181 publications. In the sixteenth century Venice retained her predominance in Italy, with 113 publishers operating, and printing three and a half times as many books as Rome, Florence and Milan together.[4]

The genius behind the Venetian printing achievement was Aldo Manuzio (c. 1450–1515), or Aldus Manutius, to give him his professional Latin name as a humanist scholar. He had started his famous Aldine Press with the specific purpose of making the Greek classics more widely available. By operating in Venice he could use the services of the several Greek scholars who had settled in the city, and the manuscripts which Cardinal Bessarion had collected there. Prominent among the Greek scholars was Marcus Musurus, with whose help Manuzio formed a Greek Academy. The poet and grammarian Pietro Bembo (1470–1547) was the librarian of the collection which Bessarion had given to the Republic, and Bembo's enthusiasm was also a support for Manuzio. Erasmus worked for a while with the Aldine Press, apparently as a humble proof-reader, although he later claimed that he read proofs only of his own work. Manuzio also printed books in Hebrew

[4] Frederic C. Lane, *Venice. A Maritime Republic* (Baltimore, 1973), p. 311.

110

characters, and illustrated his books at first with woodcuts, and later with copper engravings. The argument that printed books were less beautiful than manuscript ones would no longer go unchallenged. Manuzio designed and used italic type in 1501, the type used by the humanists, and rapidly familiar in Northern Europe as well as Italy. Roman type for print was already developed in the 1470s. Gothic type rapidly disappeared before the advance of the clearer and more classical types; only in Germany did Gothic type persist on into the twentieth century. Manuzio also invented the *octavo*, a page half the size of the *quarto* previously used, and more suitable for printed books.

Editions of the Greek and Latin classics were not the only concern of the Venetian publishers. Plays and dialogues in Italian were published, like those of the satirist, Pietro Aretino (1492–1557), whose work would be considered libellous today, and a great number of commercial handbooks, religious tracts and almanacs.

Fernand Braudel, in one of his sweeping generalizations, makes the somewhat preposterous statement that the Renaissance reached Venice only 'with the end of the sixteenth century'.[5] Even if the masterpieces of the Bellini were discounted, a consideration of Manuzio and his Greek scholars would be enough to refute the statement. The importance of printing in history is so immense that the literary nature of European civilization may be said to have depended on it, and on the fact that the first mass-production industry had the book as its product. Several centuries before Europeans were mass-producing cotton shirts, sausages or motor cars, they were mass-producing books. But what Braudel was thinking was, of course, that a greater creative activity was in progress in the fifteenth century in Florence than in Venice.

---

[5] *The Mediterranean and the Mediterranean World in the Age of Philip II* (London, 1972), vol. I, p. 133.

The Renaissance

## 3  Florence under the Medici and the Republic

Florence in the fifteenth century was in the vanguard of civilization. In terms of cultural achievement, peace and prosperity, the peak may be said to have been reached under the early Medici in the period 1434–92. In that period three of the Medici family successively ruled Florence, but the two significant figures were Cosimo, who was in control from 1434 to 1464, and Lorenzo 'il Magnifico', who ruled from 1469 to 1492.

The two men took no title, and controlled what was theoretically still a republic, with complex republican institutions. Only on very rare occasions did they take any office themselves, yet their indirect influence gave them despotic power in practice. The head executive officer, or *gonfaloniere*, had very prescribed powers, and was elected for only two months. He had to be a member of one of the seven great guilds, or *arti*. The class system, and the predominance of the class of merchants, bankers and industrialists, was thus enshrined in the constitution. The greater guilds, or *popolo grasso* (fat people) had the dominant position, but the lesser guilds, or *popolo minuto* (small people), were represented in government. Beneath the *gonfaloniere* were eight other executive officers, the *priori*, six of whom had to be from the greater guilds, but two from the lesser guilds. The *gonfaloniere* and the *priori* were together known as the *signoria*, and they held office in the great medieval palace, the Palazzo Vecchio, the work of Arnolfo del Cambio, built in 1298, in the life-time of Dante. The old aristocracy was a suppressed class, allowed only a small role by the constitution. Of the two legislative houses, the upper or *consiglio del comune* was elected on a constituency basis by the four *quartieri* – quite literally the four 'quarters' of Florence, which still exist today. The nobility were allowed seats on the *consiglio del comune*, but not on the *consiglio del popolo*, or lower house, which was confined to the *arti*.

Citizenship was restricted to members of the *arti*, who could together be summoned by the bell in the Palazzo Vecchio to meet in a *parlamento* in the piazza. The *parlamento* provided the ultimate constitutional sanction: propositions put to it by the *signoria* could be approved or disapproved by the shouts of the citizens.

These republican institutions had, of course, existed before the Medici, but they had not prevented another family, the Albizzi, becoming dominant for the long period from 1382 to 1432. The Albizzi represented the rich middle class, and it was as a representative of the lesser middle class, the *popolo minuto*, that the banker Giovanni de' Medici became prominent and was elected *gonfaloniere*. Giovanni died in 1429. His son, Cosimo, had been driven into exile in the Albizzi period, but returned in 1434, to become the virtual ruler of Florence for the next thirty years. He received the full humanist education, was familiar with Latin literature, and even knew some Greek. Yet he remained at heart a merchant banker, a somewhat grim, serious man who not only retained control of the Medici banking house, but built it up into a great international concern. But it was as a statesman that he made his mark on history. It was he rather than any other single ruler who gave Italy the peace and comparative prosperity in the mid-fifteenth century that provided the setting for the artistic achievements of the early Renaissance.

Cosimo's patronage of the arts was not simply a by-product of his wealth and dilettante interests. He was deeply involved in the work of artists, architects and scholars, as his grandson, Lorenzo, was to be. He inherited a dynamic artistic scene. One of the most significant painters of fifteenth-century Florence, Masaccio (1401–c. 1428), was almost certainly dead before Cosimo returned from exile. The revolution in painting which Giotto had started, but which had lost its steam after the plague of 1348, was revived by Masaccio. His frescoes in the Brancacci Chapel of the church of Santa Maria del Carmine in

Florence depict figures with a solidity and a three-dimensional reality which had perhaps never before been achieved in the two-dimensional medium. His figures of Adam and Eve being evicted from the Garden of Eden manage to convey the sense of a cataclysmic disaster, which even Michelangelo, working on the same theme in the Sistine Chapel a century later, failed to do.

To Cosimo's period belongs another painter for whose mention room must be found. Fra Angelico (1387–1455) was living in a Dominican monastery at Fiesole when Cosimo returned from exile, and was transferred to the convent of San Marco in Florence in 1436. His frescoes at San Marco are a delicate and wonderful synthesis of medieval Christian values and motifs with Renaissance techniques. Beatified after his death, Angelico was one of the purest products of the domestic and international peace Cosimo brought to Florence.

Fra Angelico's Madonnas with their elegant drapery, and angels with their delicately multi-coloured wings, could have been painted only in a world at peace with itself and its God. The greatest Italian sculptor of Cosimo's period, Donatello (c. 1386–1466), on the other hand, reflected the varied moods – dramatic, serene, playful, brutal – of the Renaissance. With Donatello medieval piety and humility are forgotten. The bronze equestrian statue of the *condottiere*, Gattamelata, at Padua, has often – with some reason – been taken to represent the Renaissance individual at his most overbearing: self-sufficient, arrogant, contemptuous of man and God. Yet Donatello could sculpt delightful and mischievous *putti*, or – at another extreme of the human experience – the cadaverous and horrific figure in wood of Mary Magdalene, now in the Museo del Duomo in Florence.

Donatello was outstanding in the remarkable range and sophistication of his work, but this early phase of the Florentine Renaissance produced other sculptors whose work still impresses foreign tourists: Lorenzo Ghiberti

(1378–1455), who fashioned the famous bronze panels on the doors of the Baptistery, and Luca della Robbia (1400–82), whose glazed terracotta figures constituted a new art form, and were developed into something of an industry by his nephew, Andrea.

In the republican period before the Medici came to power public competitions had been held for the execution of major works. It was as a result of such a competition that Ghiberti had been commissioned to model the doors of the Baptistery, as early as 1401. One of the greatest architects of all time, Filippo Brunelleschi (1377–1446), had won a competition for his design for the dome of the cathedral in 1420. The cathedral itself had been founded in 1296, and the dome took some forty years to build. Not only is it a thing of beauty and perfection, but claims are made that in its diameter it is still the largest dome in the world. The serene, classical churches of Santo Spirito and San Lorenzo were also the work of Brunelleschi.

So well did Cosimo de' Medici establish himself as the real ruler of Florence, the *pater patriae* as he was called, that on his death in 1464 his son Piero remained in power although he was an invalid. Suffering from some arthritic complaint, Piero was bed-ridden for much of the time. But he continued the patronage of the arts, buying manuscripts, jewels and works of terracotta. He survived for only five years, and they were dangerous, unstable years for the Medici. The period of peace had owed much to Cosimo's close personal relationship with Francesco Sforza of Milan, who died two years after Cosimo. Florence was then threatened by enemies inside and outside the state. An attempted coup almost succeeded in 1466, and was defeated partly by the alertness of Piero's son, Lorenzo, then a boy of seventeen. Three years later Lorenzo had to assume power himself on the death of his father.

His education fitted him to the task of being a Renaissance ruler. His mother, Lucrezia Tornabuoni, was a highly cultured woman, whose collection of poetry is still respected. Lorenzo was taught Greek by Argyropoulos, an émigré from Constantinople, and Marsilio Ficino, whose work in bringing a full knowledge of Plato to Western Europe was discussed in the last chapter. The distinguished humanist scholar, Cristoforo Landino, taught Lorenzo to appreciate the Latin classics and Dante. That Lorenzo would continue Medici patronage of scholarship was hardly in doubt.

That he would be a successful financier was less likely. Under Cosimo the Medici house had had branches not only in Rome, Milan, Pisa and Venice, but also in Avignon, Geneva, Bruges and London. Under Lorenzo it began to crumble from neglect. He did not watch over his branch managers with the prudence which Cosimo had shown, and the branch in London had to be closed, while the Bruges branch was sold for a small sum. But Lorenzo more than made up for his failure as a banker by his success as a diplomat. He renewed the alliance with Milan, which had been the cornerstone of Cosimo's policy, by signing a treaty of alliance with Galeazzo Sforza in 1473. He broke up the dangerous Papal–Neapolitan alliance against Florence by travelling to Naples, at considerable personal risk to himself, and securing an understanding with the ruthless Neapolitan despot, Ferrante. Meanwhile in Florence changes in the constitutional façade concealed the despotic reality of Medici power.

Among the artists patronized by Lorenzo were figures whose names would become even better known to posterity than were those of the artists patronized by Cosimo. Whether they were also more deserving is open to argument. Lorenzo virtually discovered, and adopted, an unknown boy artist: Michelangelo Buonarroti. Perhaps the supreme example of the *uomo universale*, Michelangelo thought of himself primarily as a sculptor. Yet his creations in the Sistine Chapel would alone place him in the first rank of Renaissance artists, and his deeply moving verses in the first rank of Renaissance poets. In his long life – from 1475 to 1564 (dying in the year of

Shakespeare's birth) – he stretched the art of the High Renaissance to its limits, and virtually created a new style, the Mannerist. To a wider public he is known as the architect of the dome of St Peter's, only one of his architectural triumphs in Rome. Michelangelo left Florence before his twentieth birth-day, so that none of his major works belongs to this period, but Lorenzo's discovery and protection of the young Michelangelo was not the least of that despot's achievements.

An older sculptor patronized by Lorenzo was Andrea del Verrocchio (1435–88), whose most impressive work was to be the fearsome equestrian statue of the *condottiere*, Colleoni, in Venice. Also a product of the period was Sandro Botticelli (1444–1510), whose early, serene paintings were often of pagan themes, like the 'Primavera' and 'Birth of Venus' in the Uffizi in Florence. His 'Mars and Venus' in the National Gallery in London has a gentle and astonishingly modern sense of humour: never has the theme 'Make love, not war' been better treated. After coming under the influence of the preaching of Savonarola, Botticelli abandoned pagan themes. His later, Christian compositions are increasingly tormented, having lost the serenity, clarity and balance which were the hall-marks of the early Renaissance.

Lorenzo il Magnifico died in 1492. His son, Piero de' Medici, became the effective ruler of Florence, inheriting not only the wealth and power of his father, but also the good-will felt for him by the people of Florence. But the conceited and aggressive Piero quickly antagonised large numbers of Flor-entines. The end of peace and serenity, however, was to come not because of Piero, but because of the French invasion of 1494. The French king, Charles VIII, a primitive untouched by the new learning, had been encouraged by Lodovico il Moro, who had usurped the Duchy of Milan, to take the throne of Naples. Charles entered Florence with his huge army on 17 November 1494, a grim day in Italian history. On that very day, as if to provide history with a symbolic event, Pico della

Mirandola, whose scholarship had reached the rarest heights of humanism, died of a fever.

Before the arrival of the French, Piero de' Medici had fled to Venice. When Charles left for the South the Florentines could organize a new republic. Constitutional innovations introduced by the Medici to guarantee their hold on power were scrapped. A 'Grand Council' of some three thousand members, a third of whom were to be eligible to sit in rotation for three months each, was to be the sovereign body, and was to elect the traditional executive body of nine men, the *signoria*. The man behind the creation of the Grand Council and the republican constitution was a Dominican monk, Girolamo Savonarola. Born in Ferrara in 1452, Savonarola had come to Florence in 1481, ironically under the patronage of Lorenzo de' Medici. His brilliant and hypnotic sermons constituted not only an attack on humanism but a plea for the return of the spirit of early Christianity instead of that of pagan Greece and Rome. He persuaded the Florentines to burn many works of art. But his puritanism included a condemnation of usury worthy of Marx, and a praise of democracy. By 1498 the Florentines had tired of him, and an influential party had developed against him. The Pope condemned him, and wanted him sent to Rome, but the Florentines preferred to try him themselves, for fraud and heresy. He was hanged and his body burnt in the Piazza. The historian Guicciardini commented maliciously that a greater crowd witnessed the burning even than those which had listened to his sermons.

The Medici were restored briefly from 1521 to 1527, but the period was a pale shadow of the age of Cosimo and Lorenzo. On hearing of the sack of Rome by the troops of the Emperor Charles V in 1527, the Florentines again threw out the Medici and set up a second democratic republic, but in 1529 the emperor's army besieged Florence for several months. After a supremely creative phase of his life in Rome, where he had completed his work on the Sistine Chapel, Michelangelo returned to Florence to design the city's defences. On a previous stay in Florence, from 1500 to 1504, during the life of the earlier republic, he had carved from a single colossal block of marble the 'David', a symbol of the defiant city prevailing against great odds, a youthful civilization triumphing over brute force.

When, in 1530, the Republic finally fell, Charles V restored the Medici, who were to rule Florence until 1737.

## 4 The High Renaissance: artists and their patrons in Rome, Milan, Venice and Naples

One example of the *uomo universale*, Michelangelo, has been mentioned. Another, whose fame was immense in his own day, was Leon Battista Alberti (1404–72), and another, whose name has reached wider circles over the centuries, was Leonardo da Vinci (1452–1519). Alberti was born in Genoa, but went to Florence while still a young man. He was primarily an architect, but also a writer, sculptor, mathematician and athlete. The wonderful abstract design of his marble façade of Santa Maria Novella in Florence defies definition by period or style. Leonardo's genius knew even fewer bounds. Sadly, his works of sculpture have perished, and it is perhaps a pity that several of his portraits are less well known to the general public than the Gioconda, or Mona Lisa, but his notebooks also reveal that he was an engineer, anatomist and botanist. He was a scientist and technologist born before society was ready to put his ideas into practice.

The patrons of such men could also lay claim to being *uomini universali* themselves; certainly they were often scholars. In Rome Pope Nicholas V (1447–55) had been librarian to the Medici. He built the Vatican library, and encouraged the translation of Greek works into Latin. He patronized humanist scholars, architects and painters, including Leon Battista Alberti, Lorenzo Valla, Fra Angelico and Piero della Francesca. Yet, as so often with Renaissance popes, there was another side to the coin. Nicholas destroyed pagan temples and other buildings in Rome, and was faced, at the end of his pontificate, with a bizarre revolt, led by an eccentric scholar, Stefano Porcari. The revolt was a pathetic attempt to restore the Roman Republic. Porcari was arrested and hanged.

Pius II (1458–64) had been an eminent humanist scholar before his election to the papacy, his professional name being Aeneas Sylvius. His autobiography is a strange mixture of superstitions, lies and sophisticated reflections. From being a frivolous satirist before taking holy orders, he became a devout priest and the last pope to attempt to organize a crusade against Islam.

Sixtus IV (1471–84) built the Sistine Chapel and collected an impressive group of artists to start work on its decoration. As the result of the most corrupt election in papal history a Spaniard, Rodrigo Borgia, was elected Pope Alexander VI in 1492 and was to reign for eleven years. The corruption and immorality of his court became notorious, but there was a positive side to his pontificate. Under his predecessor, Innocent VIII, the domestic administration of Rome had been weak. Alexander did something to restore law and order. The evil of his pontificate was due less to him than to his son, Cesare Borgia, who was probably responsible for the murder of his own brother, and his brother-in-law, one of Lucrezia Borgia's several husbands. But Cesare himself, by conquering Urbino, Perugia, Siena and the Romagna, did much to strengthen the independence of the Papal States. Alexander VI continued papal patronage of the arts, Michelangelo arriving in Rome during his pontificate, and carving the exquisite Pietà, now in St Peter's.

The most creative pontificate of the Renaissance was that of Julius II (1503–13). A political and military leader, Julius conducted complex diplomacy, which culminated in his creation of the Holy League with Spain and England, and effectively drove the French from Italy. His patronage of the arts was on the same grand scale as his political activity. In 1506 Donato Bramante (1444–1514) started work on the new St Peter's, and two or three years later Raphael (1483–1520) painted the beautiful series of paintings in the rooms of the Vatican. But the most powerful artistic achievement of the pontificate was Michelangelo's work on the ceiling and walls of the Sistine Chapel. His 'Day of Judgement' can be considered a pictorial equivalent of Dante's great poem, and certainly owed something to it. Looking back across two centuries, a supreme statement of the High Renaissance reflected the supreme statement of the high Middle Ages.

During the Renaissance the history of the Papacy was full of paradoxes. Liberal and open-minded intellectually and culturally, it contrasted with the closed minds of the Counter-Reformation popes who were to follow. Extremely corrupt and decadent in religious terms, it yet restored the political strength and prestige of the Papal States.

Milan in the fourteenth and early fifteenth centuries was under the harsh despotism of the Visconti. The loss of territory and breakdown of government which the duchy suffered under Giovanni Maria Visconti (1402–12) was retrieved during the long period of power of Filippo Maria Visconti (1412–47), who recaptured Pavia, Parma and Piacenza, and conquered Genoa. Only in 1528 did the brilliant admiral, Andrea Doria, re-establish the independence of the Republic of Genoa. In spite of her wars Milan enjoyed economic growth in the first half of the fifteenth century, and secured peace under Francesco Sforza, who ruled from 1450 to 1466. The first of the Sforza rulers of Milan had started his career as a *condottiere*, but married Filippo Visconti's daughter, and after controlling a republic in Milan for three years took the title of duke himself. Although a brilliant general, Francesco Sforza preserved peace through his alliance with Cosimo de' Medici's Florence.

Under Francesco the superb *castello* was built. Ludovico

Sforza, known as 'il Moro', because of his dark complexion, usurped power from Francesco's grandson in 1479. A ruthless despot, Ludovico was also a sound administrator and a generous patron of the arts. Leonardo da Vinci was a prominent figure at Ludovico's court. But Ludovico must bear the responsibility for inviting Charles VIII to invade Italy in 1494. The French subsequently turned against him, and he was to die a miserable death in the French castle of Loches. In a dungeon without light there are still marks on the walls where this cultured man, once the friend of Leonardo da Vinci, evidently tried to keep his sanity by dabbing mud markings as makeshift murals.

Venice in the fourteenth century controlled the Eastern Mediterranean and was the centre of European maritime commerce. Not only did she control the coastline of Dalmatia, where lovely little Venetian churches still stand as reminders, but her empire extended to Crete, Corfu and part of mainland Greece. In the mid-fourteenth century wars with Genoa threatened Venetian supremacy, and the Genoese reached as close to Venice as Chioggia in the war of 1379–80. Although Venice was to acquire Cyprus as late as 1489, in the fifteenth century her attention was drawn increasingly inland in Italy, though more as the result of Italian political complications than from any deliberate intent on the part of Venice.

The news of the rounding of the Cape of Good Hope by Vasco da Gama in 1499 was received with great distress by the Venetians, who immediately realized its significance: that a sea route to the Indies had been discovered, a route which would break the near-monopoly of the Venetian control of the land route via the Eastern Mediterranean. The Venetians were perhaps right to regard Vasco da Gama's achievement as more significant for them than the discovery of the American world by Europeans, but if anything they exaggerated the importance of the Portuguese discovery. While Venice lost some of her land empire in Italy in the sixteenth century, she was to remain an important Italian state until Napoleonic days.

The Venetian constitution was certainly effective, if far from democratic. By the fifteenth century the power of the doge had been curbed, and sovereignty resided in councils filled by a nobility, but a nobility which constituted perhaps 7 per cent of the population, and numbered several thousand. The Great Council held legislative, executive and judicial powers, but since it contained over a thousand members, it had to delegate powers to a Senate of sixty, and a Council of Forty. A Council of Ten dealt with foreign policy and security, and at times had a stranglehold on government. During the period of the Renaissance Venice was greatly admired by the other Italian states for her constitution, which was thought to be more nearly perfect than in fact it was.

The greatest period of Venetian art was the early sixteenth century. Deep colours and *chiaroscuro* replaced the clarity of line and composition of fifteenth-century painting, as new oil techniques were employed. Of the three Bellini, Jacopo (c. 1400–70) and his elder son, Gentile (c.1429–1507) still painted in the style of the earlier Renaissance, but Gentile's younger brother, Giovanni (1430–1516) developed the new techniques which permitted more vivid colours and a more sensuous treatment. In the last century Giorgione (c. 1478–1511) was believed to have painted a great number of paintings which are no longer regarded as his. Those mysterious small landscapes, where the human figures have become dwarfed, and which are still believed to have been Giorgione's, anticipate the romanticism – and perhaps the decadence – of a later period. By far the most renowned Venetian artist in his day was Tiziano Vecellio, whose name has been anglicized as Titian, and who was probably born about 1490, and lived until 1576. His work became increasingly vivid and dynamic, and his portraits, including those of the Emperor Charles V and

Pope Paul III, acquired a realism never before achieved in art.

In Naples there was economic growth in the fifteenth century, as there was elsewhere in Italy. The demographic setback of the fourteenth century was soon compensated for, and the population figures – especially of the city of Naples herself – started their climb to the dizzy heights they were soon to reach. The long period of Angevin rule came to an end, and the succession, which had for long been disputed between the Angevin and Aragonese houses, was settled in favour of the latter. Alfonso V of Aragon, supported by Filippo Maria Visconti, secured the Neapolitan kingdom in 1435, and in 1442 was recognized as king by Pope Eugene IV, who had previously supported the Angevin claims.

There were already Spanish settlements and Spanish institutions in Sicily; there was now Spanish power in Naples. However, Alfonso, who was to rule until his death in 1458, was known to the Neapolitans as 'the Magnanimous', and from choice became more of an Italian than a Spaniard. His reign marked a brief influence of the Renaissance in Naples. He patronized artists, architects and scholars, most significantly giving refuge to Lorenzo Valla when Valla was in danger of persecution by the Papacy. Alfonso united the thrones of Sicily and Naples, and did something to reform administration and finance.

Alfonso's reign was followed by the long despotism of his illegitimate son, Ferrante (1458–94). Despotism – sometimes brutal, but sometimes benevolent – was a characteristic of fifteenth-century Italy, but it would be an over-simplification to suggest that there was a general transition from republican communes in the fourteenth century, to despotisms in the fifteenth. Questions of sovereignty were not so clearcut in the Renaissance period as they were to become later. A despot could assert his authority over several cities, but leave the local government – a republican commune – to carry on as before. An example of such a development was provided by the careers of the Malatesta of Rimini. Of the most remarkable of this family, Jacob Burckhardt wrote: 'Unscrupulousness, impiety, military skill, and high culture have been seldom combined in one individual as in Sigismondo Malatesta.'[6]

Concentration on the main five or six Italian states must not be allowed in this book to exclude mention of the lesser despots, of whom the Malatesta were only the least appetizing. The Este of Ferrara patronized art and literature through the city's ancient university, and the Gonzaga of Mantua and Federigo da Montefeltro of Urbino were among the more enlightened. The court of Federigo's son, Guidobaldo, at Urbino, was presided over by Guidobaldo's wife, Elisabetta Gonzaga. The polished, gentle, but shrewd conversation at the court was reproduced by Baldassare Castiglione (1478–1529) in 'The Courtier', which depicts the society of a small city-state at peace with itself.

[6] Burckhardt, *Civilization of the Renaissance*, p. 21.

Chapter 5

# THE POLITICAL AND CULTURAL
# ECLIPSE OF ITALY

## *1 The foreign invasions and wars of the sixteenth century*

An Italian writer who anticipated the Europe of self-sufficient
embryonic nation states – the 'New Monarchies' of France,
Spain and England – was Niccolo Machiavelli (1469–1527).
His knowledge came from two sources: the ancient Roman
world, and his own contemporary Italian world, where secular
principalities and republics acquired a sense of identity as
independent units recognizing no higher authority, whether it
be of pope or emperor. Fifteenth-century Italy was a microcosm of sixteenth-century Europe, where powerful monarchs
nationalized their churches, and acquired a form of independence which was total in practice, and which would have
been difficult for the medieval mind to conceive.

Machiavelli's most influential work was the short handbook
for rulers which he called *The Prince*. He had held public office
under the republic, and when the Medici dismissed him in 1513
he wrote his cynical, yet perceptive, commentary on the
necessary skills for securing and retaining power. His argument took the secular spirit of the Renaissance to its most
extreme point. In his eyes *raison d'état* necessitated the
ignoring of all moral values; in his eighteenth chapter, he
wrote:

A prince, and especially, a new prince, cannot observe all those things for which men are held to be good, it being often necessary, to maintain the State, to operate against integrity, against charity, against humanity, against religion.

The first twenty-five of the twenty-six chapters of *The Prince* are written in this dispassionate spirit of *Realpolitik*. Ruthless political leaders – like Thomas Cromwell – felt immense respect and gratitude for Machiavelli's amoral sincerity and advice. Others – like Shakespeare – were to see him as a devil for the same reason. But the twenty-sixth chapter of *The Prince* is written in an altogether different tone – a tone of exalted patriotism. In it Machiavelli appeals for a native Italian prince to drive the foreign barbarians out of Italy. It was this last chapter of the book which was to give Italian nationalists a concept of Machiavelli which was strangely at odds with the impression received by people outside Italy. And even today the contrast between the Italian and the non-Italian assessment of Machiavelli is still apparent. Another idea which was to survive the sixteenth century was suggested by Machiavelli: that since the nations to the North have more brute force, the Italians must employ their greater intelligence and cunning to outwit the barbarians. Something of this outlook was to become a tradition of the House of Savoy, and was not to be entirely absent in the attitude of Cavour. Machiavelli himself, however, had no contempt for brute force. On the contrary, he believed that the strength of the lion must be combined, in the qualities of a prince, with the cunning of the fox.

If Machiavelli's *Prince*, and his *Discourses on Livy*, are works of political science, he also wrote a history of Florence, all of these in the Italian vernacular rather than Latin. But as a historian he was less original than a contemporary and friend Francesco Guicciardini (1483–1540), who wrote a history of Italy, covering the years 1494–1532. One characteristic of Guicciardini marks him out as one of the first modern historians: when he found that his own memory of an event did not accord with the evidence of the documents, he accepted the latter. With Guicciardini an important step towards a sound writing of history had been taken.

Machiavelli's hope for a native prince to drive out the foreigners was a vain one. After Charles VIII's invasion of Italy in 1494, the Italian states tried to play off the great powers against each other, but without success. If the fox showed occasional subtlety, he was not subtle enough to persuade the lion to depart. After each successive invasion, however, when the French, German or Spanish armies returned to their homelands, they took with them a knowledge and some of the new skills of the Italian Renaissance. If, in the first half of the sixteenth century, Italy was conquered militarily and politically, the end result was to be an Italian cultural conquest of Western and Central Europe.

But the foreign invasions divided, rather than united, the Italians. And it divided them not only between states, but within cities. Since the Medici in Florence opposed Charles VIII's march southwards to Rome and Naples, the republican anti-Medici party acquired the support of the French, and the domestic politics of Florence came to rely on the struggle between the great powers. Initially it was a struggle between France and the Empire, but it was to become in practice one between France and Spain. When the Spanish army entered Florence in 1512 it meant that the Medici were restored.

Charles VIII had entered Naples in February of 1495, but his rapid successes led to the formation of a strong league against him. Milan, Venice and Pope Alexander VI secured the help of the Emperor Maximilian and Ferdinand of Aragon. Charles withdrew from Italy, and died in 1498. Other barbarian invasions followed. The new king of France, Louis XII, laid claims to Milan, and secured an alliance with the Venetian Republic. In a strictly defensive spirit, fearful of the ambitions of Ludovico Sforza, the Venetians seized the opportunity to extend their land empire to its farthest extent, by the acquisition of Cremona, only some fifty miles from Milan. But their success was counter-productive. The League of Cambrai of 1508, formed to drive back the Venetians, included not only neighbouring Italian cities (Mantua and Ferrara), but also Pope Julius II, France and Spain. For a brief interlude the two great powers were aligned in Italy. Although the Venetians were defeated in the battle of Agnadello in May of 1509, most of their mainland conquests were retained. Venetian rule was efficient and enlightened, and Italian cities evidently accepted it with some gratitude.

A yet grimmer and more significant phase of the Italian wars of the fifteenth century started with the succession of Francis I to the French throne in 1515. He immediately invaded Italy and occupied Milan. He was a firm believer in the Machiavellian doctrine that a ruler must have no moral scruples in his pursuit and retention of power. Later in his reign Francis was to send many Calvinists to the stake, not because he had any religious convictions, but because he regarded Protestantism as subversive. But on the international field he was to be faced with a formidable opponent. The grandson of Isabella of Castile and Ferdinand of Aragon became King Charles I of Spain in 1517, and was elected Emperor Charles V in 1519. With his possession of the Netherlands, the Spanish settlements in the New World and his Aragonese inheritance of Naples, he could claim sovereignty over a considerable portion of the known world.

The confrontation of Francis I and Charles V was a European one, but Italy was its principal battlefield. The dynastic wars of the French House of Valois and the Austrian House of Habsburg were to devastate Italy, and wipe out many of the achievements of the Renaissance. Charles V had two aims in Italy: to assert his claims to Naples, Sicily and the island of Sardinia, and to exclude the French from the rest of the peninsula. The supremacy of Spanish infantry was established at the battle of Pavia in 1525, when the French were defeated and Francis taken prisoner. But the imperial success stimulated the creation of the pro-French League of Cognac in 1526. The League was to a great extent the result of the diplomacy of the Medici pope, Clement VII (1523–34). Although the Medici had been traditionally pro-Spanish, and Medici Florence itself still supported Charles V, the pope joined Milan in the League with France. Tragically, Italian states were now fighting each other as satellites of France or Spain.

Spanish successes led to the sack of Rome in 1527, the last of the many barbarian sackings of the city since its foundation. Rome herself had not been sacked for several centuries, but the appalling event of 1527 was only one of the many similar atrocities committed on a smaller scale on other cities since the invasions had started in 1494. An imperial army under the command of the Duke of Bourbon marched on Rome and in May of 1527 about 20,000 troops, some German and some Spanish, mostly mercenaries, broke into the city. Of the Germans some were Protestants, who were not likely to respect the sanctity of Rome, but the whole force was out of control, especially after the Duke of Bourbon had been killed in the fighting outside the walls. The pope found refuge in the Castel Sant'Angelo, the formidable fortress which had been built from the remains of the tomb of the Emperor Hadrian. A horrific massacre and unrestrained devastation ensued. Normal life came to a halt for almost a year. No one can tell how many art masterpieces were destroyed. If a date had to be fixed for the ending of the Renaissance, 1527 would have the strongest claim.

The sack of Rome did not immediately give Charles V control of Italy. On the contrary, in October 1527 the French occupied Lombardy. More important, perhaps, was control of the sea, which appeared to be safely in French hands so long as Andrea Doria, the ruler of Genoa, remained aligned with them.

But Francis I was foolish enough to quarrel with Doria, who transferred his support to Charles. In 1529 Charles was strong enough to impose the Treaty of Cambrai, by which the French renounced their claims in Italy, and the Sforza were restored in Milan. On 24 February 1530 Charles was crowned emperor by Clement VII in Bologna. Thereafter, although war between France and Spain was renewed, Italy was less continuously the battlefield. The wars were ended finally only by the Treaty of Cateau-Cambrésis in 1559, when the French were finally driven from Italy, except for the retention of Turin.

The wars in the first half of the sixteenth century in Italy had been of an entirely different nature from those of the fifteenth century. The earlier wars had been fought primarily by mercenaries, who had respected a certain trade unionism of the paid soldier, and had not killed each other needlessly. Machiavelli had complained about this, arguing that citizens should themselves fight for their republic, rather than employing *condottieri*. But when the Florentine Republic allowed him to form a citizen army – which was in practice composed of peasants, since urban Tuscans believed that fighting was something which should be done by the uneducated – his army was disastrously unsuccessful against the Spanish troops. The armies of the sixteenth century – Spanish, French or German – were far more destructive of life, whether of their opponents or of civilians. Their weapons also were more destructive. The French in particular, from the 1520s, were using a more powerful gunpowder than had ever been used before.

After the foreign invasions of the early sixteenth century there was a sharp economic and demographic decline in North Italy, partly due to loss of life in the wars and sackings, but partly also due to emigration to the South – to Rome and Naples – where employment in the building industry could be found. Some of the figures are staggering. The population of Brescia in 1505 was about 65,000. In 1517, after the French, Imperial and Spanish invasions, it had fallen to about 24,000.

The population of Pavia was about 16,000 in 1500, and only about 5,000 in 1529.[1] Pavia, of course, had been the scene of a terrible battle in 1525. Similar calculations have not been made for the larger cities, and Milan, Florence and the other cities of North and Central Italy recovered economically and demographically in the second half of the sixteenth century. But the wars and foreign invasions had left a grim and indelible mark on Italian history.

## 2 The Counter-Reformation and the Spanish period

In their relationship to the Italian Renaissance the Reformation and the Counter-Reformation can be seen as part of a single reaction. The Renaissance had been open-minded, expansive and tolerant in intellectual terms; the Reformation and Counter-Reformation were both movements of intolerance, exclusiveness and puritanism. Enthusiasm for classical studies, interest in the pre-Christian pagan world, and in the non-Christian world beyond the boundaries of Europe, tended to fade. About 1520, as a generation of Greek refugees in Italy were dying, so the study of Greek became less central to Italian scholarship. The broad-minded Christianity of the Florence of Pico della Mirandola could have come to terms with other religions and other philosophies. Burckhardt's judgement is severe, but arguable: 'Looking at Pico, we can guess at the lofty flight which Italian philosophy would have taken had not the Counter-Reformation annihilated the higher spiritual life of the people.'[2]

Italy was not, of course, so directly affected by the Reformation as Germany, France and Britain were, but, with Spain, was one of the two main centres of the Counter-Reformation. The transition in Italy from the High Renaissance period to that of the Counter-Reformation was, in a

[1] Peter Laven, *Renaissance Italy 1464–1534* (London, 1966), p. 38.
[2] Burckhardt, *Civilization of the Renaissance*, p. 120.

sense, a sudden one, so that Paul III (1534–49) cannot be defined as a 'Renaissance pope' or as a 'Counter-Reformation pope': rather was he both at once. A member of the Farnese family, he had lived in the Florence of Cosimo de' Medici, and been educated by humanists. He was made a cardinal simply because his sister was the mistress of Pope Alexander VI. He had illegitimate children himself, and made two of his grandchildren cardinals. But as pope, Paul was a fine patron of the arts. During his pontificate the building of the lovely, classical Farnese Palace was started, partly to the designs of Michelangelo. Yet it was this pope who, in 1540, issued the bull approving Ignatius Loyola's founding of the Order of the Jesuits, in 1542 approved the creation of the Roman branch of the Holy Office, or Inquisition, and in 1542 convoked the Council of Trent which made the Counter-Reformation in legislative terms.

The moving spirit behind Paul III's organization of the Inquisition in Rome was a Neapolitan, Cardinal Giovanni Caraffa. After two short pontificates, Caraffa himself was elected pope, as Paul IV. Any link with humanism was now lost. Paul IV was a fanatic, who was determined to stamp out both clerical abuses and anything which he defined as heresy. He stepped up the activity of the Inquisition. Witnesses were tortured to encourage them to denounce heretics. In 1559 the 'Index of prohibited books' was published, an absurdity that the Catholic Church was never to feel strong enough to scrap. But there was another side to Paul IV. Not only was his own life free from corruption, but he made efforts in Rome to help the poor.

Under the successor of Paul IV, Pius IV (1559–65), the proceedings of the Council of Trent were brought to a close. In the early fifteenth century the conciliar movement had attempted, in a series of general councils of the Church, to limit the spiritual authority of the pope. It had failed to do so. The Council of Trent, convoked in 1542, met for a year or two on three occasions, and completed its work in 1564. Pius IV published its conclusions in 1565. The prelates of Italy and Spain predominated at the sessions. They favoured papal supremacy within the Church, as opposed to the degree of autonomy for national churches and the supremacy of a general council which many prelates in Germany and France would have preferred. Consequently the pope was now declared to be the supreme authority in the Church, and no general council was to meet again until Pius IX summoned one in 1870 – and then it was to proclaim the doctrine of papal infallibility. Other measures passed by the Council of Trent enforced a stricter morality and discipline on the clergy, removing abuses which would have forestalled the Protestant Reformation if they had been removed fifty years earlier.

Another aspect of the Counter-Reformation was the persecution of Italian intellectuals by the Inquisition. The two most famous were Giordano Bruno (1548–1600) and Galileo Galilei (1564–1642). A Neapolitan who became a Dominican monk, Bruno lost faith in Christian dogmas, and fled first to Calvinist Geneva, where he was no safer than in Italy. He subsequently travelled to Paris, London, Oxford, Wittenberg, Prague, Frankfurt and Padua, often in considerable danger. Finally he was arrested by the Inquisition in Venice in 1592. His trial lasted for seven years, but he was eventually burnt at the stake for heresy in the Campo dei Fiori in Rome. After 1870 the Kingdom of Italy constructed his statue on the spot where he died, and where today the grim figure stands above the cheerful crowds in that lively market-place in the heart of Rome.

The thought of Galileo was of greater importance than that of Bruno. Born at Pisa, he is probably best known for his discovery that all falling bodies, regardless of weight, descend at the same speed. But already, when he was a young student of medicine, he came to doubt not only the validity of Aristotle's physics, but the whole approach of traditional, Aristotelian science, which had never been divorced from philosophy. Galileo was not concerned to speculate about causes, but to establish laws, and so gave the scientific revolution of the seventeenth century much of its character. Both in Florence in 1610 and in Rome in 1611, he was received with great honour. He ran foul of the Church by his acceptance of the Copernican astronomical system, by which the earth was held to move around the sun. He was forced to renounce his approval of Copernicus, but, unlike Bruno, he never rejected the Catholic Church; rather, it rejected him.

Not all the popes of the Counter-Reformation were obscurantist. A contemporary of Galileo, Gregory XIII (1572–85), spent huge sums on educational institutions in Rome, and introduced a reform which has influenced the lives of all of us: the reform of the calendar. The Gregorian calendar was introduced in Rome, some other parts of Italy, Spain and Portugal in 1582. Protestant Europe accepted it reluctantly and belatedly, and Czarist Russia resisted it to the end. By declaring the 5th of October to be the 15th of October, Pope Gregory had adjusted the calendar to the seasons.

In the context of the history of art Italians use the term 'Counter-Reformation' to include sentimental pictures of cherubic angels and sugary Madonnas, who seem to bear little relationship to the spirit of Loyola or the Inquisition. But the Baroque art of the late sixteenth and seventeenth centuries was by no means all sentimental, and even to call it 'decadent' is to impose a subjective standard of judgement. Rome today is, more than anything else, a Baroque city, and the art and architecture of that period contribute enormously to her beauty. The central figure was Giovanni Bernini (1598–1680). He was the son of a Florentine father and a Neapolitan mother, and since he worked in Rome he can be considered in the fullest sense to have been an Italian. Everywhere in Rome there is evidence of his genius. His architectural achievements include the colonnades in Piazza San Pietro, the Palazzo Propaganda

Fide in the Piazza de Spagna and the Palazzo Barberini. But his personality is stamped more firmly on his sculpture: the David, the Rape of Proserpine, the St Teresa of Avila and the fountain in the Piazza Navona illustrate the range of his expressive powers. There were other competent architects contemporary with Bernini, but in the visual arts far more inferior work was produced than in the preceding three centuries. Among historians and art historians it has been fashionable in recent years to deny that Italy suffered a cultural eclipse in the seventeenth century, but the work of a few artists of the stature of Bernini can hardly be said to compensate for the bulk of sentimental, posturizing and insincere products of the age which still fill Italian churches today. The cultural capital of Europe was moving from Italy to France.

A quick survey of Italian states in the period will illustrate that in political terms also Italy was in eclipse, but that in economic terms no easy generalization can be made.

In the first half of the sixteenth century North Italy suffered from the wars, while South Italy, comparatively speaking, prospered. Naples had doubled her population in the course of the fifteenth century. In 1500 it was about 100,000. By 1547 the figure is estimated to have reached 245,000, making Naples the second city in Christendom, after Paris. Yet in the sixteenth century Naples was in eclipse in political terms. She had experienced rule by foreign dynasties – the Aragonese from Spain and the Angevins from France – but she had never been annexed by a foreign power. In the fifteenth century, having the only king in Italy, Naples had been known simply as 'the Kingdom'. In 1504 she was conquered by the Spanish, and became the centre of Spanish power in Italy. She was to remain under Spanish rule for over a century, until, during the War of the Spanish Succession, she was occupied by the Austrians. The Neapolitans almost certainly resented Spanish rule, and especially the heavy taxation imposed by the Spaniards,

Map 4. Italy in 1559

although there was only one active rising. In 1647 a twenty-four year old fisherman from Amalfi, Tommaso Aniello, known as Masaniello, led a revolt against the Spanish. The revolt started as a riot among fruit-vendors in Naples. Masaniello took control of the crowd, and, astonishingly, persuaded the Spanish viceroy not only to abolish unpopular taxes, but to recognize the executive authority of Masaniello. Nine days after the rising had started Masaniello was killed by Spanish agents. The myth he had created was to be more important than the incident itself, and was to be the theme of more than one opera.

The other centre of Spanish power in Italy in the period was Milan. When the last Sforza, Francesco II, died in 1535, Milan passed under direct Spanish rule. In 1540 the Emperor Charles V voluntarily abandoned imperial claims to Milan in favour of Spain, although Milan remained in theory a fief of the Empire. The nineteenth-century Italian novelist, Alessandro Manzoni, was to give an unforgettable picture of seventeenth-century Milan under Spanish rule in *I Promessi Sposi* (*The Betrothed*), and if the picture was coloured by the age in which Manzoni was living, it is also true that the novelist can be considered a historian, since he read in depth and worked in archives in preparation for writing the novel. The plagues and the bread riots Manzoni so vividly described were without doubt part of the life of Milan, but the economic condition of Milan was by no means entirely bleak. The city was on the land route from the Mediterranean to Central, and even Eastern, Europe. Fernand Braudel points out that trade between Italy and Poland was at its peak in the second half of the sixteenth, and first decades of the seventeenth, centuries.

It is thus wrong to regard the Spanish period as uniformly retrogade economically. At the beginning of the seventeenth century Genoa and Rome, like Milan, showed economic vitality, while Livorno became at that time an important centre of international trade. Piedmont, too, experienced economic revival at the end of the sixteenth century.

The independence of the Republic of Genoa owed much to the chequered, but brilliant, career of Andrea Doria (c. 1466–1560). But Genoa had unwittingly contributed to the comparative decline of Italian maritime commerce. The Atlantic seaboard had been pioneered by Italian sailors. Genoese galleys had sailed through the Straits of Gibraltar on their way to the great market of Bruges as early as 1297, and had been followed by Venetian galleys in 1317. Genoese and Venetian merchants had virtually captured the English and Flemish markets. But in the sixteenth century the Italian share in this trade around the Western coast of Europe was declining.

The political and cultural decline of Florence after the fall of the last Republic in the early sixteenth century is undeniable. Charles V established Alessandro de' Medici as the hereditary duke in 1569, and the state was subsequently to be known as the Grand Duchy of Tuscany. In the event it was to be far less grand than Florence had been in the fifteenth century, when the Medici rulers had been common citizens. But Florence was only an extreme example of what was happening all over Italy. As real political power – and sometimes real economic power – waned, so the titles and trappings of monarchy grew. It was a misfortune for Italy that she fell under Spanish control when Spain was herself already a declining power, already being superseded by the France of Richelieu, Mazarin (who had been born in Italy – in the Abruzzi), and Louis XIV. The Spanish love of display, ceremony and exaggerated formality invaded Italy, and was adopted by the Papacy.

One part of Italy which escaped Spanish influence was the Duchy of Savoy, whose rise to the status of a European power is a feature of the history of Italy in the seventeenth century. But Savoy is sufficiently distinct from the rest of Italy to deserve a later section (5.4) on its own.

The first half of the Spanish period had at least brought to Italy the blessing of comparative peace, after the wars of the first half of the sixteenth century. Nor did Italy suffer the devastation which the Thirty Years War brought to Germany in the first half of the seventeenth century. But in the middle of the Thirty Years War, in 1627, there was a fresh French invasion of Italy. Carlo Gonzaga, duke of Nevers, claimed, not without some justification, the united duchies of Mantua and Monteferrat. The Emperor Ferdinand II (1619–37) refused to invest him, and the Spanish and Imperial forces besieged Mantua, while the Republic of Venice and Pope Urban VIII supported Gonzaga. The siege lasted for nine months, and was followed by an appalling sacking at the hands of predominantly German troops. In 1629 French and Spanish forces fought for the duchy, and in 1631 the French succeeded in securing it for Gonzaga, though mainly because of the successes of France's Swedish ally, Gustavus Adolphus, in Germany.

The War of the Spanish Succession, which lasted from 1701 to 1714, was to have a profound influence on Italian history. It started when the last of the Spanish Habsburgs, Charles II, died, and Louis XIV claimed the throne for his grandson, the seventeen-year-old boy who was to be Philip V (1700–46). The Peace of Utrecht, which closed the war in 1713, marked one of the most important turning points in Italian history. Austria acquired Milan, Mantua (which had been sold by the last of the Gonzaga to Louis XIV in 1701) and the island of Sardinia, and had her occupation of Naples recognized. The domination of Italy passed from Spain to Austria.

In the lives of the majority of people, recurring epidemics still probably played a larger role than the great political changes, except when international developments brought war to their homes. In 1576–7 there were more than 100,000 deaths in the four largest towns of Northern Italy. The epidemic of 1630 was even more terrible in its toll of lives. Some towns lost 70 per cent of their population, and most lost 25 per cent. Even in the countryside it is believed that some 30 per cent of the population died. If these figures are correct the 1630 epidemic was only less dreadful than the Black Death of 1348. The great ports were hit by a third epidemic in 1656, when Naples and Genoa are estimated to have lost 50 per cent of their population, though such was the exceptional demographic character of Naples that the loss was soon made up. Rome lost only 10 per cent of her population in 1656, which meant that the death toll there was not comparable with that caused by the sack of 1527.[3]

### 3 The Austrian period and the return to Europe

If Italy was to a degree excluded from the mainstream of European politics and thought during the Spanish period, partly because Spain was a declining power, in the eighteenth century the influence of Austria in Italy was, at least, that of a power which was fully exposed to European intellectual and political movements, and sharply influenced by them.

The Austrians occupied Naples in 1707 during the War of the Spanish Succession, and retained it in the peace settlement of 1713. They also gained Sardinia, but exchanged the island for Sicily in 1720 after the War of the Polish Succession. This war, fought from 1733 to 1738, involved an invasion by the French and the Piedmontese of Austrian Lombardy, a combination which was to be repeated in 1859 with rather more important results. The 1733 war had the effect of interrupting a few promising reform movements in Habsburg Lombardy. In Naples the consequences of the war were more striking. Elizabeth Farnese, the Italian wife of Charles V, the Bourbon king of Spain, had ambitious plans in Italy. She intended to recover both Naples and Milan. Half of the project succeeded. Her son, Don Carlos, failed to secure Milan, but his army defeated the Austrians in the South, and he established himself as Charles III, King of Naples and Sicily. He was to reign from 1735 until 1759, and his dynasty was to occupy the Neapolitan throne for a century after that – in fact, until the arrival of Garibaldi in 1860. It is a misleading common practice among historians to refer to the Neapolitan Bourbons as a 'foreign' dynasty, or more specifically a 'Spanish' dynasty. Apart from the fact that they were half-Italian even in their inception,

[3] Roger Mols SJ, 'Population in Europe 1500–1700', in *The Fontana Economic History of Europe 1500–1700*, vol. II, edited by Carlo M. Cipolla (London, 1977).

through the person of Elizabeth Farnese, the dynasty obviously became increasingly Italian – or rather, Neapolitan – as the decades passed. It would be more correct to call Queen Victoria 'German' than the later Neapolitan Bourbons 'Spanish'.

Charles III was determined to modernize Naples, and appointed as chief minister Bernado Tanucci, to introduce reforms. Tanucci had been professor of jurisprudence at the University of Pisa, and did something to rationalize the laws which had accumulated in Naples from the many systems of the past. But his reforms were intended to consolidate the monarchy, not, of course, to introduce a constitutional element, and his assault was rather on the Church than on the nobility. He adjusted Church–state relations in favour of the crown, and expelled the Jesuits – a favourite 'reform' of the eighteenth century. But his reforms were all legalistic ones. His understanding of economics was limited, and the limitation was exposed by the terrible famine of 1764, for which the Neapolitan government was totally unprepared. Tanucci's reforms had certainly not ended feudalism or poverty in Naples.

The eternal social ills of Naples were not ended by eighteenth-century reforms, but the city experienced much intellectual and academic activity. The most original writer of the century in Naples was Giambattista Vico (1668–1744). Professor of rhetoric at the University of Naples, he was an isolated figure, and the full value and brilliance of his thought have been appreciated only comparatively recently. His *Scienza Nuova*, first published in 1725, and in a revised form in 1730, lays claim to the scientific nature of history, and the cyclical nature of human development. There is an almost Hegelian quality in Vico's thought, and it is wholly alien to the later thought of the Enlightenment, which was basically confident of human progress. If Vico was essentially a philosopher, other teachers in the University of Naples were concerned with economics and law. It was a great age in the life of the University, which could well claim to have founded Europe's first chair of economics. A philosopher of law and historian, whose tragic life indicated the limitations of the Enlightenment in Italy, was Pietro Giannone (1676–1748). In 1723 – before the arrival of Don Carlos – Giannone had published his *Civil History of the Kingdom of Naples,* a strong defence of secular authority over the church. For it he had been exiled from Naples, but in Geneva he published *Il Triregno,* an even more bitter attack on papal claims. In 1736 he made the mistake of entering Piedmont, where he was imprisoned for the remaining twelve years of his life.

In 1759 Charles III succeeded to the throne of Spain. His third son, Ferdinand, a child of nine, was proclaimed King of Naples. Tanucci was the effective ruler of Naples until his fall from power in 1771. Ferdinand was by then married to Maria Carolina, daughter of the Empress Maria Theresa of Austria. She was to be a considerable influence on Ferdinand, whose reign was to last – with violent interruptions during the Napoleonic period – until 1825. It was an era of social, economic and political decline.

In Tuscany the House of Medici was in the last stage of its decadence. Its last duke, Giovanni Gastone, died in 1737. The achievements of his reign and that of his predecessor, Cosimo III, had been limited to the building of a few churches and convents. The Habsburgs seized the opportunity offered by the extinction of the Medici line to establish themselves in Florence. Francis of Lorraine became Grand Duke of Tuscany. The year before he had married Maria Theresa, who became empress of Austria in 1740, Francis himself was elected Holy Roman Emperor in 1745 and left for Vienna, turning Tuscany over to a regency. This unpromising beginning of the history of the House of Lorraine in Tuscany was to be wholly redeemed by the reign of the son of Francis, Leopold I (1747–90). It was the age of the 'enlightened despots', of those monarchs who accepted some of the doctrines of the Enlightenment. Leopold I, or Pietro Leopoldo, as he was known to the Italians, was perhaps the most enlightened of them all. He even had some respect for what, in a later age, would be called Italian nationalism, in the sense that he thought it wise to rule through Italian ministers. On his arrival in Florence he dismissed the German ministers he had inherited, while Italians, most important of whom was Francesco Maria Gianni, were retained in office. The main point under discussion in 1747 was the need to liberalize trade in view of recent bad harvests, which made the free import of grain seem necessary. Gianni, a moderate reformer, favoured the abolition of export duties, but recommended that the big landowners should not be antagonized by the removal of all import duties. Leopold moved cautiously in the direction of free trade, and imports were freed of tariffs in 1771. The growth of industry was encouraged, and the legal codes were rationalized. Leopold was convinced that the only function of the ruler was to increase the well-being and happiness of his subjects. Rarely has a ruler been so little concerned with his own prestige, and so fully concerned with the good of the people.

The Papacy was less influential in the eighteenth century than it had been in the Spanish period. Rome became the haunt of writers and artists – and simple, rich tourists – from Northern Europe, rather than of pilgrims. Even the popes themselves were influenced by the Enlightenment, and in Rome there existed an open-minded spirit which had not been in evidence since the Renaissance. The writers of the Enlightenment were, of course, basically unsympathetic to the traditions of the Papacy, and hostile to the claims of the Council of Trent, but during the comparatively long pontificate of Benedict XIV (1740–58) there was a more tolerant spirit in Rome. The Pope himself corresponded in a friendly manner with Montesquieu and Voltaire.

The spearhead of the papal offensive during the Counter-

Reformation had been the Jesuit Order. The Catholic monarchs of Europe had come to think of the Jesuits as a foreign element, opposed to the interests of the state. They had been expelled from Portugal, France and Spain, and many of them had, ironically, been obliged to take refuge in Protestant Prussia and Orthodox Russia. Benedict's successor, Clement XIII (1758–69) had spoken in defence of the Jesuits, but Clement XIV (1769–74) was under such pressure from the French Bourbons that he felt obliged to dissolve the Order in 1773. They were to be re-established in Rome in 1814 after the defeat of Napoleon.

The Republic of Venice became increasingly decadent in the eighteenth century, and was isolated politically and culturally from Europe, in a way that the rest of Italy was not. But Venice retained her independence until the arrival of Napoleon, and her beauty attracted rich Europeans, for whom she became a unique meeting-place. She also preserved peace and neutrality in the several European wars of the eighteenth century.

Milan remained Austrian from 1713 until 1859, apart from the Napoleonic period. In 1748, after the War of the Austrian Succession, Maria Theresa gave Parma legal independence under Philip, the younger brother of Charles III of Naples. The British foreign office was still giving diplomatic recognition to Parma as an independent state in 1859, although the duchy was effectively a satellite of Austria. Lombardy had some gains from the reforms of Maria Theresa, and the more radical ones of Joseph II, who was emperor of Austria from 1780 to 1790. The ownership of land was surveyed, and a tax on land was imposed which seems to have acted as an incentive to increased cultivation. Feudalism in the full sense of the term had never existed in Italy as it had in Northern Europe, but by the reforms of Joseph II some ancient privileges of landowners were removed.

The most positive aspect of Italy's history in the eighteenth century remains to be considered – her contribution to the

Enlightenment. The most influential writers of the Enlightenment were French, though a few were Scottish or English. A group of Italians in Milan, however, can be numbered among the most original and radical. Two brothers, Alessandro and Pietro Verri, worked with the Austrian authorities to introduce reforms in schools, universities and the administration of Lombardy. Pietro Verri (1728–97) was recommending free trade before Adam Smith published his *Wealth of Nations* in 1776. Verri founded a journal, which he called *Il Caffè*, explaining that coffee wakes you up and makes you ready for new perceptions. The journal was full of the new economic ideas, and in its short life had a considerable impact.

More revolutionary than the thought of the Verri brothers was that of their friend, Cesare Beccaria (1738–94), who was a criminologist rather than an economist. He was an excessively lazy man, and it was only because of great pressure from Pietro Verri that he published his little masterpiece, *Of Crimes and Punishments*. In it he seems almost to regard the concept of 'punishment' as a primitive one. Society must be protected from criminals, but should try to reform, rather than to punish, criminals. He attacks torture, pointing out that even the Romans, 'who were barbarians on more than one count', reserved torture for their slaves.[*] And he links torture with capital punishment, another barbarism inherited from a savage past.

Beccaria's book had a direct influence in the Italy of his day. In Tuscany the Grand Duke Leopold followed Beccaria's advice, and reformed the criminal code, even to the extent of abolishing the death sentence. His code of 1786 is unequivocal:

We have observed with horror how easily, in the former legislation, the death sentence was prescribed even for crimes which were not very serious ... considering that a very different kind of legislation would be suited to the increased gentleness and humanity of the

---

[*] Franco Venturi, *Italy and the Enlightenment*, edited by Stuart Wolf (London, 1972), p. 158.

present century and especially of the Tuscan people, we have arrived at the decision to abolish for ever the death penalty for any kind of offender.[5]

With Beccaria and Leopold the term 'Enlightenment' had taken on a deeper significance.

In every century of modern times Italy has produced scientists of significance for the world. The eighteenth century was no exception. Luigi Galvani (1737–98), professor of anatomy at Bologna, advanced the study of the muscles, and Alessandro Volta (1745–1827), professor of natural philosophy at Pavia, had invented the electric battery before the close of the century. The volt is named after him.

## 4 The military state of Savoy and its dynasty

The House of Savoy was to have a brilliant future. Under this ancient dynasty the Italian nation state which enjoys a robust life at the end of the twentieth century was to be founded in the mid-nineteenth century. The main themes of the dynasty's life are diplomatic and military. Its origins rested in the growth of a feudal territory. It never experienced the medieval commune, which characterized the other states of Northern Italy – Milan, Florence and Venice. Nor did it enjoy the rich cultural achievements of the Renaissance which those states enjoyed.

Nor are its origins in any sense Italian. The story may be said to start on the other side of the Alps, where a Count Thomas of Savoy had seven sons and two daughters. He supported, and was supported by, the Emperor Frederick II. He died in 1233, but his remarkable offspring showed great skill in their dealings with the powers in western Europe. Their territorial acquisitions were integrated by their nephew, Amedeo V, 'the Great' (1249–1323). By the fourteenth century, Amedeo VI (1343–83), the 'Green Count' as he was called,

---

[5] Ibid., p. 163.

from the vivid green of his clothes, controlled a fair stretch of territory which is now partly in France, partly in Switzerland, and partly in Italy. The original county of Savoy stretched westwards to the Rhône at Mâcon, and north-eastwards to Lausanne, and his lands included the Passes of the Grand and Petit Saint-Bernard and the Mont Cenis, and, in Italy, not only Aosta and Ivrea, but Turin. At one moment, in 1381, the Green Count played an important role in Turin, when he mediated between Venice, Genoa, Hungary, Florence, Padua. Aquileia and Ancona. His successor, Amedeo VIII (1383–1451), was recognized as a duke in 1416: the duchy of Savoy had started on its long career.

The subsequent career of Amedeo VIII himself was a somewhat chequered one. He was elected pope by the Council of Basle in 1439, and the conciliar party supported his claims for ten years, but he was not accepted as pope in Rome, where first Eugenius IV, and then Nicholas V, reigned as the officially recognized popes. If as 'Pope Felix V' Amedeo VIII was ultimately unsuccessful, as duke of Savoy he established firm control of the three passes over the Alps, and extended his control of Piedmont to include Saluzzo, a region which was for long to be disputed with French kings. Amedeo VIII also ruled with more sophisticated institutions – a council and an exchequer, and he even called an occasional estates general. But under his successors, Ludovico (1440–65), and Amedeo IX (1465–72), the duchy was destabilized by the French, and threatened to fall apart.

In the mid-sixteenth century the duchy was occupied by the French for almost twenty years. The Treaty of Cateau-Cambrésis in 1559, which ended the long wars between France and Spain, was a turning point in the history of the duchy. Emanuele Filiberto (1553–80) had been turned out by the French. He was now re-installed as duke, but Spanish influence was strong, and the French remained in Turin. Emanuele Filiberto introduced significant administrative reforms, and by the end of his reign the French had been persuaded to leave Turin. The reign of the next duke, Carlo Emanuele I (1580–1630) – a long one – was a period of warfare and economic neglect. The duke miscalculated badly in 1588 by occupying Saluzzo, which was a dependency of France. He believed that the French king, Henry IV, had not asserted his authority sufficiently after the French wars of religion. But Henry was not so easily going to give up French claims to Saluzzo. Long negotiations ended in a French invasion of Savoy, and reacquisition of Saluzzo, in 1600. Savoy was acquiring its diplomatic and military traditions. but remaining economically and socially backward.

After the brief, and comparatively enlightened, reign of Vittorio Amedeo I (1630–1637), French influence was again strong when the boy-king, Carlo Emanuele, needed the regency of his mother, Cristina, who was a daughter of Henry IV of France. But by the eighteenth century Savoy had become a predominantly Italian duchy, with economic and cultural links with the rest of Italy, although the court and aristocracy were still French-speaking. It still lacked a big city like Rome, Naples or Milan, but the population of Turin doubled in the course of the eighteenth century. In the War of the Spanish Succession the history of Savoy reached a turning point even more significant than that which had been provided by the Treaty of Cateau-Cambrésis. She was now treated as a state whose interests and policies were of importance to the great powers. Now at last her strategic position astride the Alpine passes was fully appreciated.

The reigning duke during this important phase of the duchy's history was Vittorio Amedeo II (1675–1730). His father died when he was only nine, so that he, too, had a period under the regency of his mother, another Frenchwoman. But he assumed full powers in 1684. During the war the loss of Turin to the French was averted in 1706 by the brilliant commander, Prince Eugène, a distant cousin of Vittorio

Amedeo. If the immediate result of the war was to make Austria supreme in Italy, there were momentous results also for the duchy of Savoy. By the Treaty of Utrecht in 1713 Savoy secured Sicily, with the title of king for Vittorio Amedeo II. He remained king of Sicily only until 1720, when he was forced to exchange it for the other island of Sardinia. Thus the dukes of Savoy acquired the title 'king of Sardinia', which they were to keep until they became kings of Italy in 1861. For the title of the increasingly important mainland kingdom to be attached to the thinly populated, semi-barbarous island was always slightly absurd, but while the title 'king of Sardinia' remained the correct one diplomatically speaking the kingdom was more usually called 'Piedmont', and that is the name by which it will henceforth be known in this history.

In acquiring the title of king, and the increase of territory, Savoy had enjoyed the diplomatic support of Britain, her ally in the War of the Spanish Succession. It was the beginning of a long tradition, which was not to be seriously broken until Mussolini's declaration of war in 1940. It suited British policy to build up a strong Piedmontese kingdom – eventually to become a maritime one – as part of the balance of power.

When Vittorio Amedeo II took over personal power at the age of eighteen, Savoy was a little state with a population of less than 800,000. Administration was fragmented. The province of Savoy itself, and Aosta, were autonomous, and Piedmont had a separate senate. The nobles and the church were large landowners, though less large than the same groups were in Southern Italy. They owned, however, the richest land, and they constituted, of course, a small minority of the population – some 10,000 nobles and 20,000 priests. The rich had tax privileges, and the system of tax farming opened the door to corruption. Vittorio Amedeo centralized the system of tax collecting, creating a single central treasury in the place of a chaos of local, feudal ones. A new rich middle class was to administer the tax system, and if they were no less corrupt than their predecessors, they were probably more efficient. Taxes were high because Vittorio Amedeo had to depend on a very large army. He needed sources of extraordinary revenue in addition to the subsidies he was paid by the British and the Dutch. It was probably his need for cash, rather than any egalitarian zeal, that led to his decision to tax the nobles, although it was loudly proclaimed that a fairer system of taxation was aimed at. The new tax system was known as *Perequazione.* It was inaugurated with a large-scale tax survey, which already stirred up local opposition. In one region forty-nine people were hanged, and many more exiled, for resisting.[6] By the time the survey was completed, and the new tax system was to be enforced, Vittorio Amedeo's long reign had come to an end, through his abdication. In 1731 the new king Carlo Emanuele III passed the edict of *Perequazione,* and abolished noble and clerical tax immunities.

In 1717 Vittorio Amedeo had preceded the tax survey by the setting up of a council of state, which resembled a modern ministry in a way that previous bodies had never done. In the field of industry the king imposed heavy taxes on imported silk products, to encourage the working of silk in his own lands rather than the export of raw silk. The reign ended on a note of personal tragedy for the king. In 1730 he abdicated in favour of his son, Carlo Emanuele, but the following year he decided that Carlo Emanuele was making mistakes, and he attempted to return to the throne. He was not allowed to do so, but was arrested, and kept in confinement until his death – an episode with a distinctly King Lear-like flavour.

The Treaty of Aix-la-Chapelle, in 1748, after the War of the Austrian Succession, provided the kingdom of Piedmont with fresh gains, including Nice. The Seven Years War (1756–63), which was fought in Asia, North America and on the oceans of the world, as well as in Europe, left Italy in peace – an

---

[6] Dino Carpanetto and Giuseppe Ricuperati, *Italy in the Age of Reason, 1685–1789* (London, 1987), pp. 140–2.

exception to her more usual role as a battleground for other nations.

Sardinia/Piedmont had not shared in the intellectual vitality of Northern Italy in the eighteenth century. Instead she had developed a strong military tradition, and a diplomatic tradition which was to be developed to its highest point of achievement by Cavour, and was a main ingredient in the 1861 Kingdom of Italy. The strength of these traditions lay partly in the fact that the kingdom had one dynasty surviving over the centuries, when the other Italian states had such varied political rulers.

Another characteristic of Piedmont which was to last until the nineteenth century was its consistent, sometimes fanatical, adherence to orthodox Catholicism, as illustrated by its war with Calvin's Geneva in the 1530s, and the massacre of the Waldenses in 1655.

Chapter 6

# *THE RISORGIMENTO*

## *1 The Napoleonic and Restoration eras, 1790–1821*

Eighteenth-century Italy had been the source of many enlight-ened political ideas, but the concept of national sovereignty had not been one of them. The monarch, whether the Habsburg emperor, the pope or a grand duke, had been generally accepted as the sovereign. The idea that the people were sovereign had been vaguely present in classical days – with their 'Senate and People of Rome' – but it had not survived into the Middle Ages. It had been revived in the eighteenth century by Rousseau and the many French pamph-leteers whose ideas could be traced back to Rousseau. In Italy the 'ideas of 1789' were not a native product, but they were quickly adopted by men who were recognized as 'Jacobins', a term which raised strong passions, whether it was used for praise or abuse.

Wars in modern times have usually had an ideological element attached to them, if only offered as an excuse for less noble reasons, or as a propaganda façade to encourage the unfortunate people who have to fight the war. The war which started in 1792 between revolutionary France on the one hand, and the Austrian and Prussian monarchies on the other, had a larger ideological element than most wars. In such a war Piedmont would have been a natural enemy of revolutionary France, even if she had not been strategically placed in the front line of resistance to this strange new force which had been hurled at the world by the citizens of Paris.

The reigning king of Piedmont in 1792 was Vittorio Amedeo (1773–96). He had close links with the French Bourbons, in that his two daughters had married the two younger brothers of Louis XVI. The youngest of the three brothers, the Comte d'Artois, one day to be Charles X of France, fled into exile after the storming of the Bastille in 1789, and brought his wife home to Turin. In 1794 he was followed by an offensive by the French army, an offensive which the Piedmontese withstood, although they had already lost Nice and Savoy to the French. Two years later the French invaded Italy in a brilliantly successful campaign, under a general of twenty-seven: Napoleon Bonaparte.

Although Napoleon was born in Corsica, claims could be made that he was more Italian than French, since both his parents came from families which had originated from the Italian mainland. But the simple fact was that Napoleon had considered himself to be a Frenchman since he had become an adult. His own very special sentiments towards Italy were almost certainly the result of his brilliant successes in 1796. After defeating the Piedmontese and the Austrians, he entered Milan, Bologna and Verona. Although theoretically only a general in the French army, he was so popular that the five men who formed the Directory and governed in Paris could not prevent him from conducting his own diplomacy in Italy, and reshaping the political map.

Bologna and Ferrara were made the basis of a small Cispadane Republic, and Milan was made the basis of a Transpadane Republic, while the ancient Republic of Genoa was given new institutions and named the Ligurian Republic, following the practice of adopting Latin names in honour of Italy's classical past. The Cispadane and Transpadane Republics were soon merged into a Cisalpine Republic, which was to have a rather longer history. A constitution, with an elected assembly, was provided for the Cisalpine Republic, and Napoleon appointed Italians as ministers, but the reality of power lay in his hands. There is no doubt, however, that the Italian professional classes regarded these new states as improvements on anything that had existed before.

The ancient Venetian Republic tried to remain neutral in the war. The elder of the two brothers of Louis XVI, the Comte de Provence, who was one day to be Louis XVIII, sought refuge in Venice under the pseudonym the 'Comte de Lille'. The Venetians at first accepted his presence – with his Italian wife – but then, fearing Napoleon's hostility, asked him to leave. But for other reasons, they had antagonized both Napoleon and Austria. Napoleon reacted in a characteristically ruthless manner. On 1 May, 1797, he declared war on Venice. The Venetian Grand Council at first prepared to resist, but, partly because of strong sympathy for the French among the Venetian masses, they accepted Napoleon's demands that their traditional institutions should be abolished. It did not save Venetian independence. In October 1797 Napoleon signed a peace with the Austrians, placing Venice under Austrian sovereignty in exchange for Austria's Belgian provinces. The Republic of Venice, which had survived for a millennium, was thus destroyed by a cynical piece of *Realpolitik*, on the part of a young French officer.

Before the end of 1797 Napoleon had left Italy, and set out on his spectacular Egyptian expedition. In his absence the 'Jacobin' movement continued, and a republic was established in Rome itself. The period 1796–9 was subsequently to be referred to as the 'triennio' – the three years which seemed to republican nationalists to anticipate the 'risorgimento'. The term 'risorgimento' had been coined by the dramatist, Vittorio Alfieri (1749–1803), who had prophesied a coming political and cultural 'resurgence' of Italy after her long years under foreign autocrats.

England had entered the war against France in 1793, and in

Map 5. Italy in 1798

1798 Napoleon was thus involved in a naval war in the Mediterranean, a war inevitably also involving Naples. Jacobin clubs and masonic lodges had been active in Naples since 1792. Conspiracies against the monarchy were uncovered – one in Naples in 1794, and another in Sicily in 1795. Several people were imprisoned, deported, tortured, or hanged. In 1798 Nelson arrived in Naples, after his naval victory over the French. The Neapolitan king, Ferdinand, took the offensive against the French, and briefly occupied Rome. But they were soon driven out; the French occupied the mainland kingdom of Naples; Ferdinand and his energetic queen, Maria Carolina, fled to Sicily; and in Naples the pro-French revolutionaries established the Parthenopean Republic. A social war of a brutal kind then developed. The liberal-minded, middle-class men who tried to run the Parthenopean Republic had advanced ideas on social reform, but acted too slowly to satisfy the *lazzaroni* – the very poor of Naples – and seemed unaware of the immediate needs of the peasants. A counter-revolutionary peasant army was formed under a priest, Cardinal Fabrizio Ruffo. Naples was sacked, much as cities had been sacked in more primitive centuries, and an appalling massacre of the 'Jacobin' middle classes filled the streets with corpses. The Bourbons returned.

In the last days of 1799 Napoleon made himself First Consul, or virtual dictator of France. In the spring of 1800 he returned with a fresh army to Northern Italy, which had been briefly retaken by the Austrians. In June he won the great victory of Marengo. Chairing an assembly to re-establish the Cisalpine Republic, he accepted the shouted suggestions of the Italian deputies that it should now be named the 'Italian Republic'. Thus, for the first time in history, the word 'Italian' was given to an existing political state, a state which did not, of course, occupy even half of the peninsula, but which was nominally sovereign and independent, even if Napoleon took the title of president himself.

When Napoleon made himself emperor in 1804, the various republics he had created in Europe were converted into kingdoms, with a new, classless, race of kings, appreciably more able than those of the old regime, though destined to survive for less than a decade. The Italian Republic became the 'Kingdom of Italy', with Napoleon as its king. He had appointed respected, and efficient, Italian ministers for the Italian Republic, and pursued the same policy for the Kingdom, except that he appointed as his viceroy a Frenchman, Eugène de Beauharnais. The relationship of the Beauharnais family with Italy was to be important in the future. Eugène was the son, by her first marriage, of Napoleon's empress, Josephine. Eugène's sister, Hortense, had married Napoleon's brother, Louis, in 1802, and was to give birth to a boy, Louis-Napoleon, in 1808. As the Emperor Napoleon III, this child was one day to liberate Lombardy from Austria for ever. At his birth, then, his links with Italy were already strong, since two of his uncles were together ruling the first Kingdom of Italy. Eugène was an intelligent and popular ruler. Venice was added to the Kingdom of Italy, and Eugène given the title of 'Prince of Venice'.

In 1796 and 1797 Napoleon had been prepared to negotiate with Pope Pius VI, when the Directory in Paris would have taken a more overtly anti-clerical line, and it was while Napoleon was in Egypt that the French had declared the pope deposed as temporal ruler, and had chased him from Rome. Not that Napoleon was soft-hearted so far as the pope was concerned. Rather was it that he saw the pope as harmless, and the Catholic religion as a stabilizing force in French society. When Austrian and Russian armies were moving into Northern Italy in 1799 Pius VI, known to the French as 'Citizen Pope', was forced to leave Italy for France. He died at Valence, virtually in captivity, in March. His successor, Pius VII (1799–1823), was to receive more brutal treatment at the hands of the French – and specifically of Napoleon – but was to outlive the First Empire. Soon after the founding of the Empire in May, 1804, the pope, much to his surprise, was invited by Napoleon to come to Paris to crown him. Napoleon and the pope had already signed a Concordat, which had partly restored the independence of the Catholic Church in France, without making it the established religion. But for the pope to travel to Paris might seem to give his blessing to the Revolution. He therefore delayed his decision, and did not

Map 6. Italy in 1810

leave Rome for Paris until September. In Paris he was treated with contempt by Napoleon, but with veneration by the crowds in the streets. The news that Pius had been treated badly in Paris was greeted with outrage in Italy, and increased popular affection for the pope, after the many years when the Papacy had seemed to be on its last legs.

The French control of Italy during the Napoleonic period provided many benefits to be balanced against considerable disadvantages. On the credit side there was the more efficient administration, and the adoption of the Code Napoléon. It was an improvement to have a simple, clearly articulated code of law, even if that code showed an excessive respect for the rights of property, no concern for the well-being of workers, and a sexist preoccupation for the authority of the father in the family. Only in Tuscany – because of the reforms of Pietro Leopoldo – had the criminal code been more civilized than the Napoleonic one. But balanced against the improvements were the increased taxes, the introduction of conscription, and the theft of art treasures: the looting was systematic, and organized on a large scale.

Another benefit brought by Napoleon, however, was the enlightened nature of the rulers he imposed on Italy. Eugène de Beauharnais has already been mentioned. When the Bourbons were driven out of Naples in 1805, Napoleon made his own elder brother, Joseph, king. Joseph had studied at the University of Pisa. He had thus had closer links with Italy than Napoleon had, and was a more cultured person. He ruled Naples for two years, through a council of state, which contained some Frenchmen, but a majority of Italians. In 1808 he was given the rather more important throne of Spain, and Napoleon made Joachim Murat king of Naples. The son of an inn-keeper, Murat had attracted the attention of Napoleon by his brilliance as a cavalry leader. Like Beauharnais, he was obliged to accompany Napoleon on the horrific 1812 expedition to Moscow, but they both left behind able ministers to rule their kingdoms in their absence.

Several of Napoleon's greatest victories had been in Italy. His defeats were to be elsewhere, and culminated in the three-day battle of Leipzig in October 1813. Murat abandoned support of Napoleon before the emperor's abdication, and so was left as king of Naples by the Austrians and their allies. After his defeat, Napoleon was an unwilling, but unguarded, exile on Elba from May 1814 to March 1815, when he again landed in France, to start the extraordinary adventure of the Hundred Days. Murat changed sides once more. Proclaiming himself king of united Italy, he led his army to the north to occupy Rome, Florence and Bologna. Only then was he halted, and defeated by the Austrians. He was court-martialled and shot, but by declaring the unity of Italy, he had added to the mythology of the Risorgimento.

The final defeat of Napoleon at Waterloo, and the settlement of Europe which was drawn up at Vienna in 1815, opened a long period of peace for Italy, as for Europe, but it was a peace accompanied by considerable political and social malaise. Austria's claims to Lombardy and Venice were accepted, and her influence was extended over much of the rest of the peninsula. The 1815 settlement restored the pre-revolutionary map and political condition of Italy, with the modifications that the ancient republics of Venice and Genoa were not restored, and Austria and Piedmont were both fortified as Italian states. Piedmont acquired the great, historic port of Genoa, which turned her into a Mediterranean power (Nice had never had much significance as a port), and a more genuinely Italian state.

The monarchs were restored with absolute powers. Vittorio Emanuele I was restored in Turin, and arrived wearing the pig-tail and clothes of the eighteenth century: a figure of fun rather than a brutal despot. Ferdinand was restored in Naples, and in 1816 declared that the mainland state and the island of Sicily were united, with the title of 'the Kingdom of the Two Sicilies', a title which it was to retain, in the language of the diplomatic world, until its death in 1860. In this history, however, it will continue to be called by the more familiar term of the Kingdom of Naples. The Central Duchies – Tuscany, Parma and Modena – all received back their absolute rulers. They were all related, in one way or another, to the Habsburgs, but were recognized as sovereign, independent, rulers by the other powers. The restoration of monarchical absolutism represented a harking back to a previous age, an age which it would have been better to forget. There was profound hostility to the restored regimes among intellectuals, the professional classes, and the many disbanded officers from Napoleon's armies, who shared the high hopes and deep disappointments of most returning soldiers after a long war.

The country to which they returned was not prosperous, and the contrast between North and South was already apparent, and was becoming accentuated. The comparative prosperity of Lombardy has sometimes been credited to the Austrians, but it owed more to the traditions of Italian engineering skills, which for ages had drained and irrigated the Po Valley, than to the administrative reforms of the days of Maria Theresa and Joseph II. Nor is the praise sometimes lavished on Austrian educational standards entirely deserved. Shortly after unification – in 1871 – 45 per cent of the population of Lombardy were illiterate. In what had been the native Italian state of Piedmont the figure was only 42 per cent.[1]

A feature of the political history of Italy during the Restoration period was the growth of the secret societies. They were composed of alienated members of the educated classes, with a strong component of retired army officers. They were strongest in the Kingdom of Naples, where they tended to oppose any regime – the French ones in Napoleonic days, the Bourbons after 1815. The most active were the Carbonari, who were prepared to adopt violent, revolutionary methods, although their aims were not extreme. They were prepared to retain the monarchy, provided a constitution was granted which would give some hope of political life. The Masons were as widespread as the Carbonari – perhaps more widespread – but were more law-abiding, and so less feared by the regime.

A leading figure in the secret societies immediately after

[1] Carlo M. Cipolla, *Literacy and Development in the West* (London, 1969), p. 19.

1815 was Filippo Buonarroti. He had taken part in the socialist rising led by his friend, Babeuf, in Paris in 1796. In the Restoration period he operated mainly from Switzerland – and later Paris – but had headquarters in Alessandria, a Piedmontese town which was always a radical centre. Buonarroti was a utopian. He aimed at revolution followed by the setting up of a communist society, where there would be no private property, but this dream he felt obliged to keep secret from all but his closest collaborators. More immediately, as an Italian (and a direct descendant of Michelangelo), he aimed at the independence of Italy from Austria.

The first revolutions led by the Carbonari against the restored regimes were in 1820 and 1821 in Naples and Piedmont. Both initially succeeded. In Naples Ferdinand I was forced to grant a constitution and to appoint liberal ministers. He would not have been able to regain absolute power without the military help of a great power. Since 1815 the European great powers had created what was known as the 'Congress System', which meant in practice an agreement that their representatives would meet fairly regularly, and always if a crisis which seemed to them to threaten peace had developed. Italy was tacitly accepted as a sphere of Austrian influence, and the Austrian Chancellor, Prince Metternich, was determined to suppress any liberal movement in the peninsula, whether it was under Austrian rule or not. He therefore invited the powers to send representatives to a congress to be held at Troppau. The Prussians and Russians were happy to comply. The British were less happy, and sent only an observer.

The 1820 congress decided on the 'Troppau Doctrine', according to which they would suppress European revolutions which threatened the peace. Although the Neapolitan revolution could hardly be so regarded, the three Eastern powers decided to meet again at Laibach in 1821, and at this second meeting Austria was commissioned to send an army to restore the status quo in Naples. The revolutionary government in

Naples put in the field an army under General Pepe, who was still to be around to lead another revolutionary army in 1848. They fought courageously, but were defeated by the larger Austrian army. Ferdinand was restored to absolute power.

Members of the Carbonari also played a part in the revolution in Piedmont in 1821. Two days after the rising Vittorio Emanuele I abdicated in favour of his brother, Carlo Felice. The crisis was complicated by the ambiguous role played by the young Carlo Alberto, Prince of Carignan, who was persuaded by the revolutionaries to take the throne in the absence of Carlo Felice, and to grant a constitution. When Carlo Felice returned to Turin ten days later, Carlo Alberto left in indecent haste. More radical revolutionaries continued the struggle for two or three weeks outside Turin, but were defeated by an invading Austrian army at Novara.

The man responsible for the defeat of the revolutions of 1820/1 was Prince Clemens Metternich (1773–1859). Italy had always been one of his main preoccupations. At the Congress of Vienna he had been quite prepared to surrender the Austrian Netherlands, but had insisted on Austrian claims to Lombardy and Venice, and had even tried, unsuccessfully, to take territory from the pope. As foreign minister, and later chancellor, of the Austrian emperor, he had decided that any glimmering of liberal or nationalist sympathies were a threat to the survival of the Habsburg Monarchy, and must be ruthlessly suppressed. A vain, but intelligent man, he suffered from the belief that the forces of the nineteenth century were threatening to destroy civilization, and that all he could do was to delay the process. He saw Italian nationalism as one of his most dangerous enemies.

## 2  Italian nationalism and the role of Mazzini, 1821–49

Enough has been said in this history to show that Italy was more than the 'geographical expression' by which Metternich described her in 1847. 'Italy' had been a cultural expression rather longer than 'Europe' had been. But Italy had not enjoyed political unity since the days of the Roman Empire. There had always been more than one sovereign authority in Italy, but there had at least been times when all sovereign authorities in Italy had been native Italian ones. This had been the case at times in the late Middle Ages and early Renaissance period – in other words in periods of great cultural achievement. In such periods there had been a clear understanding of what was meant by an 'Italian' prince, and equally what was meant when a 'foreign' prince invaded, or threatened to invade. There had even been occasional moments when there were hopes that an Italian prince would succeed in uniting the peninsula under his rule. Giangaleazzo Visconti had seemed a candidate, and had claimed to be the protector of Italy against 'barbarian nations, the enemies of Italy'. But there had always been cross-currents. Visconti had been a despot, and had been halted by the Florentine Republic, which claimed to be defending freedom and the civic virtues. And Mazzini was perhaps right to identify moments of greatness in Italian history with moments of republicanism. He was to be the first person to pursue, in a single movement, the independence of Italians from foreign rule, the political unity of the peninsula, and freedom for the individual citizen.

The nationalism of nineteenth-century Italy was part of a wider European movement, which was itself part of the Romantic reaction to the eighteenth-century Enlightenment. There had been in the eighteenth century a cosmopolitan outlook, a respect for French tastes and ideas, and a certain contempt for national differences. It was believed that rational laws and behaviour could be applied universally. But with the nineteenth century came a reaction. Just as the Romantic movement in the arts and letters proclaimed the importance of individual values, of the emotions and the imagination, so in political thought national characteristics and diversities were

felt to have a deeper significance than dispassionate speculation along purely abstract lines. Johann Gottfried Herder
(1744–1803), a prophet of cultural nationalism, had argued
that German was not only the language of the peasants, but
could become a great literary language. Italian was already a
great literary language: the basis of Italian cultural nationalism had been laid for centuries.

The revolutions of 1820/1 had already displayed a faint and
vague sense of Italian nationalism. The Piedmontese revolutionaries, if not those in Naples, had at least dreamed of
driving the Austrians out of Italy. The revolutions which
broke out in the Papal States in 1831 were not primarily
concerned with nationalist aims, but with the removal of the
judicial corruption and poor administration of the pope's
officials. In practice this meant the abolition of the pope's
temporal power in Bologna and the Legations, where the
revolt had broken out. Gregory XVI (1831–46) had just been
elected pope. His cardinal legate in Bologna had no means
available with which to resist the rising. A provisional
revolutionary government was set up, the pope's temporal
power declared abolished, and an assembly elected. One of the
revolutionary ministers noted in a private letter that the
revolution should be 'a national not a municipal' one, and
'other provinces of Italy' were invited to send deputies to
Bologna.

Metternich, however, was still chancellor in Vienna, and, in
spite of French and British protests, arranged for Austrian
military intervention. But he was perhaps less alarmed by what
had happened in Bologna than by parallel revolutions which
had broken out in the two duchies of Parma and Modena,
which were Austrian satellites. In Modena a leader of the
revolution, Ciro Menotti, was shot by the Austrians, and
became a martyr of the Risorgimento. Garibaldi was to
name one of his sons Menotti. But the revolutions in all three
regions of central Italy were suppressed by the Austrians. The

French government at the time, the government of the July Monarchy, was itself the product of recent revolution. It had loudly proclaimed that a policy of non-intervention in Italy should be respected by the great powers. When the Austrians blatantly ignored this warning the French government at first did nothing. But in 1832 they took the somewhat ineffectual step of sending an expedition to occupy the papal city of Ancona, but not to stir further, and certainly not to confront the Austrians. In practice the French were at least discouraging the Austrians from approaching Rome itself, but the time for an active military confrontation between France and Austria in Italy had not yet come. The next phase in the struggle for Italian independence and unity was to be dominated by the ideas of Giuseppe Mazzini. Born in Genoa in 1805, Mazzini was the son of a medical practitioner, and later university professor, but the first dominating influence in his life was that of his fanatically republican and democratically minded mother, who believed that her brilliant child was to be some kind of messiah of a new world. Up to a point she was right. Not only in Italy, but in places as remote as Ireland or India, his vision as a nationalist prophet was to be acknowledged by groups of young idealists.

Mazzini graduated in law in the University of Genoa, but his real interests were literary and historical. His youthful publications were impassioned defences of Romanticism in literature against Classicism. While still at school he had developed a keen awareness of a movement for Italian nationhood and political freedom. The movement was stronger in his imagination than in reality, but in the 1830s he was to do much to adjust the latter to conform with the former. Two sources of his political ideas had been the writings of Herder, which he read in French translation, since he never learnt German, and Saint-Simon (1760–1825). Mazzini, unlike Saint-Simon, was never to call himself a socialist, nor did he share Saint-Simon's Christian convictions, but Mazzini's

Plate 6. A portrait of Mazzini, painted by F. Moscheles in 1862.
Milan, Museo del Risorgimento

attitude to the French Revolution owed much to that of the French aristocratic socialist. Both men believed that the French Revolution had been triumphant in proclaiming the rights of the individual, but that it had failed to complete the message by reorganizing society along more positive lines – lines by which the individual's obligations and duties to society would be stressed, as well as his rights.

When revolution broke out in central Italy in 1831 Mazzini was in Genoa. He had joined the Carbonari, one member of whom – a government spy – reported him to the Piedmontese police. Mazzini was imprisoned for a few weeks, and in this brief spell evolved a programme for Italian nationalism. He had decided that the Carbonari were too theatrical in their manner and not clear enough in their aims. He would found a new society of young men – he would call it 'La Giovine Italia' – who would be completely dedicated to the expulsion of the foreigners and the unification of a democratic republic of Italy. On his release from prison he was sent into exile, and at Marseilles joined the numerous other Italian émigrés. 'Young Italy' was formed, and was destined to dominate the nationalist movement for the next decade.

All over Italy cells of 'Young Italy' were quickly formed, but its centres were wherever Mazzini was, or in Genoa, where several of his friends remained. As a propaganda machine the organization was brilliantly successful; as an insurrectionary body it was miserably unsuccessful. Mazzini made converts among young officers in the Piedmontese army, and his first insurrectionary attempt was in 1833 in Turin and Genoa. Before anything had been achieved the conspiracy was betrayed to the military authorities. Of the sixty-seven people arrested some were tortured and twelve were shot. Mazzini's closest friend, Jacopo Ruffini, killed himself in prison, fearing that under torture he might incriminate others. Although appalled at what had happened, Mazzini immediately started to plan another insurrection. It included an invasion by a small body of Italian exiles from Switzerland in 1834. It failed as completely as had the attempt the year before.

Mazzini was an exile in Switzerland until 1837. With a small group of German and Polish exiles he founded a society which he called 'Young Europe'. It had no immediate political significance, but showed that Mazzini was thinking beyond the creation of an Italian nation state to a united Europe. In a Swiss newspaper he explained that his nationalism was dependent on his belief in democracy; the people believed in affirming their national identity and giving it a political shape, and the voice of the people was the voice of God. In 1837 he left Switzerland for England, and was to spend the rest of his life in London, apart from brief stays in Italy in moments of hope or crisis.

At first he lived a somewhat isolated and impoverished existence in London, but after meeting Thomas and Jane Carlyle he moved into rather more prosperous and influential literary circles. Everyone who met him was impressed by the aura of deep sincerity and near-sanctity which seemed to surround him. By the force of his personality he convinced young men that the Italian cause was worth dying for. In 1844 two brothers, Attilio and Emilio Bandiera, deserted from the Austrian navy, and with only nineteen followers tried to start a rising in Calabria against the Bourbons. They were surrounded by Neapolitan troops; the peasants showed no inclination to revolt; and nine of the young men, including the Bandiera brothers, were shot. The very suicidal nature of the venture added to the powerful myth which Mazzini had nourished.

A rival movement of a quite different kind of nationalism appeared in the 1840s. A liberal Piedmontese Catholic, Vincenzo Gioberti (1801–52), published a book in Brussels in 1843, entitled *Of the Moral and Civil Primacy of the Italians.* It spoke in glowing terms of Italy's past greatness, and suggested a path for the future which would restore Italian primacy. The

Italian states, according to Gioberti, should retain their identities and their rulers, but should unite into a confederation of which the pope should be the president. Gioberti was opposed to revolution or even war against the Austrians, but his kind of very mild nationalism appealed to the practising Catholics who had been horrified by Mazzini's doctrines. The term 'Neo-Guelf movement' which is usually applied to Gioberti's followers is a little misleading, since it was not a 'movement' in the sense that the Carbonari or Young Italy had been. But influential it certainly was.

A book dedicated to Gioberti was published in 1844: *The Hopes of Italy*, by Count Cesare Balbo, who has already been mentioned for his *Sommario della Storia d'Italia*. Balbo also favoured a confederation which would preserve the independence of the existing states, but he imagined Piedmont giving military leadership to Italy, and Austria being ejected by means of diplomacy – specifically, by Austria's acquisition of Balkan territory. In some ways he anticipated Cavour's approach. The king of Piedmont since 1831 had been Carlo Alberto, who had disappointed the revolutionaries of 1821, but in whom Balbo and others were still placing their hopes.

A third of these so-called 'moderate' theorists of Italian nationalism ('conservative' would perhaps be a more accurate adjective) was Massimo d'Azeglio (1798–1866). The most experienced and sophisticated of them all, d'Azeglio had lived in Rome, Florence and Milan, as well as his native Turin, and had made a name as both a Romantic artist and novelist. He believed that the constant pressure of public opinion in favour of Italian independence would ultimately oblige the Austrians to leave Italy. He recommended what was in effect passive resistance, a revolution 'with our hands in our pockets'.

Each of these three men – Gioberti, Balbo and d'Azeglio – was to be for a short while prime minister of Piedmont after the revolutions of 1848, but it was Gioberti whose ideas were first, if misleadingly, to appear successful. In 1846, when Gregory

XVI died, the Austrians failed to get their candidate elected, but instead a little-known, saintly man, Cardinal Mastai-Ferretti, was elected pope, and took the name of Pius IX. His pontificate was to be the longest, and one of the most momentous, in the history of the Church.

Pius IX had read Gioberti's book, and was deeply conscious of being an Italian, as well as being the temporal ruler of the Papal States, which he believed to be essential for the independence of the Papacy, and which he referred to as 'the seamless garment of Jesus Christ'. Inevitably Pius was to face a crisis of identity. His first act was to issue an indemnity to all political offenders. As a result about two thousand people who had been implicated in revolutionary activity were released from prison or allowed to return from exile, provided only that they took an oath of loyalty to the pope. He then allowed a remarkable degree of political freedom to prevail in Rome, a city which had previously been one of the most repressed in Europe. He allowed an independent press to come into existence, surveyed only by a most gentle censorship board, at a time when no independent press existed in Vienna or Turin. He allowed the foundation of political clubs and noisy public demonstrations, both of which requested further reforms. But the public reaction, not only in Rome but throughout Italy, was one of extravagant enthusiasm for the pope. The cry 'Long live Pius IX' – 'Viva Pio Nono' – became a nationalist and radical slogan. Finally Pius took his most dangerous step: he permitted the creation of an armed national guard, manned and commanded by the poor people of the Trastevere, the rabbit warren of streets on the Vatican side of the river: Rome's 'left bank', on the right bank. At the opening of 1848 the pope and the people of Rome seemed to be in a close alliance for the creation of a better world.

In 1848 there were revolutions in almost every European capital. The very first, in January, was in Palermo. Before the end of the month it had spread to Naples, and Ferdinand II's newly appointed government had published a constitution.

For the future of Italy what was happening in Piedmont was more important that what happened in Naples. In 1847 Carlo Alberto had belatedly followed the example of Pius IX, and allowed an independent press to come into existence. Several newspapers were founded, among them *Il Risorgimento*, edited by Cesare Balbo and a certain Count Cavour, whose name was to be better known a few years later. They pressed for a constitution, which Carlo Alberto finally granted in March, 1848. This was the document – the *Statuto* – which was in 1861 to become the constitutional basis for the Kingdom of Italy. It read like a very monarchical document, since it detailed at length the prerogatives of the crown, and was ambiguous on the relations between the crown and parliament. But there was to be a two-chamber parliament, the upper chamber appointed by the crown, and the lower chamber elected by the literate subjects who paid a fair amount in taxes.

An electoral law, published after the *Statuto* itself, gave the vote – within this narrow franchise – to all 'Italiani' in Piedmont. It was an important concession, since there were many exiles from Naples and the Papal States who had settled in Piedmont. They had been allowed to teach in the schools and universities, and to publish. Now they could take part in the political life of the country. Having lost their original homelands, they were in a sense the first Italians.

March, 1848, was a moment of crisis for the Habsburg Monarchy. Hungarians and Czechs were threatening to fragment the empire, and in Vienna the crowds demanded liberal institutions. The Habsburg royal family persuaded Metternich to resign, much against his will. The fall of Metternich, combined with a republican revolution in Paris, encouraged the people of Austrian Milan to rise. When the troubles started in Lombardy, the Austrians placed the province under the military authority of Radetzky, the octogenarian, but still able, general. After five days of fighting – the glorious *cinque giornate* of the Milan rising – Radetzky was obliged to withdraw his regular army before a purely civilian revolutionary force. Mazzini rushed to Milan to recommend the election of a democratic republican assembly, a civic guard and a free press. Another republican leader of the rising was Carlo Cattaneo, an economist and political scientist with some depth of vision. The Italy Cattaneo dreamed of was a federal republic to which the Italy of the 1970s, with the development of the regions, was to approximate.

It was not, however, the republicans, but the Milanese conservative aristocrats who were to assert their authority in a provisional government, and they were eager to be annexed by the Piedmontese monarchy. Carlo Alberto was faced with a difficult decision. He was, with good reason, fearful of war with Austria, but it was important for him to prevent the formation of an independent Lombard republic, and if he did not go to the help of fellow-Italians there was the danger of a rising against him at home in Piedmont, especially in Genoa, with its republican traditions and Mazzinian circles.

On 23 March Carlo Alberto declared war on Austria. The day before an independent Republic of St Mark had been declared in Venice, with the Jewish lawyer, Daniele Manin, as president. The Austrian authorities had behaved in a civilized way in Venice: when the crowd released Manin from prison, the Austrians peacefully withdrew, after the loss of only one or two lives. An elected Venetian assembly voted for merger with Piedmont. Manin accepted the democratic decision, although he would have preferred to wait in the hope that a republic of Italy might emerge. On the other hand there is evidence that the peasants of the Venetian mainland, who had experienced Austrian conscription, would have been ready to form a popular army, to fight for a democratic, rather than a

Piedmontese, solution, but Manin failed to organize them, whether from inclination or negligence.

Carlo Alberto's was not the only army to confront the Austrians. The revolutionary government in Naples sent an army under the veteran General Pepe, and a smaller army arrived from the Papal States, after a rather bizarre development. Pius had given the command of a force to Giacomo Durando, an adventurer who had fought for the revolution in Spain, but the pope had then instructed the army merely to guard the papal frontiers. It was unlikely that Durando would restrict himself to so uninteresting a task. Supplied with a manifesto written for him by Massimo d'Azeglio, he had marched his army to the north to fight the Austrians.

At this moment, then, there seemed a reasonable hope that Italy could be liberated. But at the end of April things took a turn for the worse. Outraged by the disobedience of his army, Pius IX issued an Allocution on 29 April, renouncing any intention of waging war against Austria. Many people who had mistakenly imagined that the war had the pope's blessing, and who had for two years thought of him as a great national leader against the foreigner, now realized how deluded they had been. Another blow to the Italian cause followed on 25 May, when Ferdinand of Naples, with the use of Swiss mercenaries, carried out a coup against the constitutional government, and re-established his absolute authority.

Durando's army did not return to Rome, except in the shape of individual deserters carrying arms – not a reassuring feature for Pius IX. Pepe and half of his army stayed in the north to continue the struggle which their king had renounced, but they could do nothing to avert the defeat of the Piedmontese. Radetzky received reinforcements from Austria, and won a crushing victory over Carlo Alberto's army at Custozza on 24 July. The Austrians reoccupied Lombardy.

The war of the princes, Mazzini said, was over, and now the

war of the peoples would begin. Republican revolutions in the autumn drove the Grand Duke Leopold II and Pope Pius IX from their capitals. Two of the central figures of the Risorgimento – Mazzini and Garibaldi – were to play dramatic roles in the history of the Roman Republic. Mazzini was given executive powers as the most active of three triumvirs. For over three months he ruled Rome in an astonishingly tolerant manner, neither imprisoning nor persecuting any of his enemies, and introducing social measures, like progressive taxes and a rehousing of the poor. Yet outside Rome hostile forces – Austrian, Neapolitan, Spanish and French – were concentrating to destroy the Republic.

Giuseppe Garibaldi (1807–82) was placed in command of the Roman Republic's army in the field. He had made his name in wars in South America, at first as commander of an irregular naval force, and then on land as a guerrilla leader. He fought for the independence of the republic of Uruguay, where he is recognized as one of their founding heroes. He had returned to Italy in 1848 in time to fight for the revolutionary government in Milan, having been rejected by Carlo Alberto. He was now to play a far more brilliant and glamorous role in the defence of the Roman Republic.

The government of the Second French Republic, which had destroyed a socialist rising in Paris in June 1848, now set out to restore the pope. A comparatively small French force was sent to Civitavecchia, and was defeated by an even smaller Italian force under Garibaldi. Louis-Napoleon Bonaparte was elected president in December, and decided to send a much larger force to restore the prestige of the French army. With his irregular force which was only half as large, Garibaldi resisted the French for almost a month. His resistance gave him a reputation which was to stand Italy in good stead in 1860. His retreat from Rome with a few thousand men, to whom he had offered only 'hunger, thirst, forced marches, battles and death', completed the epic story, although it could make no practical achievement.

Carlo Alberto had briefly tried to renew the war against Austria, but had scarcely survived two weeks before being again defeated, this time at the battle of Novara in March. The king abdicated, entered a monastery in Portugal, and died three months later.

The Italian authority which resisted the Austrians the longest in 1849 was Venice. After the first defeat of the Piedmontese in 1848, the Republic of St Mark had again declared its independence, which survived until the summer of 1849. Only then, faced with acute food shortage caused by the Austrian siege, a serious outbreak of cholera, and an Austrian bombardment, did the Venetians surrender.

With the fall of Venice the romantic phase of the Risorgimento may be said to have ended, although it was to have a last, brief, sensational return with Garibaldi's expedition of the Thousand in 1860. In the world of music and literature the age of Romanticism in Italy had been a fruitful one. The most characteristic art form of the Risorgimento was perhaps the opera. Four composers produced operas which were performed far beyond Italy's boundaries: Gioacchino Rossini (1792–1868), Gaetano Donizetti (1779–1848), Vincenzo Bellini (1801–35), and – the most politically involved of them all – Giuseppe Verdi (1813–1901).

The nineteenth century was the age of the novel. Italy produced several lesser novelists, like Massimo d'Azeglio and Francesco Guerrazzi, but two were of a higher calibre. The single masterpiece of Alessandro Manzoni (1785–1873), *I Promessi Sposi*, went far to get a version of the Tuscan form of Italian accepted as the language which would be used by the peoples of the united kingdom. The novel is a masterly piece of narrative, yet a novel which was less well known in its day, *Le Confessioni di un Italiano* (*The Confessions of an Italian*), had perhaps greater psychological insight, and was to wear better in the twentieth century. Its author was Ippolito Nievo (1831–61), who, at the age of thirty, set sail in a ship which was never seen again.

Italian Romantic poetry reached its greatest heights with Ugo Foscolo (1778–1827), whose sonnets excel by their sheer verbal beauty, and Giacomo Leopardi (1798–1837), whose sad and deeply introspective work produces the kind of catharsis which results only from the world's greatest poetry.

### 3 Cavour and the europeanization of the Italian Question, 1852–9

The next phase of the Risorgimento was a matter of *Realpolitik*, guided to a great extent by the hand of Cavour. Mazzini and the developments of 1848 had convinced Europe that there was an 'Italian Question', although the Austrians still refused to admit it. It was the task of Cavour to place the Italian Question on the agenda of the chancelleries of the great powers.

Count Camillo Benso di Cavour was born in 1810 in Turin. He had an elder brother who inherited the title of Marquis. His father served as a minister under the Piedmontese monarchy, but his mother came from Geneva, from a family originally of French extraction. As a boy Cavour often travelled to Switzerland, where his mother's relatives provided a more interesting and varied circle than was offered by the narrow world of the aristocracy of Turin. Both parents were rich.

As a second son, Camillo was destined for the army, and sent to the Royal Military Academy in Turin. He hated the mindless discipline of the place, and was no happier after he had been given a commission in the army. Posted to frontier stations in the Alps, he eased his boredom by learning to read English (he was already, of course, bilingual in French and Italian), and by studying economic and political works. A posting to Genoa was a relief, and put him in touch with radical ideas, in the salon of Anna Giustiniani, who became his mistress, and was later – after he had left her – to kill herself.

In this period of his life Cavour regarded himself as a rebel against the autocratic regime in Turin, and his father's conservative circles. In 1835 he travelled to Paris and London, and found the moderate parliamentary regimes and the governments of Guizot in Paris and Robert Peel in London very much to his taste. He rode on the Liverpool–Manchester railway (the first passenger line in the world), which delighted him, as did the other manifestations of the industrial revolution. His readings had taught him to accept the ideas of the classical *laissez-faire* economics, and the political position he had come to occupy can best be described as that of a conservative of the left. He hated both the autocrats to his right and the republicans and socialists to his left. He loved moderation immoderately.

Virtually thrown out of the army, to his immense relief, Cavour was given one large estate and one smaller farm by his father. He embarked on the running of the estate with great enthusiasm, and was a highly successful farmer. So long as Carlo Alberto remained an absolute monarch, Cavour had no intention of taking political office. But when the *Statuto* was granted in 1848, he stood for parliament, and on the second attempt was elected. In 1850 he was given three ministries – the Navy, Commerce and Finance – in the government of Massimo d'Azeglio. He was the most energetic, and quickly became the most significant, figure in the government. He arranged commercial treaties with France, Britain, Belgium and even Austria, lowering tariffs bilaterally, but not indulging in too reckless a policy of free trade. Cavour and d'Azeglio belonged to the centre right of the Piedmontese political spectrum, though d'Azeglio was farther to the right than Cavour. In 1852 Cavour reached an agreement with the leader of the centre left, Urbano Rattazzi, who, like Cavour, was one day to be prime minister of Italy: an agreement known as the *connubio*, or 'marriage', of the two centre groups. The agreement was reached behind d'Azeglio's back, and the prime minister subsequently took offence, and resigned. Cavour was asked by the king to head the government.

Victor Emmanuel II had become king in 1849, when his father, Carlo Alberto, had abdicated. The young new king retained the constitution, if a little reluctantly. He did not at first regard his ministers as being responsible to parliament, and it was not the least of Cavour's achievements that he established the supremacy of parliament over the crown in his first few years of office. Victor Emmanuel never liked or trusted Cavour.

In 1854 the first war between great powers since 1815 broke out, when France and Britain went to the help of the Ottoman Empire against Russia. The Austrians occupied the lower Danube valley, thereby ensuring that there would be no campaign in the Balkans, and the British and French were obliged to send forces to fight the Russians in the Crimea. But the Habsburg monarchy itself remained neutral, only signing a treaty with France and Britain in the autumn of 1854, by which it agreed to put pressure on the Russians to come to terms. In the intensive and prolonged negotiations which proceeded, Cavour felt that there was a danger that Austria would enter a close alliance with the Western powers, an alliance which would leave Piedmont dangerously isolated in North Italy. Even so, he was at first unwilling to involve Piedmont in a war with Russia, and it was only after considerable pressure had been put on him by Britain, France and his own king that he agreed to military intervention. It then became the prime minister's task to convince the rest of the cabinet and parliament of the need to send Piedmontese forces to the Crimea – a task he accomplished with eloquence and success.

In the spring of 1855 a Piedmontese force of 15,000 landed in the Crimea, and fought one engagement, the Chornaya

Rechka, with some distinction. With the fall of Sebastopol the Russians decided to give up the struggle, without repeating the 1812 retreat to Moscow. A peace congress was held early in 1856 in Paris. Louis-Napoleon had proclaimed himself emperor in 1852, and the holding of the Congress of Paris in some ways marked the peak of his career, although his services for Italy were only just about to begin. Cavour's hopes fluctuated. At one moment he believed that Piedmont could extract the Central Duchies, or even Lombardy and Venice, from the congress. At other moments he was more realistic, and realized that it was unlikely that any concrete gains could be achieved. He even hesitated to attend the congress himself, and considered asking d'Azeglio to go. Eventually he went himself. In Paris it appeared that he had gained the support of the British plenipotentiary, Lord Clarendon, but this later proved a mistaken impression. For the future it was more important that he had made contact with Napoleon.

The Italian policy of Napoleon III poses problems. It is not clear if he wanted to create a united Italy, or how strong he wanted Piedmont to become. Probably he wanted a stronger Piedmont, which would be a loyal ally of France, but would not offend French Catholics by destroying the temporal power of the pope. Such an aim was incompatible with the unification of Italy, or with his avowed belief in the 'principle of nationality'. Cavour's ultimate aims were not much more clearly defined, but for the moment he was content to secure a French alliance against Austria, which was in keeping with the traditional policy of the House of Savoy: that of playing the great powers off against each other. It was by these means that Savoy had preserved her independence, and steadily extended her territory, over the centuries.

In 1857 there was an attempt by the democratic wing of Italian nationalism to seize the initiative. Carlo Pisacane, who had worked with Mazzini in the Roman Republic, hi-jacked a small Genoese ship, and, with some thirty followers, set out to start a revolution in the Kingdom of Naples. They released some three hundred men – some of them political offenders – from the convict prison island of Ponza, and landed at Sapri on the Calabrian coast. Pisacane had secretly visited Naples, and convinced himself that the Southern peasants were ready to rise. The force was defeated by the royal Neapolitan army, and Pisacane killed himself.

Unlike Mazzini, Pisacane had called himself a socialist, and had believed that the Risorgimento should be a movement of the whole Italian people, not just of the usual middle-class revolutionaries. In a sense, he had anticipated the thesis of Antonio Gramsci, the communist political philosopher of the twentieth century. Gramsci believed that whereas the French revolutionaries of 1789 had at least identified themselves with the peasants to the extent of declaring 'feudalism abolished', the bourgeois revolutionaries of the Risorgimento failed to secure an alliance with the masses, but instead ultimately accepted the hegemony of the Piedmontese monarchists. Pisacane's aims may have been sound, but his methods and expectations had been tragically mistaken.

In 1857 Mazzini had made one of his clandestine visits to Italy, and had intended to start a rising in Genoa to synchronize with Pisacane's in the South. His attempt was bungled, and had to be called off. In retrospect it can now be seen that republican attempts were not likely to succeed, and that the best hope for Italian independence lay in the machinations of Cavour.

After the Congress of Paris, Cavour kept in touch with Napoleon III through several intermediaries. Most important of them was a cousin of the emperor Prince Jérome-Napoléon, nicknamed 'Plon-Plon', who was very pro-Italian. Then there were Cavour's private secretary, Costantino Nigra, who stayed for periods in Paris; Napoleon's doctor, who treated Cavour when he was in Paris, and became a friend; and finally the nineteen-year-old Countess Castiglione, who slept with

Napoleon, having been despatched to Paris for that purpose, though not – it should be said – against her will.

But it was an event which had nothing to do with Cavour's plottings which, unexpectedly, furthered his ends. Felice Orisini was a Mazzinian exile in England who had, like so many Mazzinians, quarrelled with his mentor. In January of 1858 he and four accomplices arrived in Paris with outsize bombs, which they had had made in England. Three of the bombs were thrown at the Emperor and his Empress, Eugénie, as they arrived outside the opera. Apart from a glass splinter in Eugénie's eye, the two were unhurt, but seven people were killed, and over a hundred injured. On the face of it, it seemed an incident unlikely to increase Napoleon's affection for the Italians. But since he had evidently already decided to support the Piedmontese against the Austrians, he used the trial of Orsini to further that end. Probably prompted by Napoleon's chief of police, who had visited him in his cell, Orsini at the trial had a letter read by his counsel, declaring that he had wrongly assumed that Napoleon was an enemy of Italy, but that he now appealed to the Emperor, 'from the foot of the gallows', to secure Italy's independence.

Of Cavour's agents in Paris, the one who proved the most effective was Nigra. In the summer of 1858 he told Cavour that the emperor was planning a meeting. Cavour was conveniently at hand in Geneva when Napoleon, who was in the little spa town of Plombières, just across the border from Switzerland, invited Cavour to visit him. At Plombières one of the more momentous alliances of the nineteenth century was forged, the one which was to start the process which would stop only with the creation of an independent Italy.

By the terms of the Plombières agreement the two countries were to wage war on Austria, after the duke of Modena had been provoked into an aggressive diplomatic exchange with Piedmont, an exchange which would make a Piedmontese attack on Modena appear justified in the eyes of the great powers – with the exception of course of the Austrians, who would go to war to defend their satellite. France could then enter the war, since Cavour would have provided Napoleon with an excuse. The real reason for the war would be a redrawing of the map of Italy. Piedmont was to be enlarged into a North Italian Kingdom, with the acquisition of Lombardy and Venice; there was to be a Central Italian Kingdom, consisting of the three Central Duchies and a large slice of the Papal States; the Kingdom of Naples was to remain intact. The whole peninsula was to be formed into a confederation, under the presidency of the pope – to compensate him for the loss of so much of his territory, Napoleon said. France, in return for fighting a major war, was to acquire Savoy from Piedmont. A hundred textbooks have taught thousands of schoolchildren that Nice was also to be ceded to France, but in fact at Plombières Cavour had politely protested at Napoleon's request for Nice, and the matter had been left open. The whole arrangement was to be sealed by a marriage treaty between Piedmont, in the person of Victor Emmanuel's fifteen-year-old daughter, and France, in the person of Prince Jérome-Napoléon, the emperor's middle-aged cousin.

Cavour's policy now was to start a war of nerves with Austria, which would ultimately lead the Austrians into making a false move. One step in the process was Victor Emmanuel's speech opening parliament for its first session in 1859. The king's speech, drafted by Cavour, submitted to Napoleon, and even improved a little by the king himself, declared that Piedmont could not 'remain insensible to the cry of pain (*il grido di dolore*) which comes to us from so many parts of Italy'. Although Plombières had been a secret agreement, about which even the French foreign minister had been ignorant, everyone suspected that Napoleon and Cavour were considering war with Austria. But by no means was everyone happy with such a prospect. Napoleon himself changed his mind from one moment to the next, and the British government launched a peace offensive, aimed at arranging a congress on the Italian Question. But with the increase of tension both the Austrian and Piedmontese mobilized their armies. At the eleventh hour the British government, through its indefatigable foreign secretary, Lord Malmesbury, almost succeeded in pressing both governments to demobilize. The Austrian government undermined his efforts by sending an ultimatum to Turin in April, 1859, demanding a promise, within three days, of Piedmontese demobilization. Cavour replied, very correctly, within the three days, that he could not accept such a request.

The Austrians had blundered, but Cavour's diplomacy had been brilliant. Although there is no doubt that Piedmont, backed by France, was in spirit the aggressor, Cavour had made it appear as though the Austrians were the guilty party. The Austrians confounded their diplomatic blunder with a military one. They were slow in attacking the Piedmontese before the arrival of French armies. But the common habit of non-Italian historians of referring to the conflict as 'the Franco-Austrian War' is misleading. The French forces involved were less than twice as numerous as the Piedmontese, and Piedmont paid for the war in financial terms. All wars are horrible, but this one, although limited in space and time, was perhaps more horrible than most. In the two major battles of Magenta and Solferino the casualty rate was appalling. The numbers involved were greater than in the Crimean War, and a characteristic of the battles was the great number of wounded and dying who littered the battlefields, and for whom no provisions seemed to have been made. It was as a result of these battles that in 1864 the philanthropist, Henri Dunant, founded the Red Cross.

The two battles were defeats for the Austrians, but not overwhelming defeats. For military and humanitarian reasons alone Napoleon might have decided on peace, but there were other pressing reasons. Prussia had remained neutral, but with other states of the German Confederation had mobilized a

Plate 7. A fan with a patriotic scene. 1859. Milan, Museo del
Risorgimento

larger army on the Rhine than the French army which was
fighting in Italy. And in Central Italy there were developments
over which Napoleon had no control. At the outbreak of war a
major demonstration in Florence, mostly of the urban lower
classes, had persuaded the Grand Duke Leopold II to depart
for Vienna. The group which eventually gained control under
the grim, authoritarian figure of Baron Bettino Ricasoli
(1809–80), wanted Tuscany to be merged with Piedmont.
There had also been revolts in the other Central Duchies, and
in the Papal Romagna, and the provisional governments which
seized control in those places equally wanted annexation by
Piedmont. The Central Italian Kingdom that Napoleon had
planned at Plombières seemed to be forgotten, while Piedmont
seemed likely to be rather larger than had been planned.

With all these considerations in mind, Napoleon decided on
peace, and in a one-hour meeting with the young Austrian
Emperor Francis Joseph he signed the armistice of Villafranca.
Its terms were in several respects reactionary. The grand duke
of Tuscany, the duchess of Parma and the duke of Modena

were all to be restored to their thrones. Venetia, which had not been occupied by the Franco-Piedmontese forces, was to remain Austrian. There was to be an Italian Confederation, of which the pope was to be president, and in which the Austrian emperor, as the sovereign of Venice, would evidently be represented. The one feature which was a positive one from the Italian point of view was that Piedmont was to annex Lombardy.

Mazzini had warned Cavour that the peace would be dictated by France and Austria somewhere on the Lombard plain, and that Cavour would be far away. Mazzini had been proved right. Even the agreement of Victor Emmanuel had been sought only after the armistice had been signed. The king accepted the *fait accompli*, but Cavour, in an uncontrollable rage, bitterly abused the king, and resigned. Yet most of the Villafranca settlement was to remain a dead letter. The rulers of the Central Duchies were not to be restored: Palmerston in London talked wildly of going to war to prevent such a step. The pope renounced any intention of becoming president of what he called 'a federal Italian republic'. In the long term the important and definitive feature of the settlement was that Lombardy had been liberated from foreign rule. Never again was she to come under foreign sovereignty. And Cavour would be back. Garibaldi, in the uniform of a Piedmontese general, had led a force of his volunteers in the war. As always, they had performed brilliantly. Garibaldi was as furious as Cavour at the terms of Villafranca. But he, too, would be back.

## 4 Garibaldi and achievement of unity. 1859–61

Reference has already been made to Garibaldi's campaigns in South America, Northern Italy in 1848 and 1859, and his defence of the Roman Republic. Something more must now be said of the man.

He was born in Nice in 1807 of humble parents, who had

themselves come from the Ligurian coast to the east of Genoa. His father was a fisherman, and Giuseppe himself went to sea at the age of fifteen. At this early age he experienced fights with pirates, and sailed as far to the East as the Crimea. He thus had little formal education, but evidently developed a habit of reading, and by his early twenties had come across the nationalist ideas of Mazzini. The combination of a tenderness of heart, total sincerity and honesty, and exceptional physical courage gave him the kind of personal magnetism which made women of all classes love him, and men of all classes follow him in circumstances of acute danger. He himself had no consciousness of class, showed no deference for monarchs or nobility, and equal respect for the poorest of his companions.

Garibaldi was the kind of hero needed by Italy at this stage of her history, but before the sailing of his Thousand in May of 1860 there was a period of indecision.

Cavour was out of office from July 1859 until January 1860. In his absence two strong men held the initiative: Ricasoli in Florence, and Farini in Modena. Luigi Carlo Farini (1812–66), one day to be briefly prime minister of Italy, had been born a subject of the pope, and was now in control of Parma and the Papal Romagna as well as Modena. He united them into a temporary unit, which he called Emilia. For the time being both Ricasoli and Farini were dictators, but held that role only until the timid Piedmontese government should feel strong enough to annex the territories concerned. The successors of Cavour in Turin were too nervous to act until Napoleon's attitude became clearer. At Villafranca the emperor had seemed to have abandoned Piedmont, having helped her to win Lombardy, and to have reached an understanding with Austria. He was now trying to organize a congress to discuss the future of Italy. In December 1859 an anonymous pamphlet appeared in Paris, entitled *Le Pape et le Congrès*. It was public knowledge that the author, La Guérronnière, was an unacknowledged spokesman for Napoleon. The pamphlet recommended the pope to resign himself to the loss of the Legations (the part of the Papal States centred on Bologna, administered formerly by papal legates, and now controlled by Farini), and persisted with the idea of an Italian Confederation, whose army would guarantee the pope's independence. Needless to say the pope did not accept Napoleon's advice, but the Austrians decided against attending a congress, which in the event was never held.

In Italy another element had entered the scene in the shape of the National Society, a comparatively small, but influential, group of people. The two most prominent members of the Society were Giorgio Pallavicino, a rich nobleman, and Daniele Manin. Pallavicino, like Manin, had been a republican, and, also like Manin, had been imprisoned by the Austrians. But both men had come to the belief that the Italian nationalist cause was now best represented by the Piedmontese monarchy. Although they were not close to either Cavour or Garibaldi, they were in touch with both, and formed a link between the two men, who were in general terms so remote from, and hostile towards, each other. Perhaps the most important function of the National Society was its influence on Cavour: it pushed him towards a realization that Italy could be united.

Assemblies in Tuscany, Parma, Modena and Bologna had voted for union with Piedmont in the autumn of 1859. When Cavour returned to office he did not immediately arrange for Piedmontese annexation of this considerable area, because he wanted to ensure the good-will of Napoleon – or, at least, not to incur too much ill-will. Although there was no recognized connection between Piedmontese annexation of the central Italian territories on the one hand, and French annexation of Savoy and Nice on the other, Cavour believed that only by accepting the latter could he risk the former. Both sets of annexations could be justified by plebiscites. As a constitutional device Cavour was not at first fond of the plebiscite by universal suffrage, which had a flavour of democracy and

Mazzini about it, but he realized that in the circumstances it could be employed usefully. Ricasoli in Tuscany and Farini in Emilia were pressing for annexation, and in March arranged for plebiscites. All men over twenty-one could vote in favour of union with Piedmont or 'a separate kingdom'. They voted overwhelmingly for the former.

At the same time Cavour was bribing Napoleon by the gift of Savoy and Nice. A secret treaty was signed by Victor Emmanuel and Napoleon, with a promise that plebiscites were to be held in Savoy and Nice; and the plebiscites were in the event held in April, again with overwhelming majorities voting for what, in this case, was a *fait accompli*. The result of the plebiscite in Savoy was probably a valid expression of public opinion, since the people of Savoy were more French than Italian in character, in spite of their long link with the ducal dynasty, but Nice was another matter. In 1860 there were more people in Nice who spoke a Ligurian dialect of Italian than there were French-speaking inhabitants. The vote may have been swayed by the activity of French agents and the large French armed forces which were in Nice, on their way back from the war in Northern Italy.

Paradoxically Cavour, and even Victor Emmanuel, were less distressed at the loss of Savoy and Nice than was the British government. Palmerston, the prime minister in London, and Lord John Russell, the foreign secretary, were jealous of French influence in Italy, and alarmed at the thought of the French expanding their frontiers. They were both old men, who could remember Napoleon I, and the fears that he might conquer the world. Napoleon III had no such intentions, and Cavour was young enough, and realistic enough, to recognize the true nature of the emperor's ambitions. But one Italian, who had been born in Nice and elected to parliament as her deputy, was understandably outraged that she had been given to a foreign power: Giuseppe Garibaldi.

It was with a view to preventing the French annexation of

Nice that Garibaldi first collected a force – which was to be the famous Thousand – at Quarto, a place on the coast just to the east of Genoa in the spring of 1860. Fortunately he was dissuaded from this desperate plan, mainly by a Sicilian, Francesco Crispi, who was to play a central role in Italian history for the rest of the century. Early in April revolution had broken out in Palermo, a mainly working-class rising, which was, however, suppressed in two weeks. Other risings in the countryside had not been wholly suppressed, and Crispi eventually persuaded Garibaldi that they could be made the nucleus of a national movement, if the name of Garibaldi were to be thrown into the cauldron. The thousand young men who had assembled at Quarto came from all over Italy. They were not interested in supporting a minor rising against the king of Naples; they were determined to create Italy. They sailed on 6 May in two small ships. Only when they were at sea did Garibaldi reveal that they were to fight for 'Italy and Victor Emmanuel'. To Garibaldi this meant a democratic monarchy. He was prepared to give up his republicanism in order to unite Italy, but he would not be happy with the conservative constitution Carlo Alberto had granted Piedmont.

The Thousand landed, unopposed, at Marsala, on the west coast of Sicily. The Neapolitan general in command in Sicily foolishly did not send the whole army available to destroy the Thousand. But the force which he sent was nevertheless larger, and far better equipped, than Garibaldi's. The Thousand had to depend to a great extent on their bayonets, yet routed the Neapolitans in the battle of Calatafimi, charging uphill with the only cover provided by the small terraces on the steep slopes. Calatafimi was not a major military victory, but psychologically its effect could hardly have been greater. A purely Italian force, unconnected with any existing state, and unsupported by a foreign ally, had defeated the army of an ancient kingdom. In a very direct sense it was a victory of the future over the past. The ranks of the Thousand were now swelled by volunteers from all over Italy, and elsewhere in Western Europe.

But among European governments only the British reacted favourably, by insisting that there should be no foreign intervention, and that the Italians should now be allowed to work out their own destiny. Cavour had allowed the Thousand to assemble at Quarto only because to have arrested and disarmed them would have been too unpopular. It so happened that in the first week of May elections were being held in Piedmont for a parliament which would have to ratify his treaty with France over Savoy and Nice. To have arrested Garibaldi might well have lost Cavour the majority he needed. He had evidently hoped, however, that Garibaldi would not sail, and assumed that, if he did sail, he would be defeated by the Neapolitans, as Pisacane had been defeated in a not dissimilar expedition three years before.

After Calatafimi, Garibaldi had the larger task of occupying Palermo. He did so only after bitter and bloody fighting, and was then glad to reach a truce with the Neapolitans, a truce arranged by the British admiral, Mundy. Garibaldi made better use of the truce than did the Neapolitans, and was soon ready to continue the conquest of Sicily.

Cavour was now pressing for a Piedmontese annexation of Sicily, but he had no means of forcing Garibaldi to accept it. He could only send an agent, Giuseppe La Farina, to Sicily from Turin. La Farina was a Sicilian, and a member of the National Society. In Sicily Garibaldi was leaving political control in the hands of his own Sicilian, Francesco Crispi, who was bitterly opposed to Piedmontese annexation. La Farina and Crispi were not likely to reach an understanding, and when La Farina began arrogantly proclaiming Piedmontese annexation, Garibaldi had him arrested and sent back to Piedmont. At this point Cavour's influence was clearly at a low ebb: he had lost the initiative to the forces of the revolution.

By the end of July 1860, after much bitter fighting, Garibaldi was in control of the whole of Sicily. It has been argued that Cavour would have liked the Piedmontese fleet to prevent Garibaldi from crossing to the mainland, had it not been for the presence of the British navy. Certainly Napoleon was unhappy at Garibaldi's apparently irresistible advance. The British Mediterranean command had been a close ally of the Kingdom of Naples in Nelson's day, but already by the 1820s a more liberal generation of British naval commanders had appeared, and in 1860 the British navy shared the enthusiasm of Lord John Russell at the Foreign Office for Garibaldi and the Italian cause.

Garibaldi crossed the Straits of Messina without opposition. The royal Bourbon army put up less resistance on the mainland. The royal family soon evacuated Naples, and withdrew with the greater part of their army to the northern extremity of their kingdom. Ferdinand II had died in 1859. The new king, Francis II, introduced a constitution – the one which had been granted, but very soon withdrawn, in 1848 – only when Garibaldi was in possession of most of Sicily. Although he appointed supposedly liberal ministers, it was too late for Francis to secure the loyalty of his people. Garibaldi entered Naples, amid great rejoicing, on September 7.

Cavour had tried to organize a pro-Piedmontese revolution in Naples, but had found no support. He desperately needed to recapture the initiative. Garibaldi was making no secret of the fact that once he had defeated the Neapolitan army he would march on Rome. There was a French force in Rome, and although it was smaller than the army Garibaldi now had under his command, it could rapidly be reinforced from France. Cavour and Napoleon both had to weigh two dangers against each other – the danger of doing nothing while Garibaldi invaded the Papal States, and the danger of a pre-emptive invasion by Piedmont. Costantino Nigra, in Paris, wrote to Cavour to the effect that Napoleon would not oppose action by Piedmont. It was a gamble, but Cavour had gambled before in politics, as he had always enjoyed gambling with cards, in the casinos, and on the stock market. On the spurious grounds that revolution was breaking out in the Papal States, orders were given for a Piedmontese invasion. Pius IX had taken steps to modernize his army since his restoration after the defeat of the Roman Republic, and a tough, but ultimately fated, resistance was offered by the papal forces to the much larger Piedmontese army at Castelfidardo, in the hills above the Adriatic. The Piedmontese were careful not to go too near Rome itself, but to have fought the pope's forces in their own territory was shocking enough in the eyes of the Catholic powers of Europe. The great powers – including France – broke off diplomatic relations with Piedmont. The exception was Britain, whose government managed to radiate sympathy equally for the Piedmontese and for Garibaldi.

After Castelfidardo Victor Emmanuel joined the Piedmontese army, which continued its march to cut off Garibaldi. The largest army in Italy was still that of the Neapolitan Bourbons, which was perhaps 50,000 strong. The Piedmontese numbered about 33,000, and Garibaldi's 'Southern Army', as it was now called, was smaller still. The final battles against the royal Neapolitan army were fought in the broad valley of the Volturno. At first Garibaldi suffered a defeat, but he displayed his ability to control a considerable army by winning a final victory. He had developed into something more than a guerrilla leader.

Victor Emmanuel and Garibaldi, and their two armies, met on 26 October. On the surface the meeting appeared a friendly one, with the soldiers of the two armies fraternizing cheerfully, but the underlying tension was real enough. Garibaldi had wanted to be appointed governor, or 'dictator', of the Neapolitan provinces for one year, until a genuinely Italian government could take over, but this had been refused. For his part, he had refused all honours or cash rewards. He could already have taken his pickings from the wealth of Naples, but preferred to

Map 7. The unification of Italy

depart with nothing, for the somewhat desolate island of Caprera, off the coast of Sardinia, which he had made his home.

Cavour preferred to remain in Turin, and to appoint men to govern the South for him. Already a few days before the Piedmontese army arrived, plebiscites were held in what had been the kingdom of Naples. All adult men could vote 'Yes' or 'No' to the proposition: 'Italy One Victor Emmanuel'. They

195

voted so overwhelmingly in the affirmative that it is difficult not to feel a little sceptical about the elections. The majority of people voting would never vote again, since it was to be many years before more than a minority – the literate and the rich – would have the vote.

On 27 January 1861 the first parliament of the kingdom of Italy was elected according to the *Statuto* of Carlo Alberto, now extended to the greater part of the peninsula. It met on 18 February in Turin, and on 17 March proclaimed Victor Emmanuel II 'king of Italy'. No pope or prelate crowned the king, who was to be an essentially secular and parliamentary monarch. The ideals of Cavour were to be orthodoxy in the new kingdom, but Cavour was not to live long to propagate them. He died of a 'fever', according to the contemporary diagnosis, on 6 June 1861, at the age of fifty. The king was present towards the end, and recorded some of the prime minister's delirious ramblings. Evidently Cavour was worried about the acquisition of Naples by the kingdom which he had helped to create. The Neapolitans, he said, were intelligent, but corrupt. It would be necessary to cleanse them of their corruption. But they should not be ruled by martial law – 'anyone can rule by martial law' – rather they would be cured by ten years of freedom.

In the event Naples and Sicily were to get martial law rather than freedom. Brigandage had been endemic in the South for many decades, but something much more, and much more terrible, than brigandage developed after 1860. Great numbers of disbanded Neapolitan troops took to the hills, either to continue a guerrilla war in support of the Bourbons, or simply to escape the law. In October of 1860 several towns on the Neapolitan mainland were occupied by pro-Bourbon forces, after they had driven out small Garibaldian detachments. Cash for this counter-revolution was provided from the Papal States, where a refuge could also be found for the so-called 'brigands'. The civil war, like most civil wars, was an extremely bitter one. Atrocities were committed by both sides, the new authorities burning down whole villages, and the counter-revolutionaries literally crucifying their victims. Not for some five or six years did the war come to an uneasy close, and lawlessness on a big scale has never disappeared from the sad island of Sicily.

Chapter 7

# FROM UNIFICATION TO FASCISM, *1861–1922*

## *1 The first years of unity and the era of Depretis and Crispi, 1861–96*

By 1861 the epic phase of the Risorgimento was over. The Kingdom of Italy had been created, and although one major war of independence was still to be fought, the main task now was to integrate and standardize institutions, so that the new kingdom could become a genuine nation state. Benedetto Croce argued that this task was more difficult than the more dramatic ones which had preceded it. The institutional unification was not made any easier by the fact that there was no man of vision to carry it through. Cavour was dead. Mazzini refused to recognize the conservative monarchy as the Italy for the creation of which he had devoted his life. Garibaldi thought only of securing Rome, and although – unlike Mazzini – he accepted election to the Italian parliament, he was out of sympathy with the new regime.

The men who had to carry through the institutional unification were the party of the Right, the successors of Cavour. The state they created combined parliamentary institutions of a British kind with administrative institutions of a French kind. Administration was to be strongly centralized, with the country divided into prefectures and sub-prefectures, with prefects and sub-prefects appointed in Turin. It was the system Napoleon I had made common throughout much of Western Europe, and it has survived in Italy, as in France, until this day, although with significant modifications.

Administrative methods were perhaps a less deep-rooted part of tradition than was the educational system. Napoleon I had centred education on the university in Paris. The Italians in 1861 also centralized schools and universities on the capital, Turin, through a ministry of education. It was not an easy task, since Turin had no university with the long traditions of the great universities of Bologna, Padua, Ferrara, Pavia or Naples. That the creation of a single educational system was not carried out with even more friction than in the event was experienced owed much to the appointment by Cavour – just before his death – of Francesco De Sanctis, a distinguished literary figure and himself a product of the University of Naples. De Sanctis believed his own university as fine as any in the world, but was also an Italian nationalist, who wanted a national system of education. He ensured that educational authority stayed in Turin, but that it was lightly and discreetly exercised.

To integrate the armed forces created even greater difficulties than did the integration of education. There were in existence at the end of 1860 three separate armies; the Piedmontese, the Neapolitan, and Garibaldi's Southern Army. The Tuscans had never had a military tradition, and their army was very small, but the Neapolitan and Southern Armies had just concluded a war against each other. While the ordinary Neapolitan soldiers deserted in great numbers to join the 'brigands', their officers were welcomed into the ranks of what was now the Italian army. Their loyalty might have been – but evidently was not – considered suspect, surely more suspect than that of Garibaldi's officers. Yet only a few of the officers of the Southern Army, many of whom had been in the original Thousand, were given commissions in the army of the new kingdom. Such insensibility on the part of the authorities in

Turin provided Garibaldi with his main grievance against them. But in spite of him a large, single, Italian army was quickly created, and if its record in the war of 1866 was a poor one, it must be remembered that it had then been in existence as a united force for only five years.

To create an Italian navy was even more difficult. By far the largest navy in Italian waters had been the Neapolitan one, which in 1860 had been demoralized and scattered. At least it had not passed under Austrian control, but an integrated Italian navy could not really be said to exist in 1866.

That Turin became the capital of Italy in every sense in 1861 raises the question of whether the process of unification had not been rather one of Piedmontization. The king certainly still called himself 'Victor Emmanuel II', although there had never been a 'Victor Emmanuel I' of Italy and Carlo Alberto's constitution was to be the starting point for an evolving Italian one. But for some years eminent figures from other parts of the peninsula had been settling in Piedmont, and they were to play a prominent role in the life of the kingdom of Italy. Cavour's successor as prime minister was the Tuscan, Bettino Ricasoli, and the ministers appointed in the first governments came from several different Italian regions.

Garibaldi, however, certainly believed that Piedmontese – and, specifically, Cavour's – influence was too strong in the new kingdom. When the first Italian parliament met, Garibaldi, who had inevitably been elected a deputy, was on Caprera, but he returned in April 1861 to intervene in a debate on the army. His ideal was a people's army in which all male citizens would serve, and which would be large enough not only to defend the fragile new state, but to liberate Rome and Venice without much loss of life. He was loudly cheered from the galleries when he spoke in parliament, but was bitterly attacked by other deputies, especially when he led a verbal onslaught on Cavour. He condemned Cavour as an evil influence on the king, and declared – correctly – that Cavour had been opposed to the expedition of the Thousand. It was a sad episode in the life of the first Italian parliament, but there was some truth in what Garibaldi had to say.

In 1862 there was to be a more violent clash between Garibaldi and the new authorities. In March of that year Ricasoli resigned – mainly because of his failure to retain the king's confidence – and Urbano Rattazzi, the Piedmontese lawyer who had, ten years before, celebrated the *connubio* with Cavour, became prime minister. Rattazzi, whether intentionally or not, led Garibaldi to believe that the government would allow him to take Rome. He therefore collected together a small force of volunteers in Sicily, and moved them across to the mainland without hindrance from the government. Only then did Rattazzi order steps to be taken to halt Garibaldi. A royal force met Garibaldi's at Aspromonte in the toe of Italy, and a few shots were exchanged. Garibaldi was quite badly hurt in the leg, and for five weeks was imprisoned, before receiving the king's pardon. Some of the blame for the incident fell on Rattazzi, who resigned at the end of the year.

So long as there was a French occupation of Rome and Garibaldi was capable of forming an irregular force, the Italian government had grounds for feeling apprehensive. But in September 1864 Napoleon III took steps to ease the situation. He and the Italian government reached an agreement – henceforth known as the 'September Convention' – by which the French force was to be withdrawn from Rome within two years, and the Italian capital moved from Turin to Florence. Napoleon believed, not altogether logically, that if the Italians moved their capital once, they would not do so again. But there was a more realistic motive for moving the capital: if there was to be another war with Austria, Florence would be a better capital in strategic terms, since it would be on the far side of the Apennines in the event of an Austrian advance.

For four years, from 1866, Florence was to be the capital of Italy. The people of Turin reacted with violent rioting, while

Florence was prepared for its grand role by splendid landscaping in the region of the Piazzale Michelangelo. Parliament was housed in the magnificent Palazzo Vecchio, and the king in the beautiful Palazzo Pitti.

In her Third War of Independence, fought over six weeks in 1866, Italy had a great power as an ally – indeed, rather, more than just an ally, since Prussia provided the decisive victory over the Austrians. In April of 1866 the Italian government signed a treaty with Bismarck, with the approval of Napoleon: Italy was to go to war with Austria, with Venice as the reward, if Prussia declared war within two months. Bismarck ensured that he would have an Italian ally, and that Austria would have to fight a war on two fronts, by declaring war on 14 June.

The war was a disaster in military and naval terms for Italy, since she was defeated on land at Novara, and on sea at Lissa. The defeats were the fault less of the army and navy as a whole than of their commanders. At Novara the order for a general retreat was given when the army was far from beaten, and at Lissa the Italian admiral at first tried to avoid a battle, and was then defeated by a smaller and older Austrian fleet. Although it had spent considerable sums on both the army and the navy, the attempts to create integrated, efficient services by the Italian government had not yet succeeded. But in far-away Bohemia the Austrians were firmly defeated by the Prussians at the battle of Sadowa, and the Habsburgs were obliged to cede Venice. A day or two before the war Napoleon had negotiated an agreement with Austria by which Venice would first be ceded to France, and Napoleon would then pass it to Italy. The acquisition of Venice had thus come about in an unsatisfactory manner, but at least the Venetians were no longer under foreign rule. All that now remained to complete unification was Rome, and the surrounding patrimony.

Once again, in 1867, Garibaldi assembled an irregular force for an attack on Rome. Again Rattazzi was prime minister, and

again Garibaldi mistakenly assumed that the Italian government approved his action. At least this time it was left to the
French to defeat Garibaldi, at Mentana, but once more
Rattazzi's policy had been ambiguous. Rome was finally
secured for Italy only when Napoleon III became involved in
his last war, the Franco-Prussian War of 1870. As soon as war
broke out, in August, Napoleon, needing all the troops he could
get, withdrew his force from Rome. The government in
Florence debated what their policy should be, but no further
debate was needed when the French lost the battle of Sedan,
Napoleon himself was taken prisoner by the Prussians, and the
Second Empire came to an end. The Italian army now fought
its way into Rome, breaching the walls at Porta Pia. The pope's
army, no longer supported by the French, resisted, with the
result that forty-nine men of the Italian force, and nineteen
papal soldiers, were killed. But Rome at last could be made the
capital of Italy.

Pio Nono (Pius IX) had refused to recognize the Kingdom of
Italy. He was now deprived of the last shreds of his temporal
power, and even his palace, the Quirinale, was occupied by the
king of Italy. The Italian parliament passed a 'Law of
Guarantees', which promised that its army would defend the
independence of the pope and provide him with a pension. But
it was a unilateral declaration, having no force in international
law, and it stopped short of recognizing the pope as the
sovereign of an independent state: for this the papacy would
have to await Mussolini. Pius refused to recognize the Law of
Guarantees, and left his pension untouched. Instead he retired
north of the river, and declared that he was 'the prisoner of the
Vatican'. Another step he took was to be of importance for the
more immediate future of Italy. He declared, in a document
known as the *Non expedit*, that no Italian should vote, or play
any political role, in the new godless kingdom of Italy. The
ruling had the paradoxically beneficial effect for Italian
political stability that it prevented the emergence of a right-

wing clerical party, which might have aimed at the destruction of the monarchy in the name of the pope. Meanwhile the spiritual authority of the pope in the Catholic world had been strengthened by the Vatican Council, which had been called in 1869, and which declared the dogma of Papal Infallibility in 1870 – the very year when the pope lost his temporal power.

From 1861 to 1876 Italy was ruled by the Party of the Right. It was an age of austerity, high taxes, and desperate, if unsuccessful, attempts to balance the budget. The peasants were burdened with crushing taxes, which led to riots, and a violent insurrection in Sicily in 1866. The Party of the Left, under Depretis, at last came to power in 1876. Agostino Depretis (1813–87), originally a follower of Garibaldi, had been a prominent leader of the Left in opposition ever since 1861, but by 1876, at the age of 63, he had become a somewhat cynical opportunist. His attitude to politics was summed up in the phrase, 'Justice for everyone; favours for friends': at least he was not a hypocrite. He was the author of the policy which came to be known as *trasformismo*, or 'transformism'. It consisted in retaining power by offering places in the government to men who would otherwise have been political opponents, and giving honours – or concessions in their constituencies – to parliamentary deputies who voted as Depretis wished them to vote. By these means Depretis kept a parliamentary majority.

The term *trasformismo* is sometimes used in a more general sense. Gramsci pointed out that a ruling class in Italy had tended to retain hegemony because sections of the opposition were continually splintering away to join those in power, and the process has continued in an even more obvious manner since Gramsci's day. It may be said to have originated with Depretis.

From 1876 until 1887 Depretis was hardly ever out of office, either as prime minister (which was usually the case), or in another important ministry. For six months in 1879 he was prime minister, minister of the interior and foreign minister at the same time. The main achievement in domestic policy during this period of rule by the Left was an extension of the franchise, in 1881, which more than trebled the electorate. It gave the vote to virtually all literate males, but in view of the still high rate of illiteracy, Italy was still far from attaining universal male suffrage.

The main step of foreign policy by the government of the Left was the signing of the Triple Alliance with Germany and Austria in 1882. Italy's relations with France were unhappy, mainly because the French had, in 1881, annexed Tunis, where there was a larger group of Italian residents than of French residents, and which seemed of greater strategic importance to Italy than to France. By the terms of the Triple Alliance, Germany and Austria would come to the help of Italy if she were attacked by France. But equally in the event of Germany being attacked by France, Italy would assist Germany, and all three powers would assist each other in the event of any of them being attacked by two other powers. In a sense the signing of the Triple Alliance by the government of the Left implied a final rejection of republicanism, by an alignment with the two monarchist powers of Central Europe. Although Mazzini had died in 1872, Bismarck had still feared that a republic might be established in Italy, and that such a regime would join forces with republican France. Garibaldi, with a legion of his volunteers, had fought for the young French republic in 1870, after the fall of the Second Empire. His death, in 1882, just before the signing of the Triple Alliance, seemed to mark the end of an era.

Depretis took another step of which Garibaldi would not have approved: he started the movement of Italian imperialism in Africa. Garibaldi had said that if Italy ever began to exploit other peoples, he would go to their aid against his fellow-countrymen. But Depretis was not an imperialist in the sense that his successors were to be. His move into Africa was limited to the acquisition of Assab and Massawa on the Red Sea, in 1885, and was little more than an attempt to assert Italian prestige after the French had taken Tunis.

A more constructive aspect of the rule of the Left was the desperate attempt to eradicate illiteracy, The Act of 1877 made elementary education compulsory. At least in the North it was successful, but there were enormous variations of illiteracy from one region to another. In Piedmont, the most literate part of Italy, it fell from 42 per cent in 1871, to 32 per cent in 1881, to 18 per cent in 1901. In Lombardy it was a little higher, the figures for the illiterate in the same years being 45 per cent, to 37 per cent, to 22 per cent. In Tuscany, rather surprisingly, the illiterate were appreciably more numerous at all stages, the figures being 68 per cent, 62 per cent, and 48 per cent. But the real contrast comes when the figures for the South are given: in Calabria, for the same three years, the illiteracy figures were 87 per cent, 85 per cent, and 79 per cent.[1] The educational reforms of the united kingdom, and the considerable expenditure on the building of schools and the employment of teachers, had made little impact in the deep South. The explanation seems to be that the South was simply too poor to benefit. Even when children were taught to read and write, they forgot the skills, because the society in which they worked was too primitive for literacy to have any relevance.

Depretis died in 1887. His achievements in parliamentary and social reform had been limited, if not entirely negligible. But they had been marred by his corrupt methods.

His successor as prime minister was the Sicilian, Francesco Crispi (1819–1901). Garibaldi's political organizer in 1860, Crispi had held office under Depretis, and could claim to have

---

[1] Cipolla, *Literacy and Development*, table facing p. 18.

already done much for Italy. Although he was sixty-eight years old, he had lost none of the turbulence of his personality. His anti-clericalism was expressed in educational reforms which abolished compulsory religious education in primary schools, and in the erection of the statue to Giordano Bruno on the spot where he had been burnt at the stake in the Campo dei Fiori. Leo XIII had been elected pope on the death of Pio Nono in 1878, and was on most issues a moderate and conciliatory man, but he over-reacted to the unveiling of Bruno's statue, and talked of leaving Rome.

In his first ministry, from 1887 to 1891, Crispi inherited a colonial policy which had just resulted in the battle of Dogali, in which five hundred Italian troops had fought a savage battle against thousands of Ethiopians, a battle resulting in the heroic death of almost the entire Italian force. The excitement over Ethiopia was not of Crispi's making, but he was determined to avenge Dogali, and sent considerable reinforcements. An Italian protectorate over what was to become Italian Somaliland was established, and Eritrea was colonized. But Crispi's fall from office in 1891 was due less to uncertainties over his African policy than to a growing economic crisis.

His second ministry, from 1893 to 1896, was torn by yet more acute crises. He ruthlessly suppressed peasant movements in his native Sicily, and inaugurated savage laws against the growing movements of socialism and anarchism. But he was eventually destroyed by disaster in Africa. The war in Ethiopia was renewed on a larger scale, and in 1896 an Italian army – mostly of African troops under Italian officers – was defeated by a massive Ethiopian force in the battle of Adua. Crispi resigned, and died, forgotten and in poverty, in 1901. To some extent he was a scapegoat for military disaster, but the element of megalomania in his personality had led to an overplaying of every step of his policy. In his exuberant oratory, and his imperial ambitions, he anticipated Mussolini.

## 2 *Giolitti's building of democracy, 1892–1914*

There could hardly have been a greater contrast in personality than that between Crispi, the volatile, excitable Sicilian, and a much younger man in his government, a man who was to have more positive achievements than Crispi. Giovanni Giolitti was born at the other extremity of Italy, at Mondovi, in the foothills of the Alps. The essential pragmatist, Giolitti was prepared to adjust his policy to the changing mood of the public, and to what was possible in terms of domestic and international politics. Always avoiding confrontations, this shrewd, quiet man was to achieve results which would have been beyond the powers of Crispi.

Giolitti's carreer as a political leader straddled the dark days of social suffering and unrest at the turn of the century, the First World War and the coming to power of Mussolini. The first government which he formed was a short-lived one, in 1892/3. After the fall of Crispi's last government in 1896, there was a period of mounting unrest, which can be best decribed as class warfare of an exceptionally bitter kind. It took the form of bread riots, strikes, confrontations between angry crowds and the police, the imposition of martial law, and considerable loss of life, during a coalition government under the Marquis di Rudiní, from 1896 to 1898. The troubles culminated in the events of May 1898 – the *Fatti di Maggio* – when Rudiní ordered the army to move into Milan. Opponents of the government – socialists and clericals alike – were arrested for wholly inadequate reasons. During the *Fatti di Maggio*, military tribunals handed out sentences totalling 3,000 years of imprisonment.[2]

Rudiní's government was followed by the even more authoritarian prime minister, the general Pelloux, who

[2] John A. Davis, *Conflict and Control. Law and Order in Nineteenth-Century Italy* (London, 1988), p. 351.

resigned in 1900, after failing to get drastic emergency regulations through parliament. Democracy, by the skin of its teeth, was surviving.

Victor Emmanuel II had died in 1878, and was succeeded by his son, Umberto. The new king established a more extravagant court than that of his father, who had preferred a simple domestic existence. In 1900 an anarchist in the USA took boat for Italy, and assassinated Umberto in Monza. The assassination was only the most dramatic achievement of the Italian anarchist movement, which was also, of course, a European movement resulting in assassinations of several ruling figures. The new king of Italy, Victor Emmanuel III, was to bear the heavy responsibility of asking Mussolini to form a government in 1922. He was to reign until 1946.

Widespread strikes continued until 1903, when Giolitti formed his second government, which was to last until 1905. A general strike was called in 1904. Giolitti's policy was to keep the government strictly neutral as between strikers and employers, and not to use the police except in moments of extreme necessity. He believed that to use the police or the army could only exacerbate the crisis, but to carry through his policy required a particular kind of courage, a kind not usually recognized as such by the law-and-order brigade.

Giolitti's support in parliament came on the whole from the centre left. In the general election of 1904 there was a swing to the right, a backlash against socialist industrial action, and a reflection of the impatience of many middle-class Italians with Giolitti's passive methods. Pope Pius X (1903–14) had lifted the *Non expedit*, so that Catholics were permitted by their Church to vote for the first time. Many devout Catholics had, of course, already been voting, and Giolitti in his memoirs recalled one parish priest who had been encouraging them to do so. But now that the *Non expedit* had been formally lifted, the impact on the election was marked. Socialists and radicals did badly in the elections of 1904.

Giolitti was out of office until May 1906, but was then prime minister until 1909. In this, his third, ministry he trimmed his policy to attract the Catholic voters. By a law of 1908 local councils were allowed to provide religious instruction, according to the Catholic faith, if parents so requested. Giolitti's political method now involved attempts to attract specific groups of voters, in the manner adopted by American presidential candidates later in the century. But parliamentary history in these years was overshadowed by an appalling natural disaster. One of the worst earthquakes in history destroyed Reggio Calabria and Messina, and left some 150,000 dead.

Giolitti's fourth ministry, from 1911 to 1914, was his greatest. In the age of imperialism he carried through a successful imperialist exercise, but more to be praised was his radical programme of parliamentary and social reform.

The war with Turkey for the acquisition of Tripoli was deliberately intended to satisfy the nationalist group of voters. Diplomatic preparation for the war was careful and had a touch of Cavour's genius about it. Italy was still a member of the Triple Alliance, and Turkey had become something of a protégé of Germany, yet Germany's assent for Giolitti's war was obtained. The contrast between the thorough diplomatic preparation for this war for Libya in 1911 with Crispi's erratic steps in foreign and imperial policy, and with the later follies of Mussolini, is striking.

But the people to whom Giolitti's war was intended to appeal were very different in temperament and aims from the prime minister himself. The Futurist movement was revolutionary in the arts and literature, and ultra-nationalist politically. The central figure of the movement, Enrico Corradini (1865–1931), denounced humanitarianism, pacifism, individualism, and what he saw as the Christian slave mentality. He defined Italy as a 'proletarian nation', which had been denied the benefits of the richer nations, and would have to establish a place in the world through hard labour, struggle and war. In all this he anticipated not only Fascism, but Nazism. He operated through a journal, the *Idea Nazionale*, and his novel, *La Guerra Lontana* ('The Distant War'), struck the same note. But if Corradini was little more than a brash, if original, journalist, there were more creative figures in the Futurist movement. Carlo Carrà was a far from negligible artist, and on the fringe of the movement was the poet and novelist, Gabriele d'Annunzio (1863–1938), whose work was to transcend the somewhat hysterical writings of the others. The Futurist Manifesto, written by Filippo Marinetti (1876–1944), and published in *Le Figaro* in 1909, glorified speed, violence and warfare.

These men were really the natural enemies of Giolitti's parliamentary liberalism, but he was intent on getting votes, and the war with the Ottoman Empire won their support. He was also influenced by the French moves to acquire Morocco, which could be used to justify compensation in North Africa for Italy. Thus the Italian acquisition of Tripoli in October, 1912, which ended the war with the Ottoman Empire, could be hailed as a sign that Italy was no longer a 'proletarian nation'.

Giolitti, however, should be remembered not for his excursion into imperialism, but for his building of Italy into a democratic and socially conscious nation. In June 1911 he introduced a parliamentary reform bill which gave the vote to all literate men who had reached the age of twenty-one, and to illiterate men who had either completed military service or reached the age of thirty. In other words something approaching universal male suffrage was granted. The passing of the bill increased the electorate from about 3,000,000 to about 8,500,000. While it is true that universal male suffrage had been introduced in the Habsburg Monarchy and Bismarck's Germany, this had been for assemblies to which the executive governments were not responsible. Italy, on the other hand, was now, like the French Third Republic, a full democracy, in which the executive government was responsible to parliament. Britain, it must be remembered, was not to have universal male suffrage until 1919.

Giolitti's social legislation was as forward-looking as his parliamentary reform. It included a public health act, workers' insurance against accidents, the limitation of child labour, and old age pensions: a programme not unlike that of the contemporary government in Britain, the government of Asquith and Lloyd George.

In the general election of October, 1913, Giolitti and the Liberals did well, but Giolitti preferred to control government through his parliamentary majority, without being in office himself, and resigned. The productive period of his career was over. Ahead lay his neutralism during the First World War, and his disappointments and mistakes which accompanied the advent of Fascism. But before the war he had turned Italy into a democracy, with the nucleus of a welfare state. His methods had been somewhat unprincipled, but if ends can ever justify means, these ends can surely be said to have done so.

### 3 The First World War: neutrality, intervention, and victory, 1914–1919

At the outbreak of the war in July, 1914, Italy's international position was a complicated one. There was certainly no reason for her to go to war as an ally of France, and her membership of the Triple Alliance with Germany and Italy had become little more than a formal one. Italy had four principal reasons for not going to war as an ally of the Central Powers, and they were ultimately likely to become reasons for her entering the war as an ally of the Western democracies.

In the first place, Italy had been let off the hook so far as the terms of the Triple Alliance were concerned, since Austria had already broken those terms. After the assassination of the Grand Duke Franz Ferdinand the Austrians had presented their ultimatum to Serbia – thereby opening the possibility of war – without informing their Italian ally.

Secondly, there was the question of the South Tyrol, or as the Italians called it, the Alto Adige. South of that region, around the town of Trento, was the Italian-speaking Trentino, and the Italians could claim that its 'redemption', or liberation, was an uncompleted part of the Risorgimento. The northern half of the region, around the towns of Bolzano and Merano, was German-speaking, but was on the Italian side of the Alps, and the Italians could therefore claim that it was necessary for their national security. The Austrians rejected both claims, and consistently refused to cede any further territory.

Thirdly, the British and French fleets in the Mediterranean would constitute a grave danger for Italy if she entered the war on the side of the Central Powers.

Fourthly, there were popular demonstrations in Italy, encouraged by the nationalists, against Austria.

There were also at least three reasons for Italy maintaining a strict and permanent neutrality – for never entering the war on either side.

In the first place the population as a whole seemed to favour neutrality. Giolitti, although not in office, still commanded much support in parliament and the country, and he was a convinced neutralist. Just as he had maintained neutrality in the confrontation of workers and employers, so did he want Italy to maintain neutrality between the warring powers. There was certainly no life-or-death motive for Italy to enter what promised to be a major, and perhaps devastating, war.

Secondly, devout Catholics, in particular, favoured neutrality, Pius X had been elected pope in 1903. In 1904 the French Republican government had declared the separation of Church and state. Pius was bitterly antagonized by the French action. The Italian Church would be strongly opposed to a war as the ally of 'atheist' France against Catholic Austria.

Thirdly, the Left in Italy, for once in agreement with the

clericals, wanted neutrality. The Second International, of which Italian socialists had been members, had recommended workers to offer at least passive resistance – perhaps by a general strike – to any attempt by their governments to make them fight a war against fellow-workers in other countries. However, moderate socialists, like Leonida Bissolati, could envisage a time when an alliance with the Western democracies would be justified.

There was a danger in neutrality: a quick German victory, which seemed likely in the first weeks of the war, could leave Italy in an unenviable position; on the other hand, if Britain and France won the war, Italy would be isolated in the Mediterranean. Neutral countries are never very popular at the end of a great war.

In the first week of September, 1914, a German advance threatened to reach Paris. It was halted by General Joffre's French army on the Marne, and the German armies were rolled back, until the ghastly stalemate of the trenches was reached, and the war of attrition began. Joffre subsequently said that if Italy had been allied to Germany in September 1914 he would have had to deplete his army on the Marne, the Germans would perhaps not have been held, and Paris might have been lost. As it was, the French had moved the government from Paris to Bordeaux. The balance had been a very fine one in 1914, and Italian neutrality had been far from irrelevant. The Austrians' refusal to surrender a miserable tract of territory in the Alto Adige probably cost them their empire.

The Italian prime minister when the war started was Antonio Salandra, who had served in the right-wing government of Pelloux, and is described by Giolitti in his memoirs as a 'Conservative', but who was generally considered to be a Liberal in 1914. Salandra had no intention of entering the war as a member of the Triple Alliance. The Marquis Antonio Di

San Giuliano, a Sicilian nobleman, had been foreign minister since 1910. He was more sympathetic towards Austria than was Salandra, and had hoped in the past to make Italy's membership of the Triple Alliance more genuine and more active. But the Austrians had not made life easy for him, and in 1914 he reluctantly accepted neutrality. His death in October 1914 made it more likely that Italy would be able to come to terms with the Western democracies.

San Giuliano's successor at the foreign ministry was the dour Baron Sidney Sonnino, who had been prime minister briefly on two occasions. He, too, had been an enthusiast for the Triple Alliance in the past, but was now becoming convinced that Italy should enter the war as an ally of France and Britain, after negotiating favourable terms. The fact that he was the son of an English mother had less to do with his policy than his chilling sense of *Realpolitik*.

The decision by Salandra and Sonnino to enter the war was something of a conspiracy between them, concocted in the face of parliamentary, Giolittian, and probably popular, opposition. A treaty was signed in London on 26 April 1915 by which Italy agreed to enter the war within a month as an ally of the Entente powers of France, Britain and Russia. At the end of the war Italy was to obtain the Trentino, the Alto Adige, central Dalmatia, and – much more important – the great port of Trieste.

An unfortunate effect of the debate on neutrality or intervention was that Giolitti and the neutralists, who had in the end failed to keep Italy out of the war, were discredited, and branded by the Futurists and nationalists as pacifists, or virtually as traitors. In the Socialist movement there was an even stranger development. The editor of the Socialist newspaper, *Avanti!*, was the young Benito Mussolini. He had started his career as an orthodox Marxist, opposing the Libyan war – even by carrying out acts of sabotage – and threatening revolutionary acts if Italy entered the capitalist war in 1914. But already in October he was recommending in the pages of *Avanti!* an abandonment of complete neutrality in favour of the Western powers. This abrupt change of attitude obliged him to resign from *Avanti!*, and found his own newspaper, in November, the *Popolo d'Italia*, in which he recommended war. He was expelled from the Socialist Party, and now led a group of interventionists, who were to form a nucleus of the Fascist Party. The *Popolo d'Italia* was certainly financed by French, British and Russian money, but the charge that Mussolini had been bribed by the French to change his policy has never been substantiated.

Italy's war was no less bitter than that fought by the French, Germans, Russians and British. But the Italian and Austrian counterpart of the muddy trenches of the Western front was the grim range of the Carso, where the sharp rocks cut through the soldiers' boots. General Cadorna, the chief of staff, was not without military ability, but tried to impose an impossibly hard discipline. Continually sacking commanders for cowardice or incompetence, he came to be hated by officers and soldiers alike.

The Austrians launched an enormous offensive in 1916, but it was held by the Italian armies, with appalling losses on both sides. The collapse of Czarist Russia increased the pressure on Italy, as German troops from the Russian front came to reinforce the Austrians against the Italians. The offensive in 1917 by the Central Powers at first seemed to threaten disaster. It broke through the Italian lines at Caporetto, and a retreat continued almost to Venice. The Italian forces rallied on the Piave, but not before Cadorna had foolishly and publicly charged his troops with cowardice. He was replaced in command by General Armando Diaz, who rapidly became a more popular leader.

British and French troops were sent to Italy as reinforcements, but they did not arrive until after the Italians had themselves halted the Austro-German advance. On October 30, 1918, Italy finished her war with the devastating victory of Vittorio Veneto, which did something to repair the damage done to national morale by the rout after Caporetto.

Salandra had been succeeded in June 1916 as prime minister by the seventy-eight-year-old Paolo Boselli, who was succeeded in his turn by Vittorio Orlando, who was Italy's chief plenipotentiary at the Conference of Versailles in 1919. Italy's second plenipotentiary was Sonnino, who had remained foreign minister throughout the war. They hoped to obtain from the peace settlement more than Sonnino had been promised by the Treaty of London. In the event they obtained less. They were mainly preoccupied by the question of Fiume, a predominantly Italian town, which had not been promised to Italy by the Treaty of London. Today's Reka, Fiume was an Adriatic port on the borders of Istria and Croatia, with a rural hinterland which was ethnically Slav. To the south, much of the Dalmatian coast, which was also ethnically Slav, had been assigned to Italy by the Treaty of London. But the USA had not been a signatory of the Treaty of London, and the American president and plenipotentiary, Woodrow Wilson, could see no reason for Italy's acquisition of any part of the eastern seaboard of the Adriatic beyond Trieste.

Thus Orlando and Sonnino could not claim Fiume by the terms of any existing treaty, but persisted in citing the Treaty of London to support their claims in Dalmatia, and for concessions in the Ottoman Empire. Bissolati and the moderate socialists recommended them to forget about the Treaty of London, which was simply a piece of the old out-dated diplomacy, and concentrate on demanding Fiume along democratically nationalist principles. Instead Orlando and Sonnino tried to have the best of both worlds, and extracted no sympathy from the other victorious powers.

Even so, Italy's gains in 1919 were impressive:

In the first place she gained the great port of Trieste, which was, with Strasbourg, which was acquired by the French, one of the two largest cities to be gained by any of the victorious powers.

Secondly, she acquired an excellent frontier by her annexation of the South Tyrol, or Alto Adige.

Thirdly, the destruction of the Habsburg monarchy, Italy's traditional enemy, meant that in one sense she did not need such an effective frontier anyhow.

But the Italian government and public were disappointed at the peace terms, and the myth of the 'mutilated peace' was born. Gabriele d'Annunzio exploited the myth to carry through an outrageously daring adventure. He had already made a name for himself as an air-force pilot. He had flown over Vienna in an unarmed plane, carrying with him only his violin (from which he was inseparable), and composing Futurist-type manifestos under the address 'The skies of Vienna'. In September, 1919, with some two thousand deserters from the Italian army, he led a motorized column into Fiume, and declared it an independent republic, until such time as the Italian government felt strong enough to take the town over. It was the kind of defiant and lawless act which was later to characterize Fascism. It lacked only the violence and brutality which Mussolini and his thugs were to add to the mixture.

## 4 Socialist failure and the advent of Fascism, 1890–1922

The Socialist movement has been mentioned in passing in the last two chapters; it must now be considered for its own sake.

A founder of the Socialist Party in 1892 was Filippo Turati (1857–1932), who had also founded the immensely influential Milanese review, the *Critica Sociale*, the year before. A sensitive and non-violent man, Turati hoped to unite the Socialist movement, and to reconcile Marxism with his own deep respect for parliamentary democracy. As a model he took the Social Democratic party in Germany, which had working-class support, but operated within the parliamentary context, and was already a considerable force in the country before the retirement of Bismarck in 1890. Another reformist socialist, and an exact contemporary of Turati, was Leonida Bissolati (1857–1920), who was editor of the Socialist journal *Avanti!* from 1896 to 1904, and elected to parliament in 1897. These two men partly succeeded in bringing together the intellectual, journalistic and working-class strands of Italian Socialism.

There had briefly been a workers' party, the *Partito Operaio Italiano*, founded in 1885, and dissolved by the government of Depretis in 1886, but it had been exclusively for 'manual workers of both sexes, either in the fields or in the workshops, who are wage-earners and directly dependent on their bosses, entrepreneurs or capitalists'.[3]

A pure Marxist, having nothing to do with workers' movements or trade unions, was a professor at Rome, Antonio Labriola (1843–1904). A Neapolitan, Labriola was at first a Hegelian, but discovered Marx in 1890, and corresponded with Engels. He translated the *Communist Manifesto* into Italian for the first time, and was to be an influence on Croce and Gramsci. He could well claim to have been the founder of Marxism in Italy.

Depretis had greeted the early dawn of working-class politics in Italy with alarm. In the 1890s Crispi was to confront it with savage repression, ruthlessly putting down workers' and peasants' risings. From 1900 a rift began to appear in the Socialist movement, between the 'maximalists' and the 'minimalists'. Once maximum and minimum programmes had been

---

[3] Martin Clark, *Modern Italy 1871–1982* (London, 1982), p. 77.

defined there were bound to be clashes as to which should be pursued. But there was sufficient unity for fifty-two Socialist deputies to be elected to parliament by 1914, and a million people to have voted Socialist.

The Socialist cause was blurred by the existence of the anarchist movement, which has already been noticed in connection with the assassination of Umberto I. After the war there was a revival of anarchism, when the leader, Enrico Malatesta, returned from exile in London in 1919. He had tried, of course without success, to start a peasant rising north of Naples as early as 1877. For ten months in 1897 he had been back in Italy, addressing meetings in Ancona, and condemning the reformist tendencies of Italian Socialism. He was an uncompromising insurrectionist, but rejected Bolshevism in favour of the total freedom of anarchism.

Another wild man of the Left was Amedeo Bordiga, who was calling himself a 'communist' by 1919, although still in the Socialist Party. An engineer from Naples, Bordiga founded a journal in 1918, which he called *Il Soviet*. He warned Socialists not to compromise the proletarian struggle by participating in elections or parliaments, but to prepare to seize power by force.

More original and complex in his thought and aims than either Malatesta or Bordiga was Antonio Gramsci (1891–1937), who published the Communist journal, *Ordine Nuovo*, in Turin. A hunchback from Sardinia, Gramsci was an unlikely political leader, and secured his leading role of the communist wing of the Socialist Party by sheer intellectual mastery. He explained that the ruling class held its position not only by economic, military or police powers, but by imposing its own cultural and intellectual values on the whole of society – an imposition which he termed 'hegemony'. The only way in which the masses could escape from the hegmony of the ruling class was for the workers and peasants to take over the running of their own economy and society – peacefully whenever possible. This meant in practice that the workers should occupy the factories, and the peasants take over the land. Gramsci found that there were already in existence, in the Fiat motor car factories in Turin, Workers' Councils, which could be turned into Soviets on the Russian model. He was to use these councils for one of the more remarkable – if unsuccessful – Socialist experiments of the twentieth century.

After the war Italy was still a predominantly agricultural country, but modern industry was growing in the North. By 1914 only 55 per cent of the population was still engaged in agriculture, but that 55 per cent were mainly poor peasants: many of them were killed in the war, or suffered grave hardships during and after the war. Official hints that they would be given their own land after the war were not honoured, with the result that the peasants in several regions occupied uncultivated land.

Significant though developments on the land were, what happened in the cities was of greater immediate importance. Industrial wealth was centred in the triangle Turin/ Genoa/Milan, and in this region trade unions were growing dramatically. The largest trade union was a Socialist one, but a Catholic one, appealing to the peasants, was almost as large, and there was a considerable anarcho-syndicalist one. With widespread strikes, occupations of the land by the peasants, and – most important – occupation of the factories by the workers, there seemed therefore, in 1920, to be a strong possibility that a Socialist revolution would succeed.

The government of Francesco Nitti, an economist who had been minister of finance during the war, was in office from June, 1919, until June, 1920. Nitti tried to assert control through tough police action, but the social upheaval continued. When Nitti's government fell, Giolitti formed his last ministry, which also lasted exactly a year – from June, 1920 to June, 1921.

Giolotti was seventy-eight in 1920. He attempted the tactic

which had worked so well before the war: that of preserving the neutrality of the government in industrial disputes, and even when the workers occupied the factories. In September, 1920, the factories were occupied by the workers throughout most of Italy, by the process which had started with the Fiat works in Turin. If not elsewhere, in Turin something like a new proletariat society was emerging, with the population sympathizing with the workers, and the shopkeepers supplying them with goods free, or at a discount. The workers claimed that they were producing more cars than they had done under management and employers, but the cars were not marketed: they simply piled up on the assembly lines.

Giolitti refused to use force, and for the moment the old magic seemed to be working. He believed – rightly – that merely by occupying factories the workers could not bring about a revolution. He would have been more worried if government buildings had been occupied, or, at least, public buildings like post offices or railway stations. Lenin had seized power by storming the Winter Palace. Even the Easter Rising in Dublin in 1916 had taken the form of an occupation of the central post office, and the British imperial government had felt obliged to shell the place.

Eventually the factories returned under the old management with a promise from Giolitti that some form of workers' councils would remain in existence to represent trade unions – a promise which was not to be fulfilled after Giolitti had fallen from power.

The Socialist revolution of 1920 had failed. In a sense it had never developed into a genuine revolution at all. The Socialists had never attempted to seize central political power. But there were other reasons for the failure. Giolitti's tactics were one of them, and a Fascist backlash – taking the form of armed fighting in the streets against strikers and Socialists – was another.

Benito Mussolini was born in 1883, at Predappio, near Forlì, in the Romagna. His mother was a primary school teacher, and his father a blacksmith. He may have subsequently exaggerated the poverty of his childhood, but his background was humble enough. His father, however, had become a leading figure in the local Socialist Party, and Benito himself was a prominent Socialist until his expulsion from the party over the policy which he adopted on intervention in the war. The influence of his early Marxism never entirely left him, though as a motive for hating the middle class, rather than as a feeling of sympathy for the workers.

But the extreme nationalists had a more important influence on Mussolini than the Marxists had. He was attracted by the image created by Corradini and Marinetti of war and violence as cleansing forces in a sick world. The social forces which rallied to his Fascist movement were like those which were later to rally to Nazism in Germany – especially, in the towns, the small tradesmen and shopkeepers, who lacked identification with the trade union movement. But fascists also came from a variety of different social groups. On the whole they were not, as Mussolini was, deserters from other political movements. Rather they were people who in the past had felt no interest in politics, and now felt only a vague, ill-informed contempt for politicians. A Fascist, Agostino Lanzillo, wrote: 'Fascism has mobilized its forces from the twilight zones of political life, and from this derives its unruly violence and the juvenile exuberance of its conduct.'[4]

The Fascist Party was founded in 1919, but was not a serious force until 1920. Its doctrine was always incoherent, and no attempt was made to define it until an article was included in the 1932 edition of the *Enciclopedia Italiana*, written by Mussolini himself and by the idealist philosopher, Giovanni

---

[4] Quoted by Adrian Lyttleton, *The Seizure of Power. Fascism in Italy 1919–1929* (London, 1973), p. 67.

Gentile (1875–1944), who had accepted Fascism and was made a senator and minister of education by Mussolini. The article spoke in very abstract terms of the spiritual nature of Fascism, and had little bearing on political realities. In practice Fascism represented a force *against* Socialism and parliamentary Liberalism, rather than *for* any idea of its own. The only faintly positive element in the Fascist philosphy was the concept of the Corporate State, which will be considered in the next chapter.

The Fascist reality in the streets was provided by the *arditi*, gangs of strike-breaking thugs, whose existence led to much arson, street-fighting and loss of life. It was against this background that the Fascist March on Rome was to take place in 1922.

Chapter 8

# THE FASCIST DISASTER, 1922–45

## 1 The establishment of the dictatorship, 1922–9

The general elections of May, 1921, were held among scenes of great violence. About a hundred people were killed. In spite of controlling whole areas, and smashing up socialist meetings, the Fascists won only thirty-five seats. The outward trappings of Fascism, like the black shirt and the Roman salute, were already being adopted, and were giving the movement some spurious glamour.

There were short-lived governments, under Ivanoe Bonomi (from July 1921 to February 1922) and Luigi Facta (from February to October, 1922). These Liberal leaders could not agree to form a coalition together, nor with Giolitti. Nor did they have any success in forming a coalition with the Socialists, or with the democratic Catholic party, now known as the *Popolari*. It is easy in retrospect to say that a coalition of all democratic parties should have been formed to keep the Fascists out, and that it would have been comparatively easy to have done so, but no one in 1922 knew, of course, that a Fascist regime would survive for twenty-three years, and bring immense suffering and disaster to Italy.

In 1921 Italian Socialism began its long tradition of splitting into contending groups. Lenin had recommended that the Italian Socialist Party (the *Partito Socialista Italiano*) should change its name to the 'Communist Party'. At the party congress in January 1921 about a third of the members, including Bordiga and Gramsci, voted to accept Lenin's advice, and the Italian Communist Party (the *Partito Communista Italiano*) was born, with Gramsci's *Ordine Nuovo* as its daily newspaper. The Socialist Party also suffered secessions to the right, when Turati formed a reformist, minimalist, party.

Mussolini on the other hand was becoming more of a realist. He had to persuade big business that he was their most effective weapon against Socialiam. To do this he had to shed some of the radical and exotic character of his past. In particular he had to give up his republicanism, not only to reassure the rich, but – more obviously – to reassure the king. Equally important, he had to secure the sympathy of the army. His ambiguous relations with the Freemasons helped him to get in touch with high-ranking army officers. Leaders of the Freemasons had contributed to Fascist funds, seeing Fascism as an ally against their Socialist enemies. Yet Mussolini was soon to break with the Freemasons, as early as February 1923 forbidding members of the Fascist Party to become Masons. It was typical of him to use any available contact for the moment, but to reject it brutally when it had served its purpose.

But in 1922 the old political leaders could not be ignored. Mussolini kept in touch with Nitti, Giolitti and other Liberal leaders. His seizure of power was made possible through a combination of these contacts and his threat of a violent *coup*. The March on Rome was thus not the only – or even the main – element in Mussolini's coming to power. But equally it was not irrelevant to it.

Mussolini made no secret of being in command of a large, illegally armed body. He reviewed some 40,000 Fascist militia in Naples on 24 October 1922. The March on Rome started from several points, while Mussolini remained in Milan, waiting for a call to office from the king. He continued to negotiate with a great variety of people – d'Annunzio, Giolitti, Nitti, Orlando, Salandra and Facta – and it is possible that he would have taken office with any of them, given the right conditions.

A considerable royal army surrounded Rome, and could probably have halted the march of the inadequately equipped and badly fed Fascist militia, if ordered to do so. But the March was effective as a piece of psychological warfare, a colossal bluff. Until the evening of 27 October Victor Emannuel was determined to resist the Fascists, but that evening he changed his mind and refused to order martial law. The reasons for his change of mind included: the control exerted by the Fascists over many points of the provinces; the fear of civil war; the evident unreliability of the prime minister, Facta; and finally doubts about the loyalty of the army. Marshal Diaz, the war hero, was mainly responsible for convincing the king that the army could not be trusted, but ultimate responsibility lay, of course, with the king himself. There were flaws in his character: he was a deeply pessimistic man, a solitary, who had little confidence in humanity in general. In his weakness he asked Mussolini to form a government.

In a sense, then, Mussolini came to power constitutionally, though only in a somewhat deceptive sense. The cabinet which he formed was a coalition, with six or seven posts being given to non-Fascists, but he kept for himself the posts of minister of the interior and foreign minister, as well as the premiership. The semblance of legality partly explains the apathy which greeted Mussolini's advent to power in many circles. Another explanation of the apathy was the lack of knowledge of the aims of Fascism, not least by its own followers. Giuseppe Bottai, a close companion of Mussolini in these early days, and later minister of education, said in his diary: 'everyone has his own Fascism', by which he meant that everyone interpreted Fascism in a way in which it would be most acceptable to him or her. Others believed that Mussolini was only a temporary expedient.

In the event, he was to create the first Fascist regime in

history. One of its basic characteristics was the merging of the party and the state, so that the leader, or *duce*, of the party became the leader, or *duce*, of the state. In the same way a 'Fascist Grand Council' was created, with authority not only in the party, but for the state: in other words, it was a second cabinet. Another consitutional innovation was an electoral law which laid down that the party which secured most seats in a general election should be rewarded with two-thirds of the seats in parliament. The law, combined with a great deal of violence and intimidation of the public by the Fascists, persuaded people to vote for Mussolini in the general election of April 1924. The Fascists won 64 per cent of the votes, which gave them 374 seats. The new law had not even been needed.

The next month a crisis broke which threatened to destroy the regime. Giacomo Matteotti, a reformist Socialist, who had just been elected to parliament, made a courageous speech condemning Fascism. A week or two later he was kidnapped and murdered. Whether Mussolini was personally responsible for the murder has never been proved or disproved, but in an astonishing statement to parliament he declared: 'I, and I alone, assume the political, moral and historical responsibility for all that has happened.' The statement was evidently intended to placate the more extreme and violent members of the party, who knew that Mussolini had been shaken by the sense of moral outrage which swept the country after the murder. For some months Mussolini adopted a low profile, and waited for the immediate impact of the murder to be forgotten, until it was possible for him again to assert his authority both over the country and the wild men in the party.

The non-Fascist minority in parliament reacted to the crisis by withdrawing for an indefinite period from the chamber. This protest move was known as the 'Aventine secession', since it emulated a move by the *plebs* of ancient Rome to the Aventine Hill. It was a weak and ineffective protest, and seems to have strengthened the resolve of the king to leave Mussolini in office.

In 1925 a much more thorough dictatorship was imposed. For the first time in history the term 'totalitarian' was used, Mussolini employing it with pride, and claiming that the Fascist regime was completing the work of the Risorgimento by removing all divisive forces in the state. No longer were there to be divisions of class or political parties. In practice some limitations on totalitarianism remained. The monarchy and the Church were both to retain their independence from the regime. But non-Fascist political parties were dissolved. The Catholic party, the *Partito Popolare Italiano*, had at first given its conditional support to Fascism, but members of the Party who had taken office with Mussolini in 1922 were thrown out in May 1923. Don Luigi Sturzo, leading the left wing of the party, resisted Fascism bravely, but Pius XI helped Mussolini by denouncing Sturzo and his followers.

Mussolini did not suppress the press outright, but simply removed non-Fascist editors from their posts. Luigi Albertini, the distinguished editor of the influential *Corriere della Sera*, was replaced by a Fascist, and – rather surprisingly – offered the embassy in Washington, which he refused. Elected local governments were replaced by officials appointed from Rome. In 1926 a political police force, OVRA (*Opera Vigilanza Repressione Antifascismo*), separate from the Fascist Militia, was formed. Italy was now a one-party state, and in most respects a totalitarian one. Fascism tried to provide its own working-class cultural and leisure institutions. The *Dopolavoro* (entertainments in workers' clubs), or *Case dei Fascisti*, were well attended in some parts of Italy, though not everywhere.

The leaders of the opposition to Fascism either went into exile, like Luigi Sturzo, Gaetano Salvemini, Pietro Nenni, and Palmiro Togliatti, or were imprisoned, like Antonio Gramsci, who was sentenced to twenty years, and released only in 1937 when he was dying.

The most sophisticated concept for the removal of social and political division in Italy was the Corporate State. Corporations consisting of representatives of employers, workers, and professional groups were to be elected to give advice to the political government. The theory was that in a modern, industrialized country one's sense of identity was less with a geographical location than with one's occupational group. The corporations were eventually to elect representatives to a central congress, which would replace the old political parliament as an advisory body to the government. Parliament was indeed deprived of any real significance in 1928, but Mussolini soon lost interest in the idea of the Corporate State, especially when, in the thirties, he decided to build an African empire.

One measure taken by Mussolini was destined to survive, and is still in existence: the Lateran Pact of 1929, with Pope Pius XI. By it, Mussolini recognized the temporal power of the Papacy, which, since 1870, united Italy had refused to do. The Vatican was thus recognized as an independent state, and the Catholic religion as the 'sole religion of state' in Italy. For his part, the pope recognized the kingdom of Italy – which no pope had ever done – and Rome as the capital of Italy. But Mussolini's alignment with the Papacy destroyed the argument that he was the heir to the Risorgimento.

## 2 Isolation and triumph in foreign policy, 1925–36

The Italian Fascist regime was a new phenomenon in world history, but it was not at first recognized as such by the other European governments. Mussolini tried to disarm criticism of his kind of totalitarianism by declaring that 'Fascism was not for export', although he was soon to boast that it was a new ideology which would change the world. His first treaties of alliance were with small states rather than with great powers. In 1927 he signed a treaty with Hungary, a state which, like Italy, wanted to revise the terms of the Versailles Treaties, but for Hungary to be a revisionist state made more sense, since she had been on the losing side in the war, and her rulers were, if anything, more bitter than the Austrians at the break-up of the Dual Austro-Hungarian monarchy.

In 1928 Mussolini signed a treaty with the independent African empire of Ethiopia – an ironical early step in view of what was to come. Also in 1928 he signed a treaty with Greece, an early crisis over Corfu in 1923 having been partly forgotten. Finally, in 1930 he signed a treaty with Austria. But the great powers had been sympathetic to him, and had not reacted unfavourably to his coming to office. Fascism seemed far less alien and less dangerous to accepted values than Bolshevism.

Yet Mussolini himself recognized Soviet Russia in 1924. He had hoped to be the first power to do so, and had been furious at being beaten at the post by Ramsay MacDonald's first Labour government in London. Lenin had expressed admiration for Mussolini personally, and in 1924 Mussolini was still talking occasionally of Fascism as a mediating force between Communism and capitalism, just as the Corporate State, with its industrial tribunals, was supposed to be a mediating force between employers and workers.

But this kind of talk was for home consumption only. Abroad in the 1920s Mussolini tried to behave in a normal, respectable, bourgeois manner, observing the diplomatic niceties, and in 1929 appointing Dino Grandi as his foreign minister. Grandi was a cautious, conservative man, who, as foreign minister and later as ambassador in London, tried to tone down Mussolini's extravagances. In the 1920s, then, Fascist Italy had no enemy among the great powers, but equally she had no close ally.

The first major foreign crisis faced by the regime was over Austria in 1934. The little republic which had emerged in Vienna from the 1919 settlement was ruled by a clerical right-wing government under its Chancellor Dollfuss, and had become a client state of Italy. Mussolini provided cash and moral support for the ruling party. To the right of Dollfuss was a Nazi party, which had close links with the newly appointed chancellor of Germany, Adolf Hitler. On July 25, 1934, a Nazi gang occupied the broadcasting house in Vienna, had an announcement made to the effect that Dollfuss had resigned, and then proceeded to kill him. That the crime was an act of aggression against Italy as well as against Austria was underlined by the fact that the wife of Dollfuss was at the time of the tragedy visiting Mussolini in Rome.

Although the Nazis failed to take over after the death of Dollfuss, the danger had not immediately passed. Hitler gave signs of planning to invade Austria, as he would certainly have done had the coup succeeded. Mussolini's response was to send considerable troops to the frontier, making it clear that Italy would resist a German invasion of Austria. Hitler took no further action for the time being. It is ironical that Mussolini, who was eventually to come so completely under Hitler's control, was the only European ruler who ever made Hitler stop in his tracks.

Mussolini himself was already becoming more interested in Africa than in Central Europe. The nucleus for an Italian African empire already existed in the two colonies of Eritrea and Somalia, but they were separated by the independent African empire of Ethiopia, the prize which Crispi had failed to obtain, and on which Mussolini now had designs. He hoped and assumed that the British and French governments – the 'super powers' in Europe before the rise of Hitler – would not oppose him. In 1906 they had recognized an Italian sphere of influence in Ethiopia. The concept of 'spheres of influence' was no longer, after the First World War, a respectable one, but the frontiers of Ethiopia were by no means clearly marked, and if Mussolini was looking for an incident which would give him a justification for war with Ethiopia, he would not have long to wait.

The opportunity presented itself in December, 1934, when

an Ethiopian force attacked an Italian unit at a place called Ual Ual (a phonetic spelling, sometimes – probably less accurately – rendered as 'Wal Wal'). According to the Italian army's own maps Ual Ual was about eighty miles inside Ethiopia, but at the time British troops were also nearby, and inside Ethiopian boundaries, without being too concerned about, it and certainly not expecting to be attacked. Mussolini took some months to build up an effective force, but began a massive invasion of Ethiopia in October of 1935, with numbers reaching some 400,000 by the anniversary of Ual Ual.

Mussolini's motives for going to war with Ethiopia were mixed. There was the simple thirst for glory, prestige, and revenge for Crispi's defeat at Adua in 1896. But there was a slightly less juvenile preoccupation. Mussolini was obsessed with demography. He believed that France, and even Germany, were decadent powers, because they had declining populations. Indeed the Germans, he said, were happy if you gave them enough motor cars and sausages. Italy had a growing population, but she had suffered from what the Futurists had called a 'haemorrhage' of people through emigration. The movement of mass emigration had started soon after unification. According to the 1871 census at least 400,000 Italians were living abroad. Emigration to America was only 20,000 a year in the 1870s, but had reached 205,000 a year by 1888. In 1891 there were nearly one and a half million Italians living on the other side of the Atlantic. This first wave of emigration had been largely from Northern Italy. The next wave came from the South, and was yet more impressive numerically. The number of emigrants per year from 1898 to 1914 sometimes reached 750,000.[1] Mussolini's belief that mass emigration was an economic loss for Italy, and justified the colonizing of new lands, was thus understandable. But while Italians were happy to settle in developed communities in

[1] Clark, *Modern Italy*, pp. 32–3 and 165–7.

America, it was less likely that they would want to settle in Africa.

Four days after the Italian invasion of Ethiopia began, the Council of the League of Nations denounced Italy as an aggressor, and a few weeks later voted for the application of sanctions – that is, an embargo on the sale of arms to Italy, and a boycott of Italian exports. The Fascist regime made great efforts to survive sanctions, efforts which were surprisingly successful. Italy was helped, however, by the fact that the USA, having never ratified the Treaty of Versailles, was not a member of the League. Oil, which was now an essential war material, continued to flow into Italy in spite of President Roosevelt's appeal to the great oil companies to stop supplying the aggressor nation.

Italy's use of modern, mechanized armies, bomber planes, and the ruthless employment of poison gas, eventually brought victory in Ethiopia. On 9 May 1936 Mussolini could proclaim the Italian annexation of Ethiopia, and Victor Emmanuel III its 'Emperor'. For the Duce this was not just the extension of a colonial empire, but the rebirth of the Roman Empire. The extravagance of his oratory was equalled only by his audacity in adopting a new calendar. The year 1936 of the Christian era was the year 14 of the Fascist era.

Italy's isolation during the Ethiopian war had been more apparent than real. The British, and still more the French, government had been reluctant to give up a possible ally against the growing might of Nazi Germany. The Western democracies chose to ignore the tyranny Fascism had imposed upon Italy, and the Duce's praise and adoption of brute force. Fascist Italy had forged a wholly independent policy, regardless of the opinion of the League of Nations, or in the world at large. And independence, arrogance and amorality seemed for the moment to be paying dividends.

## 3 The alliance with Germany: neutrality and entry into the Second World War, 1936–40

Mussolini had successfully resisted Hitler in 1934. The South Tyrol, or Alto Adige, as it had officially become since its annexation to Italy in 1919, had remained a point of possible friction with Austria, and Hitler initially encouraged Austria to demand that these German-speaking lands be returned. But Mussolini certainly had no intention of returning them, and Hitler was eventually to give up claims to the Alto Adige when bigger issues were involved.

One of the bigger issues was the Spanish Civil War. Following the outbreak of the war in the summer of 1936, the Italian and German governments, who were both hostile to the legitimate, democratic government in Madrid, drew closer together. In a speech in Milan on 1 November Mussolini first used the phrase 'Italo-German axis', a phrase subsequently adopted by Hitler. Galeazzo Ciano, who had married Mussolini's daughter, Edda, and been made foreign minister, had visited Berlin in October, signed a general agreement with the German foreign minister, Von Neurath, recognizing the two countries' hostility towards Bolshevism and support for the rebel generals in Spain, and had then visited Hitler at Berchtesgaden. The two dictators provided aircraft to enable the rebel general, Francisco Franco, to move his rising from Morocco to Spain itself. Thereafter Italian intervention in the Spanish Civil War was on a bigger scale than German intervention, and on a much bigger scale than the intervention of Soviet Russia on the side of the government. Entire Italian military units were moved directly from Ethiopia to Spain.

In August 1936 the Italians occupied the Spanish island of Majorca, to use as an air and naval base in the war. Sympathizers of the Spanish republican government in Majorca were massacred. In spite of the blatantly obvious intervention of the Italian government, Mussolini hypocritically joined twenty-seven other governments – including Germany – in accepting the general principle of non-intervention proposed by the British government. A conference met in London to consider how non-intervention could be imposed, but Dino Grandi, the Italian ambassador, and the German ambassador, managed, by raising endless procedural points, to prevent any firm steps being taken.

Another Italy took part in the Spanish Civil War – the Italy of exiles, Liberals, Socialists and Communists – in support of the republican government. In March 1937 Spanish republican forces were supported by an Italian anti-Fascist battalion in the battle of Guadalajara, in which four of Mussolini's divisions were routed. In a very real sense this struggle between Italians and Italians was a rehearsal for the resistance to Fascism at the end of the Second World War. One of the Italian anti-Fascist leaders, Carlo Rosselli, and his brother, the historian, Nello Rosselli, were murdered in France by Italian Fascists in June 1937. Other men who were to survive and lead the left in Italy after the Second World War – the Socialist Pietro Nenni, and the Communists Palmiro Togliatti and Luigi Longo – also fought in Spain against Franco.

Mussolini's motives for supporting Franco were partly, of course, ideological: the war was an aspect of the struggle against European Socialism. But he evidently also hoped that he could extract some territorial reward, especially since he was already in *de facto* occupation of Majorca. Such an outcome was prevented by British diplomacy. During the Ethiopian war Mussolini had come to see the British as the potential enemy in the Mediterranean, in spite of the fact that the British government's attitude to the League of Nation's policy of sanctions had been somewhat ambivalent. The young British foreign secretary, Anthony Eden, had become something of a *bête noire* in Italy, and it was ironical that it was now Eden who arranged what was known as the 'Gentleman's Agreement' with Italy. By the 'Gentleman's Agreement' both Britain and

Italy renounced any territorial gain which might have resulted from the Spanish Civil War.

Mussolini was, at least, on the winning side in the Spanish Civil War, but the price he paid for firmly aligning Italy with authoritarian dictatorships against democracy would in the end lose him his independence. He was now a close friend of Hitler, and ready to accept the German annexation of Austria in 1938. As a young nonentity in the early 1920s Hitler had been an ardent admirer of Mussolini, and he was still – in 1938 – deeply grateful for Mussolini's moral support. Mussolini, for his part, did not yet have any inkling of the extent to which he would, before very long, fall under the influence of Hitler. There was even a brief moment when it seemed that Britain and Italy would draw closer together. Anthony Eden's resignation from the foreign office in 1938 enabled the prime minister, Neville Chamberlain, to indicate friendlier relations with Italy, although Eden's resignation had been mainly in protest at Chamberlain's tendency to adopt a foreign policy of his own, without reference to the foreign office, rather than because of any specific difference of opinion. The momentary improvement in Anglo-Italian relations did not, anyhow, come to anything.

That Mussolini was in effect already falling under the influence of Nazism was illustrated in the summer of 1938, when the Duce introduced anti-semitic laws. Racist legislation had already been introduced in the Italian African colonies, but the Jews in Italy had not been persecuted in recent decades. On 3 August regulations were introduced expelling Jews who had come to Italy since 1919, forbidding marriages between Jews and gentiles, and depriving Jewish teachers of their jobs.

In the Czech crisis of 1938 Mussolini at first supported Hitler, but then assumed the role of mediator. He was in effect chairman at the Munich conference, and made it easier for Chamberlain to give his approval of German annexation of the Sudetenland. Mussolini suddenly, and rather unexpectedly, found himself praised as a peace-maker. At every railway station on his trip back to Rome crowds cheered him as the saviour of Europe from war. It was not a role which he played with much enthusiasm or conviction.

When, in March of 1939, Hitler's troops marched into Prague, thereby destroying the Munich agreement, Mussolini was given no prior warning. Ciano commented in his diary: 'What weight can be given in the future to those declarations and promises which concern us more directly? It is useless to deny that all this worries and humiliates the Italian people.'[2] Partly as compensation for Hitler's unilateral move in Central Europe, the Duce decided on the conquest of Albania. The move was not quite so dramatic as Mussolini had intended it to be, since Albania had been recognized as a sphere of Italian influence since before the First World War. Nor did it embitter relations with Hitler. On the contrary, a close, offensive Italo-German treaty, the Pact of Steel, was signed in May.

It could be argued that Italy broke the Pact of Steel when Britain and France declared war on Germany on 3 September, and Italy remained neutral. But Hitler had hoped to conquer Poland without involving Germany in a war with the Western democracies, and he was far from eager for Italian assistance, even when he knew that he had started a European war. Still, the neutrality of Italy in the first months of the war bore an uncanny resemblance to what had happened in 1914–15.

During the phoney war in the winter of 1939–40 Italian neutrality was correct and complete. News bulletins on the Italian radio provided the best and most impartial account of events. The Italian forces were totally unprepared for war in 1939, so soon after Ethiopia and Spain, and in spite of massive expenditure on the armed forces, and especially on the navy. They were no better prepared in the spring of 1940, but France was then defeated, and Britain appeared to be on the point of

---

[2] *Ciano's Diary 1939–1945*, edited by Malcom Muggeridge (London, 1947), p. 45.

defeat. Even so, Italians did not enter the Second World War with enthusiasm. Insofar as public opinion can be assessed, it would seem that the Ethiopian war had been considered a national war, with Italy pitting her strength against the rest of the world for legitimate reasons; war against France and Britain in 1940 was, on the other hand, a party war, having little to do with national interests.

## 4 Defeat and the collapse of Fascism, 1940–5

The military record of Fascist Italy in the Second World War was an abysmal one. Mussolini had a grand plan: having made the Mediterranean into an Italian lake, he would break out into the bigger world of the oceans, by defeating the British, and forcing his way through the Suez Canal or the Straits of Gibraltar. Yet is is never clear whether his grand plan was a piece of propaganda, or whether he sincerely believed it feasible. More immediately he was prepared to accept Ciano's plans for a forward policy in the Balkans, but Ciano had never wanted the war, and recommended an advance into the Balkans rather to discourage a possible German advance than as a means of securing a final Axis victory. Ciano always found it difficult to conceal his distaste for the Germans.

Late in October, 1940, the Italians attacked Greece from Albania, but early in December the Greeks won an appreciable victory, and invaded Albania. Hitler immediately sent sufficient reinforcements to halt the Greek advance, and in the spring of 1941 a massive German army was to occupy Yugoslavia and Greece. Even in the secondary war zone of the Balkans, Fascist Italy seemed incapable of operating without German support. In North Africa Italian defeats were on an even larger scale. In August 1940 the Italians conquered British Somaliland, and in September invaded Egypt, but their successes were short-lived. In the winter of 1940/1 the British invaded all parts of Italian East Africa, and a comparatively small army under Sir Archibald Wavell drove the Italians out of Egypt, and eastwards across the Libyan desert. Mussolini's Roman Empire crumbled with remarkable speed. In this massive fiasco only two elements in the Italian forces earned some praise from the British. Their fighter aircraft, although out-dated in other respects, showed great powers of manoeuvre, and their radio signals units – in the tradition of Marconi – were efficient. But radio communications are no substitute for the morale of an army. In North Africa, as in the Balkans, the Italians had to be rescued by the Germans, and from the spring of 1941 Italy was playing a very minor role in Africa.

Italy's final defeat in the Second World War was decided by the defeat of Germany – by Hitler's miscalculation in invading, the USSR, and by the entry of the USA into the war in December, 1941. The army of some 3 million men with which the Germans invaded Russia on 22 June 1941 might well have been assembled and put into motion earlier, if Hitler had been free of preoccupations in the Balkans – preoccupations to some extent unwittingly forced upon him by Mussolini.

By 1942 the defeat of Italy already appeared likely. Virtually her whole merchant fleet had been destroyed; there was a desperate food shortage; allied air raids on North Italy were growing in intensity; the population was turning firmly against a war for which they had never felt much enthusiasm. Primo Levi, the writer who was later to give such a brilliant account of his life in Auschwitz, described how he and his circle of young anti-Fascist friends viewed the war in the autumn of 1942 in Milan. They endured with 'malicious joy' the rationing and the cold caused by the coal shortage, and they accepted, without questioning, the nightly bombing raids by the British. They had come to believe that the Germans and the Japanese were invincible, but now suspected that the Americans were invincible also, and since the Western Allies were in control of the air, perhaps Fascism was really doomed. They felt totally detached from the war, from the 'stupid and cruel games of the Aryans'. But in December, with the beginning of the Resistance, anti-Fascist leaders began to appear; Levi and his friends began to realize that the stupidity and evil of Fascism had to be fought. Names previously unknown reached their ears: Gramsci, Salvemini, Gobetti, the Rosselli.[3] So there were new heroes, heroes as real as Garibaldi had been, and Gramsci and the Rosselli had been victims of Fascism even before the monstrous folly of Mussolini's war had started.

In March, 1943, there were large-scale strikes in the factories in Turin and Milan. The workers, remarkably united in their strike action, were undeterred by the hundreds of arrests which were made. Meanwhile the Germans were being driven back in North Africa by the British Eighth Army which had advanced from Egypt, and by an Anglo-American force – including the British First Army, one of the unsung armies of the war – which had landed in Morocco and Algeria in November of 1942. The zones of fighting were coming perilously near to Italy, and in April, 1943, Mussolini visited Hitler, to secure more help for the defence of Italy. He believed that Hitler should negotiate a peace with Stalin, so that the full German strength could be devoted to the southern defences of Europe, and the war in Africa. Hitler had lost a huge army at Stalingrad in January, and must have realized that any attempt to negotiate with the Russians would be futile. There was, anyhow, a contradiction in Mussolini's argument. Far from discouraging the war in Russia, as early as June 1941 he had pressed Italian troops on Hitler as a contribution to the Russian campaign. An appalling number of Italian troops were to die on the Russian front, fighting a Fascist war which was in no sense Italy's.

---

[3] Primo Levi, *Il Sistema Periodico* (Turin, 1975), pp. 131–4.

Mussolini's visit to Hitler in April 1943 was a fruitless one. The Duce was by now a very sick man. Precisely what his illness was cannot now be known, but photographs show that his once rotund face had become emaciated, and his eyes had acquired an unhealthy stare. He suffered from acute stomach pains. Ironically this man, who had been so proud of his physical vitality, now looked much older than his sixty years, and the year 21 of the Fascist Era was also to be its last.

On 10 July 1943 British and American forces landed in Sicily. Mussolini agreed, reluctantly, to a meeting of the Fascist Grand Council, which had not met for some time. The meeting took place on 24 July. The Grand Council contained several men who had been close to him from the beginning of his period of power, but who had come to believe that he must go. Galeazzo Ciano had always shown more foresight than Mussolini. After the fall of France in 1940, when few British people could, in their hearts, have felt certainty of an ultimate victory, Ciano, sitting in his office in Rome, believed that Britain would defeat Germany in the end. Another member of the Council, Dino Grandi, had also felt more apprehension at Italy's prospects than Mussolini. Both Ciano and Grandi, operating in the diplomatic world, had been painfully exposed to reality. A third member of the Council, Giuseppe Bottai, who had for a while been minister of education, had also regretted the alliance with Germany. He had always been interested in the few vaguely positive features of the Fascist regime, in particular in the idea of the Corporate State. It was Bottai who was to leave a vivid account of the meeting of 24 July, in his remarkable memoirs, *Vent'anni e un Giorno* ('Twenty Years and a Day').

The meeting went on all night, and took the form of a violent confrontation between the Duce and his critics. A motion from Grandi, bitterly condemning Mussolini's conduct of the war, and – more significantly – his imposition of a dictatorship, secured nineteen votes against seven, with one abstention. The next day, after an audience with the king, Mussolini was arrested, and power was returned to king and parliament. In a sense the wheel which had tragically started to turn when Victor Emmanuel III had asked Mussolini to form a government in 1922 had now completed its full circle.

## Chapter 9

# *ITALY SINCE THE SECOND WORLD WAR, 1945–80*

### *1 The resistance and the establishment of the Republic, 1944–7*

After dismissing Mussolini, and having him arrested, Victor Emmanuel appointed a Fascist general, Marshal Pietro Badoglio, prime minister. Regarded as a hero during the Ethiopian war, Badoglio had previously been governor of Libya, but had never been close to Mussolini. On becoming prime minister he declared that the war would continue. For his long delay in coming to terms with the Allies he was to bear a heavy responsibility. Only on 13 October 1943 – eleven weeks after his appointment – did he declare war on Germany. Italy then became a 'co-belligerent', since the Western powers were not ready to consider her a full ally. By then Hitler had poured his armies into Italy, occupying Rome on September 11. The Italian army had found itself in an ambiguous position, with some generals being reluctant to resist the Germans, and none prepared to do so without clear orders from Badoglio's government, or reliable promises of help from Allied head-quarters. For the muddle and delay Italy was to pay a terrible price in human suffering, and the world war was almost certainly prolonged.

Mussolini had been kept in detention in a hotel in the Abruzzi mountains. On 12 September a German air-force unit carried out a dramatic rescue – or kidnapping – of the dismissed Duce. The wretchedly sick man had earlier said that he wished only to be left in peace, but he was now to be provided with a small Italian state by Hitler. The state was called the 'Italian Social Republic', but more familiarly known as the 'Republic of Salò', since it was at Salò on the shores of Lake Garda, that its ministry of culture was based. Somewhat pathetically and belatedly Mussolini had returned to a few of the instincts of his youth: a hatred of monarchy and the middle class. Large firms were either to be nationalized or run by committees on which workers would have 50 per cent of the places. But Mussolini's latter-day Socialism did not get very far in practice, and although in theory he was now president of two-thirds of Italy, in fact the Germans – or more specifically the SS – were in control.

Mussolini's resurrection as Duce gave him the opportunity to revenge himself on the men who had voted him out of office on 25 July. A peculiarly wicked deceit was practiced on Ciano. He and Edda were invited to Munich for a Mussolini family reunion. Subsequently he and four others who had voted against Mussolini on 25 July were tried, condemned to death, and shot in January 1944. Not surprisingly, Edda never spoke to her father again.

Hitler still professed personal affection for Mussolini. He assured him that they were the 'two best hated men in the world.' It was a relationship of a kind. But politically Hitler treated the Republic of Salò with contempt. The South Tyrol and Trieste were annexed to Germany, and a small death camp was constructed at Trieste – the only one ever to exist on Italian soil. Great numbers of Italian Jews were rounded up and sent to the death camps in Poland. The enormous evil of Nazism had reached Italy.

But Italy was soon to be saved from the twin evils of Nazism and Fascism by two great movements: the Liberation, by an immense invading force from many lands, and the Resistance, a native rising of selfless heroism.

The first Allied landings to be made on the European

mainland were in the far South of Italy. But throughout the winter of 1943/4 the Allies were held on the Gustav Line, which included Monte Cassino. The ancient and beautiful Benedictine abbey was destroyed by Allied bombing, but after that the Germans had fortified the hill by the spring of 1944. The Allied army facing the Germans on the Gustav Line included British, American, Canadian, South African, and French units. A Polish infantry unit eventually stormed Monte Cassino in May, while British armour – notably the 6th Armoured Division – dug its way northwards in the stinking ditch of corpses that was the Liri Valley. The Germans had ill-advisedly named a line to the north of the Gustav Line the 'Adolf Hitler Line'. It fell with surprising ease. The Allies almost succeeded in cutting off the major German army south of Rome, but Field-Marshal Kesselring extracted it with with consummate skill. From May 1944 to May 1945 the Allies dragged what Churchill called the 'hot rake of war' up the Italian peninsula. All bridges and most roads were destroyed by the Germans as they retreated. Most buildings in the countryside and small towns were shelled beyond repair. Italy had not experienced such devastation for centuries.

Less destructive was the native movement of liberation – the Resistance. Even before the arrival of the Allies there had been an insurrection in Naples, and the German garrison had surrendered. That devastation was less in the big cities than in the countryside was owed partly to the work of the Resistance. In Rome on 9 September 1943, two days before the Germans occupied the city, a Committee of National Liberation was formed. It consisted of six anti-Fascist groups, the nuclei of future political parties: the Christian Democrats, Communists, Liberals, Democratic Labour (right-wing Socialists), Action Party (of whom more later) and Socialists. But the reality of power at that time still lay with the monarchy, which was supported by the Allied armies south of Cassino. Churchill, in particular, favoured recognition of Victor Emmanuel and

Badoglio. The reality of power in the North still lay with the Germans. Rome was a no-man's land, and the CNL more an aspiration than a political force.

It was in the North that large Italian partisan forces were formed in the course of 1944. Here the four main groups – the Communists, Socialists, Christian Democrats and Party of Action – worked in considerable harmony. They did not dwell on their different visions for a future world, but were concerned only with defeating the Germans and Fascism. Of the four groups the Communists acquired the best reputation for correctness of behaviour towards the civilian population. When Allied troops arrived in 1945 the peasants in the North assured them that the red-scarfed partisans (the Communists) never looted, and were incorruptible. The Party of Action consisted mainly of non-Socialist, republican intellectuals. The name 'Party of Action' was the one Mazzini had used in the 1840s and 1850s, and this group a century later respected Mazzinian values. They were not to survive long after the war as a political party.

Milan and other cities of the North were liberated by the partisans before the arrival of the Allied armies. It has been calculated that 35,000 partisans died in the Resistance, and 21,000 were seriously wounded.[1] The difference between the two figures is interesting. The Germans usually killed partisans, who were not, of course, protected by the Geneva Convention, and could not be regarded as prisoners of war. It takes considerable courage – perhaps a touch of madness – to fight with a civilian insurrectionary force against the disciplined might of an existing state, especially a state as ruthless as Nazi Germany. In this sense, if in no other, the Resistance could be regarded as a second Risorgimento.

The German army corps in Italy surrendered to the Allies on 1 May 1945, before the end of the war in Germany itself.

---

[1] G. Quazza, 'The Politics of the Italian Resistance', in *The Rebirth of Italy 1943–50*, edited by S.J. Woolf (London 1972), p.28.

The Salò Republic disappeared without trace, and Mussolini himself tried to escape with his mistress, Clara Petacci, a few days before the German surrender. They were caught by Communist partisans on the shore of Lake Como, at Dongo, and shot. Their bodies were taken to Milan, and hung in the Piazza Loreto, so that no one could deny that the Duce was dead. Mussolini's death was thus surrounded by less mystery than Hitler's.

Italy's entry into the war as a co-belligerent on the side of the Western powers was rewarded in two ways. In the first place Italy, unlike Germany, was to remain a single state. In the second place, while she lost her African empire, she did not lose a great deal of territory in Europe. French claims in the West were rejected, and the Alto Adige was returned to Italy. She lost Fiume to Yugoslavia, but Italians showed a more realistic attitude to the possession of this small town than they had in 1919. Triese, however, was a different matter. There was no doubt that the great port was mainly inhabited by Italians, but South Slavs lived in the hinterland. It was consequently decided to leave the city under Allied occupation, and considerable friction was to last over Trieste for several years.

The parties which had fought the Resistance, and formed the CNL, were almost inevitably to share power in first Italian governments after the war, while the Allied occupation of Italy continued. In 1945 there were three coalition governments. The seventy-one year-old Liberal, Ivanoe Bonomi, was prime minister from December 1944 to June 1945, when Ferruccio Parri of the Party of Action, a partisan leader, took over. In December 1945 Italy acquired her first Christian Democrat prime minister in the person of Alcide De Gasperi, who retained power until 1953. Communists were members of these governments until 1947, and in these early days after the war both Communists and Catholics were prepared to share power with each other, and with the other main parties.

248

In May 1946 Victor Emmanuel III reluctantly accepted his share of responsibility for bringing Fascism to power, and abdicated in favour of his son, Umberto II. The next month a constituent assembly was elected. By then it had become clear that Italy needed the support – both economic and diplomatic – of the USA, and a consequence was the success of Christian Democracy in the elections. Before the constituent assembly could draw up a constitution one basis for it was laid down. A popular referendum was held to see if Italians wanted to retain the monarchy. The referendum gave a clear, but not overwhelming, victory to a republic over the monarchy. In the South there was still strong support for the monarchy. The house of Savoy, which had come from the far north-west, was at the end, ironically, more loved by the peoples of Naples than those of Turin or Milan.

So an Italian Republic had at last come into being. Mazzini's dream had been fulfilled, though the new republic, for some years in the hands of a clerical party, was to be unlike anything Mazzini would have recommended Of its constitution, however, he might well have approved. Published in December 1947, it was a complex, but ultra-democratic one. It took effect on 1 January 1948, and was approved in the constituent assembly by a large majority, with the three largest parties – the Christian Democrats, the Communists and the Socialists – voting for it. It was designed to prevent any return to Fascism, or, indeed, to monarchy. The President of the Republic was to be elected indirectly, mainly by parliament, and his main task in practice was to nominate a potential prime minister, who must then form a government, which must secure parliamentary approval within ten days. Parliament was to be – is – elected by proportional representation, which ensures in practice that a single party is very unlikely to have a monopoly of power. Although parliament seems to be the sovereign body, it can be argued that the 'people' are sovereign in that a popular referendum can introduce measures in parliament, and can challenge much parliamentary legislation. The creation of regional governments was also an important limitation of the power of central government, although less of a limitation than some had hoped. The autonomies of the regions were at first put into practice only in the most independently minded areas, like Sicily or the Val d'Aosta, but in the 1970s regional governments were to begin to control much expenditure and administration.

The new era was symbolized in May 1948 by the election of Luigi Einaudi as President of the Republic. Born in 1874, Einaudi was an economist and professor of the science of finance at the University of Turin. Immensely respected as a person of integrity, he was a quiet man with a limp: the exact antithesis of the loud showman who had bedevilled Italian history for so long.

## 2 The economic recovery and the predominance of Christian Democracy, 1947–58

After the devastation of the Italian campaign the Italian economy recovered remarkably quickly. Already in 1946 trade was recovering. In the first four or five years after the war there was rampant inflation, which could well have led to other evils, but inflation was halted by 1950. Alcide De Gasperi must take some of the credit for this. He used the radio effectively to persuade Italians to avoid inflationary behaviour, and for once persuasion seems to have had some effect. But Italy was also fortunate in the discovery of resources of fuel. Throughout the life of the united kingdom of Italy – including the Fascist era – there had been a shortage of raw materials. Now oil was discovered in Sicily and the South, and – as early as 1949 – in the Po Valley. In the 1950s natural gas was also discovered. Exports of industrial products began to grow, and were helped immensely by the high standards of Italian design. Without

Plate 8. A new Italy: the Palazzo della Civiltà del Lavorno, known as the 'Square Colosseum', designed by Giovanni Guerrini and others

doubt the long and rich traditions of Italian art had something to do with this.

Economic help also came from outside. The American offer of Marshall Aid, intended to bolster Western countries against Communism, was readily accepted by the Italian governments, and from 1949 to 1953 cash flowed into Italy from the New World. Some of it was used for the building of modern railway stations, which were almost certainly more beautiful than any which existed in America, but this extravagance was overlooked.

But there was a negative side to the economics of the post-war period. There was acute unemployment, bringing with it the unusual social malaise and divisiveness. The poverty of the South persisted, and led to a massive migration of poor southerners to the North. In the elegant and sophisticated centre of Turin a great number of desperately poor families from Calabria and Puglia settled, and their presence was, almost inevitably, resented. In the South itself poverty was exacerbated by the organized crime of the Mafia. In Sicily in particular the Mafia was the only native authority, which – in a perverse kind of way – could therefore be trusted. As this history has shown, the sovereign governments of Sicily had always been remote and alien. Since the fall of the Kingdom of Naples in 1860 this had become true of the southern mainland as well. The Mafia, with its murders, brutality, and primeval customs, was, at least, familiar.

The political scene in 1947 was dominated by the party of Christian Democracy (the DC). With the disappearance of Fascism and the monarchy, the only remaining traditional authority was the Church. Pope Pius XII had been elected in 1939, and was to live until 1958. He was still there, then, in the Vatican, ruling the little state that Pius XI had acquired by his deal with Mussolini. But the Christian democrats were much more than an appendage of the Church. Having played so prominent a role in the Resistance, they had earned the right to be considered as something more than a purely clerical party. They included people who had worked with the Fascists, but also people with decidedly leftish views. They were almost a microcosm of the Italian political world. The origins of the DC lay with the *Partito Popolare* of the pre-Fascist period, and the left-wing of the *Popolari* had been disowned by the Papacy. The fact remained that with the Christian Democrats in power no friction with the papacy was likely to remain. On the contrary, the Church regarded the DC as a close ally against Communism, although De Gasperi had no intention of allowing the DC to become a confessional party.

To the right of the Christian Democrats was the Liberal Party. It was a matter of some moment whether the rich industrialists would look to the Liberal Party for support, or to the Christian Democrats. In the event the Liberal Party were too far to the right – and so lacked popular support too obviously – to make them a viable choice for receiving patronage from big business. Thus the Christian Democrats secured the support of the industrialists as well as the Church: a formidable combination. The Liberal Party survived, but has always been considered more conservative than the Liberal Party in Britain, and has no relationship at all with the concept of a 'Liberal' in the USA.

It is reasonable to ask the question: 'What had happened to all the Fascists?' in the post-war period. Part of the answer was simply that popular support for Fascism had been fading rapidly since 1940, but there was one political party, the *Uomoqualunque*, or Everyman Party, which attracted many former Fascists. It was populist, strongly anti-Socialist, and appealed to people who resented the influence of the parties who had fought the resistance. But the *Uomoqualunque* were not to retain a following for long.

The man who emerged as undisputed leader of the Christian Democrats, Alcide de Gasperi, had been born a subject of the Emperor Francis Joseph, in 1881 in the Trentino, and had actually sat as deputy in the parliament in Vienna. In 1921 he had been elected as a member of the Popular Party in Rome, and in 1926 had been imprisoned by the Fascists for sixteen months. With excellent credentials, he was an austere man, like Einaudi a sharp antithesis to Mussolini, though in a totally different manner. In his first, coalition, government the foreign minister was the leader of the Socialist Party (the PSI), Pietro Nenni, and the minister of justice was the leader of the Communist Party (the PCI), Palmiro Togliatti. These two were to be leaders of the left-wing parties for some years. They were sharply contrasted in personalities and backgrounds. Nenni, born in 1891, had been editor of *Avanti!* in 1920, and had gone into exile in France in 1926. An exuberant man, he was a dedicated Socialist, but more interested in forming a 'third force' of Socialist governments in Western Europe than in having links with the USSR. Togliatti, born in 1893, was almost as austere a figure as De Gasperi. He had left Italy before the advent of Fascism, but in 1936 had settled in Moscow, as secretary of the Third International.

Another party which was to play a significant role in Italian politics for some years was the Social Democrats. They had split away from the Socialists, primarily because of a basic disagreement on foreign policy, the Social Democrats rejected Nenni's concept of a 'Third Force' and supporting an alliance with the USA and Britain. The leader of the Social Democrats was Giuseppe Saragat, who made a considerable contribution to the drafting of the constitution. He had insisted upon the principal of proportional representation, which was to be partly responsible for the wide range of political opinion which has always been expressed in the Italian parliament, but also for the shortness of the lives of governments.

In 1949 De Gasperi took Italy into NATO, in the face of strong opposition from the Socialists and Communists. He had excluded Communists from the government in 1947. The government formed in May of that year had included Carlo

Sforza of the Republican Party as foreign minister, and Saragat. The Italian public were concerned about the fate of Trieste, and knew that they needed the diplomatic support of the USA to resolve the question in their favour. But the electoral results made it impossible for the Christian Democrats to rule alone. De Gaspari was happiest with the support of the centre-left parties – the Republicans and Social Democrats – either for the the formation of coalition governments, or for voting support in parliament. Alternitavely, he could depend on support from the centre-right Liberal Party.

The most serious problem facing the governments of these years remained that of the South, and the Christian Democrat governments at least made determined attempts to solve it. A fund – the *Cassa del Mezzorgiono* – was created to finance development in the South. It was placed in the hands of Amntore Fanfani, one of the more dynamic figures in the DC. Born in 1908, Fanfani belonged to a younger generation than De Gasperi. He had not opposed Fascism, or gone into exile, and had even written a vaguely racist article in a Catholic journal in his younger days. He was minister of labour and social security from 1947 to 1950, minister of agriculture from 1951 to 1953, and secretary of the party and prime minister on several occasions after 1954. He was in office when the 'Economic Miracle' got under way.

But before the advent of the Economic Miracle, in the early 1950s, the Communists seemed to be gaining ground in elections, and a new extreme right-wing party, the *Movimento Sociale Italiano* (MSI, or 'Missini') was founded. The Missini managed to avoid breaking the anti-Fascist laws, but did not conceal their nostalgia for what they regarded as the glorious past of the 1930s, when Italy had conducted an independent foreign policy, and built up an empire. The Missini never became a mass movement, but secured a few seats in parliament.

The Economic Miracle started in 1956. In it a large role was played by the *Ente Nazionale Idrocarburi*, or ENI. Originally simply a public corporation for the exploitation of hydrocarbons in the Po Valley, ENI became a huge nationalized concern, under its director, Enrico Mattei, a man as dynamic as Fanfani. Besides exploiting oil and natural gas, ENI produced chemicals, textiles and machinery, and published its own very successful newspaper, *Il Giorno*, which supported the left wing of the Christian Democrats. Mattei made enemies, but ENI maintained its central role in the Italian economy, and in 1976 was the seventh largest industrial concern in Europe. Mattei himself died in an air crash in 1962, inevitably giving rise to rumours that his enemies had disposed of him.

Private industry also, of course, contributed to the Economic Miracle. Fiat and Olivetti exportrf their products with great success. There was a large increase in steel production. Hundreds of miles of *autostrade* were built, the *Autostrada del Sole* being the great show-piece, running as it does the whole length of the peninsula.

Not only was Italy a founder member of the European Economic Community, but the document giving birth to the organization was signed in Rome in 1957. There were immediate benefits from the Treaty of Rome. Already by 1958 unemployment figures were falling. Not surprisingly the Christian Democrats did well in the general election in 1958, and Fanfani became prime minister for the second – but not for the last – time.

### 3 Communism in Italy and its relations in Western and Eastern Europe since 1956

While the Christian Democrats were dependent on help from the USA, economically and politically, after 1949 the opposition of Nenni's Socialists and Togliatti's Communists to Italy's membership of NATO meant that they were both likely to look for sympathy from the Soviet Union. But Stalin's policy towards Italy since the fall of Mussolini had been one of *Realpolitik*. He had given diplomatic recognition to Italy while Victor Emmanuel III was still king and Badoglio prime minister. The Western powers had now themselves established diplomatic relations with Italy, although they thought of her as their protégé; they were suspicious of Stalin's intentions. Togliatti had returned to Italy from Moscow in 1944, and had at once taken up a pragmatic policy. He recognized the monarchy and the Lateran Treaty. He was determined not to offend the Church needlessly. Rather he believed that king and pope were irrelevant to the growth of Communism.

The very considerable grass-roots support for the PCI, coupled with the moderation of its policy, might have been expected to lead to Communist electoral triumphs. But Communist fortunes were undermined by American policy: by the Marshall Plan, which seemed to suggest that prosperity depended on friendship with the USA, and by American support for Italy's claims to Trieste, in opposition to the claims of Communist Yugoslavia. Nor did the ambivalent policy of the USSR in the 1950s help matters.

In the first years of peace any sign of excessive wealth or social injustice would be greeted with the jocular threat that 'Baffoni' – the man with the big moustaches – would come, and sort things out. But Stalin died in 1953. Baffoni had not come. The rich were still rich, and the poor were still poor. In the event, Stalin had done little to help the PCI, and it was not surprising that few tears were shed in Italy when, in 1956, Khruschev announced a policy of de-Stalinization at the Twentieth Congress of the Russian Communist Party in Moscow. Denunciation of Stalin's 'cult of the personality' was welcome with all but the oldest of the comrades. Togliatti had certainly never made a cult of his own personality; such cults had been out of fashion in Italy since Mussolini. But in the same year as that of the Twentieth Congress, the rising in

Hungary was followed by a brutal repression, and Nikita Khruschev showed that he was capable of action of a kind of which Stalin would have wholly approved. The repression of Hungary was an acute embarrassment to the PCI, and the Italian Socialist Party reacted by moving closer to the Social Democrat Party, who were part of the governing coalition with the Christian Democrats. The ground had been cleared for the Christian Democrats, in the 1960s, to admit the Socialists into the coalition, by what was called the *apertura alla sinistra*, the 'opening to the left'. The Communists could then charge the Socialists with betrayal of the left, and corruption – with a new form of 'transformismo'. But the PCI itself was moving away from dependence on Moscow. In public statements Togliatti implied that Stalin's faults had been deeper ones than a mere 'cult of the personality'.

The Italian Left was temporarily helped in 1960 by a blunder of the Christian Democrats. Fernando Tambroni became the head of a Christian Democrat government which ruled without the support of other parties in the cabinet, but which needed votes in addition to the Christian Democrats in parliament. The Italian Social Movement – the Missini – had secured one and a half million votes in 1953, and in 1960 still had twenty-four deputies. It was with these neo-fascist votes that Tambroni tried to govern. When the Missini attempted to hold a party congress in Genoa, complete with Fascist salutes and talk of the value of violence, the left-wing city experienced a mass rising, in which about a hundred people were injured. The Missini threw bombs, and risings followed the one in Genoa in several other Italian cities. Tambroni was forced by his own party to resign, but not before the Left had captured something of the spirit of the Resistance.

The 1960s was an era of left-wing hopes, and of hopes of détente, in Italy as in the rest of the world. In 1958 the son of a peasant had been elected pope, and had taken the title of John XXIII. He was at once one of the wisest men ever to occupy the papal throne, and one of the wisest statesmen of the twentieth century. His wisdom is expressed in a single, but long and majestic, encyclical, published just two months before his death in 1963, the encyclical *Pacem in Terris*. Unlike the usual papal encyclical, this remarkable document is concerned not only with the Catholic world, but with humanity as a whole. It is an appeal for peace, and good sense in the world at large. Without explicitly referring to the Communist world, it clearly implies that communism, even though based on a false philosophy, may be the right form of social organization for certain peoples at certain times. Above all there is no point in waging war against an ideology like Communism, because it is subject to change, and war against it would solve nothing. In 1961 he had already published an encyclical, *Mater et Magistra*, which had appealed for social justice and workers' rights, but *Pacem in Terris* was of universal significance, and praised the United Nations and its Declaration of Human Rights.

In the Italian context John XXIII clearly approved of the 'opening to the left', and although he was equally clearly not trying to increase the Communist vote, his encyclicals had that effect, as did the audience which he gave to Khruschev's son-in-law, the editor of *Izvestia*.

Togliatti died in 1964. the Communists were by then the only major party which had not shared in government since 1947. Yet throughout the life of the Republic they had had the largest 'card-carrying' membership – larger than the DC. Political parties in Italy since the Second World War have been far more a part of society, and far more permanently integrated with society, than political parties in Britain or the USA, or indeed other Western countries generally. The PCI, in particular, had had its own sub-culture, with regular, well-attended, fêtes, the *Feste dell'Unità*, organised by the Communist journal, *L'Unità*.

The 'opening to the left' finally blossomed in December 1963 in the government of Aldo Moro, who accepted as his deputy prime minister the seventy-two-ear-old Nenni. The increase in Communist votes in April 1963 had driven the left wing of the DC, led by Moro and Fanfani, to seek the alliance with the PSI. By 1968 Moro had been prime minister of the centre-left coalition on three occasions. In that year the formation of student revolutionary societies was greeted with rather more sympathy by Moro than by the PCI, although Luigi Longo, who had succeeded as Communist leader on Togliatti's death, admitted that if there was no understanding between the students and the PCI it must be partly the latter's fault.

The Russian repression of the Czech regime of Alexander Dubček, and his attempt to introduce "Communism with a human face' in 1968, was, in the eyes of Western Communists, a far more objectionable act than the repression of the Hungarian rising in 1956 had been. Dubček could not be considered a counter-revolutionary; he was not even a nation-alist in the sense that some of the Hungarians had been; and he had had no intention of leaving the Warsaw pact. The Italian Communists had no hesitation in condemning the Russian action.

In another important matter the PCI aligned themselves with Western Europe: they accepted membership of the European Community. They wanted radical reforms of the Community, but were prepared to fight for them from inside the organization. In the late 1980s they gave strong support to the Community's Social Charter, which laid down guarantees of workers' and trade union rights. From the 1970s they had even given up opposition to Italy's membership of NATO. With the coming of Gorbachev these pro-Western policies were more acceptable even to hard-line members of the party.

A logical complement to the PCI's eagerness to be regarded as a West European institution was the idea of 'Eurocommun-ism'. Enrico Berlinguer succeeded Luigi Longo as leader of the Party in 1972. In a year or two the concept of Eurocommunism was being floated. In 1975 the PCI joined the French and Spanish Communist parties in joint declaration of their independence from the Russian party, and their respect for multi-party societies, freedom of the press, of religious belief, and the other liberal-democratic principles. Yet Eurocommunism never led to a very active co-operation between the various Communist parties of Western Europe.

Berlinguer was a 'new man' in every sense. He had been a parliamentary deputy only since 1968. He had come to the fore in the Communist Party purely because his intelligence and imagination had been quickly recognized. In 1976 he remarked to a journalist that he felt safer with Italy in NATO, since it assured his independence from Moscow. In domestic politics he came to believe that the PCI could not remain in opposition indefinitely: it must seek a 'Historic Compromise' with the Christian Democrats, and enter a coalition government. But it takes two sides to reach a compromise, and by 1989 no such coalition had emerged. Even so in the 1970s the PCI usually supported the government in parliament. Its moderation also seemed to be paying dividends: in 1976 it had 34 per cent of the national vote, its highest percentage ever. After 1976 it declined slightly, but the PCI remained the largest communist party in Western Europe.

With the apparent failure of Eurocommunism Berlinguer coined a new phrase: the 'Euroleft', which would include Socialist as well as Communist parties. The idea was reminiscent of Nenni's 'Third Force' of the late 1940s, or, looking farther back still, the Popular Front of the 1930s. President Mitterand of France did not reject the concept of a Euroleft, but did nothing much about it.

The moderate stance of the PCI led to the formation of terrorist groups to the left, notably the formation of the Red Brigade. The most important victim of the Red Brigade was Aldo Moro, who was contemplating a movement towards the Historic Compromise. In 1979 he was kidnapped. His colleagues refused to pay ransom money, on the grounds that to do so would encourage the epidemic of kidnappings which had broken out. His wife pleaded with them in vain. Subsequently his dead body was found in a car boot in Rome.

But even more horrific terrorist outrages came from fanatics of the right than from the Red Brigade. In the first four months of 1980, twenty people were asassinated by Fascists, and in August of the year eighty-four people were killed on the railway station at Bologna by a bomb explosion.

# Epilogue: From the First to the Second Republic: Italy 1980–2001

Within a few years of the late Harry Hearder completing this book, both the Christian Democrat and Communist parties ceased to exist. This epilogue continues his history of Italy up to the end of the twentieth century, covering the meltdown of the post-war political system, and the new political forces that emerged from this.

The 'economic miracle' led to the advent of a secular, consumer society whose stress on individualism challenged the collective sub-cultures underlying both Communism and Christian Democracy. The 1970s saw the enactment of a series of civil reforms, notably the legalisation of divorce and abortion, championed by the tiny Radical party. These were passed through the combined support of 'lay' parties in the governing coalition (such as the Socialists), and the Communist opposition outside it. The Christian Democrats sponsored national referenda against divorce in 1974 and abortion in 1981, but on both occasions the populace voted in favour of reform – the first explicit rejection of the Christian Democrats at the polls. In the 1980s, as its popularity declined, the DC became increasingly reliant on its strongholds in the south.

The Communist vote also fell throughout the decade, reflecting both internal and global developments. In 1981, Berlinguer declared that the Soviet-backed military coup in

Poland was proof that the Soviet revolution had run its course, but this only intensified the need for the PCI to elaborate a new strategy – a task neither Berlinguer, who died in 1984, nor his successors were to prove up to. Following the fall of the Berlin wall in 1989, the party declared its intention of changing both its name and its character. Two years later a new Party of the Democratic Left (PDS) was launched, although a tenth of the PCI membership left to set up a Communist Refoundation party.

Pluralism increased within the political structures of the country. In 1970, twenty-four years after they had been promised in the constitution, regional governments were finally instituted across the country. A 'red belt' of Communist administrations sprang up in the central regions of Emilia-Romagna, Tuscany and Umbria, but the overall effect of the reform was to increase the importance of smaller parties with the creation of a series of power-sharing administrations.

In 1981, Giovanni Spadolini, the rotund leader of the diminutive Republican party, became the first non-Christian Democrat Prime Minister since the establishment of the Republic, leading a coalition government of five parties – Christian Democrats, Socialists, Social Democrats, Liberals and Republicans. Although he only remained in office for seventeen months, the *pentapartito* (five-party) alliance lasted more or less intact until 1992. While the Christian Democrats remained by far the largest party within the *pentapartito*, it was the Socialists who were in the ascendant – progressively increasing their share of the national vote. After the 1983 elections, their forceful leader, Bettino Craxi, was installed as Prime Minister.

Craxi's period of office coincided with an economic boom that set the tone of much of his administration. In 1985, he won a referendum that broke the so-called *scala mobile*, a national wage-indexing mechanism. This victory over the unions formed the foundation of a policy that saw inflation rates fall from 15 per cent p.a. in 1983 to 4.6 per cent p.a. in 1987. The Socialists became identified with business as the Italian economy expanded at a rate of over 2.5 per cent p.a.

Much of this growth occurred in the small and medium-sized family firms that are the most dynamic element in the contemporary Italian economy. These have been particularly successful in former areas of small peasant farming such as the Lombard hills, the central regions of Tuscany and Emilia, and, above all, in the northeast where the Veneto has been transformed from a peripheral zone into the fastest developing region in Italy. Frequently small enterprises are organised into 'industrial districts' in which several firms concentrate on the same product – for example taps, valves or shoes. This enables them to share information, support common overhead costs, and even exchange both work and workers in a manner reminiscent of that in which peasant farmers would swap labour and resources amongst themselves.

Small firms are less hampered by laws governing the labour market that make it expensive to hire new staff, and extremely difficult to lay them off. Consequently large enterprises often sub-contract work to smaller ones, which cope with the extra load either by making use of their own family, or by hiring temporary workers from the so-called 'black economy', notably immigrants, whose existence (and earnings) remain undeclared to the state. Craxi celebrated when, in 1987, it was claimed that, by taking an estimate of the activity in this sector into account, Italy had overtaken Britain as the world's fifth largest economy. Talk of this triumph receded after Mrs Thatcher tartly suggested that the two countries' contributions to the EC budget be adjusted accordingly.

Craxi's strong personality was reflected in his style of rule. He stood up to the Americans in 1985, after the US Air Force forced a plane carrying Palestinian terrorists to land at its base in Sicily, insisting the prisoners be handed over to the Italian authorities. His talk of the need for a powerful French-style

President (a role he clearly wanted for himself) led newspaper cartoonists to portray him in a black shirt striking Mussolini-like poses.

One incident captures the atmosphere of the period. The satirical comic Beppe Grillo used his spot on a state television show to poke fun at Ayatollah Khomeni, infuriating the Iranian authorities. Italian diplomats responded that Grillo was exercising the freedom of speech associated with democracy. Soon afterwards, Grillo performed a routine mocking the enormous size of the retinue that accompanied Craxi on his visit to China. He was dropped immediately from the show and did not work on state television again for the best part of a decade.

The Christian Democrats forced Craxi to agree to a pact stipulating that he would pass the premiership to one of their number for the second half of the government's period in office. When the time came for the handover, he refused to go, leading to the collapse of the government in 1987. Following new elections, the *pentapartito* was re-formed with the Christian Democrats supplying the premier. Craxi now formed a pact with two key DC politicians, Giulio Andreotti and Arnaldo Forlani, that became known as the CAF after the first letters of their surnames. After Forlani became party secretary in 1989, he and Craxi installed a government led by Andreotti that held office until 1992.

The CAF came to epitomise the stultifying nature of Italian politics – a battle over place and position, rather than political principle. There was nothing new in this; the administration simply perpetuated practices that had developed over the history of the Republic. What was different was the degree to which the Italian public became alienated from this system – eventually providing the moral support necessary to bring it down.

Political parties in the Italian Republic had assumed the role of employment agencies, acting as channels of social mobility for their members and voters. They exercised a discretionary control over appointments and careers in the public sector, using these to reward supporters who, once in office, returned the favour by granting requests made by the party regarding the assignation of contracts, or the appointment of other clients.

The result of this use of the public sector was a considerable expansion in its dimensions and costs, without a concomitant increase in its efficiency. A major attraction of public-sector jobs was that they were covered by special employment norms making the holders of such positions virtually unsackable providing they turned up for work. This was hardly an onerous imposition, as many posts only required their holders to work in the mornings. Often such positions entitled the holder to retire after a few years' service and pick up a so-called 'baby pension' from the state. These phenomena help explain the notoriously poor performance of Italian state bureaucracy and public institutions such as the post office.

Of course many people in the public sector performed their jobs properly, having succeeded in passing the highly competitive recruitment contests that also lent themselves to behind-the-scenes manipulation by party agents. The Sicilian investigating magistrates Giovanni Falcone and Paolo Borsellino, for example, achieved world renown in 1986 for using the testimony of the 'supergrass', Tomasso Buscetta, to obtain the convictions of a large number of Mafia leaders at a so-called maxi-trial in Palermo. Yet even in the justice system, policemen and magistrates who took too close an interest in certain issues might find themselves isolated through a lack of support from above. Corruption inquiries would be dropped and convictions 'adjusted' on appeal.

Politics was primarily concerned with the distribution of the resources of the state to party clients, rather than projects for the government of the country. The contest between the political parties became one over the division of positions within state institutions and developed its own particular vocabulary: *lottizzazione* referred to struggles between parties to obtain particular positions, while *consociazione* referred to the informal agreements formed between parties to co-operate and regulate the dividing up of resources. One obvious instance of both practices was RAI – the state television and radio company – where the three main channels of the service reflected roughly the DC, PSI and PCI viewpoints.

By demanding that entrepreneurs paid backhanders (*tangenti*) to those who awarded them public contracts or permits, political parties were able to finance their ever-escalating operations. These illicit commissions were often divided up on the basis of *consociazionismo*. Contracts were awarded not to the lowest tender, but to the highest payer, who then recouped the bribe through excessive charges, or by failing to complete the work.

Key political contests took place behind closed doors. It was clearly an advantage for parties to be members of the ruling coalition as this provided greater access to resources – one reason why the *pentapartito* stayed together. Small parties exercised disproportionate influence within the system, as their votes were often critical for keeping a coalition in power and were therefore well rewarded. By 1987, there were fourteen parties represented in Parliament.

The public face of politics was one of stagnation. The Radicals resorted to sponsoring a series of provocative candidates for election, notably the pornographic actress La Cicciolina, who was elected in 1987. Politics simply became a vehicle for publicity – in the 1992 elections, regular politicians shared the television studio with representatives of the Housewives' League against Football, Omar the Magus, and the 'adult' entertainers of the Party of Love.

Meanwhile both the public and hidden costs of Italian politics were escalating. Public debt rose, partly as a result of increased spending on health and welfare, but also because of the continuing expansion of the public sector to accommodate political clients (many of whom were, of course, 'pensioners'). The adoption of monetary convergence criteria for admission to the European single currency highlighted how unhealthy the Italian fiscal situation had become. In 1992 the budget deficit amounted to 9.9 per cent GDP compared to the target of 3 per cent while overall public debt stood at 103 per cent of GDP when the target was 60 per cent.

Attempts to deal with the problem concentrated on increasing tax receipts but this disrupted an implicit bargain in the Italian economy whereby a degree of 'tax forgiveness' was extended to business and the self-employed in the expectation that the savings from this would be invested in Treasury bonds. In 1984 and 1992 shopkeepers, who were declaring lower incomes than their employees, went on strike against anti-evasion measures such as compulsory use of cash registers.

The rates at which *tangenti* were calculated also rose under the CAF, reflecting the intensity of competition between the parties and an increase in the overall number of their clients. When the economy entered a recession, the spiralling costs of taxes and *tangenti* provoked dissent amongst hard-hit entrepreneurs, especially in those northern regions that had been most successful during the earlier Craxi boom. Protest movements developed in the form of various local political leagues that claimed they wanted to secede from the Italian state. In 1989, these came together in an alliance known as Lega Nord (the Northern League) led by the Lombard senator, Umberto Bossi.

Bossi presented himself as the antithesis of an Italian politician, dressing scruffily and talking in a down-to-earth, direct language, in direct contrast to the elegant equivocation of most politicians. His message was simple: northern taxes were paying to prop up the south and finance a bloated state. Crude to the point of racism, the League's rhetoric none the less captured popular sentiment – never more so than in its prophetic 1992 electoral slogan 'Thieves of Rome, it's over'.

And for the CAF it was. At the general election of April 1992, the League polled 8.7 per cent of the votes, a massive increase on the 0.5 per cent gained by its component elements in 1987. All the main parties lost votes. Those for the DC fell to 29.7 per cent, the PSI to 13.6 per cent and the PDS to 16.6 per cent. The *pentapartito* could no longer command a majority in the parliament. There was no coalition capable of representing the Italian people. Eventually President Scalfaro appointed a 'government of transition' including six ministers drawn from outside politics (so-called technicians) led by Giuliano Amato, the former Socialist Treasury minister who was known as a financial expert rather than a political leader.

The *tangentopoli* or 'bribesville' scandal now assumed a whirlwind momentum, laying bare the hidden structures upon which Italian politics had been based. The scandal started in February at an old people's home in Milan, run by a Socialist appointed nominee who was arrested red-handed with a suitcase of money passed to him as a *tangente* by the cleaning contractor. The investigating magistrate, Antonio Di Pietro, used a law allowing preventive detention to arrest those he suspected of participating in the bribery chain and place them in the city's antiquated San Vittore prison. The strategy was highly effective at persuading pampered politicians to break the silence that had surrounded the system. By May most of those involved in governing Milan, the Socialists' showpiece city, were under investigation, as the hidden story behind the party's success became clear. At the end of the year, Craxi himself became the subject of a judicial inquiry focussing on bribes paid to build the Milan metro system. He eventually fled to Tunisia, was convicted in absentia, and died as a fugitive from justice in 2000.

It did not take long for the scandal to spread into the other parties of the *pentapartito*, as magistrates throughout Italy applied Di Pietro's methods. Seven ministers in Amato's government were forced to step down owing to judicial inquiries being opened against them as part of the so-called 'Clean Hands' investigations. At the end of 1993 over 1,000 individuals were the subject of investigations, 500 of whom had been placed in preventative custody.[1] Nearly all the major faction leaders in the DC and PSI were involved. The Enimont case, involving what Di Pietro called the 'mother of all *tangenti'* – paid to allow the Montedison chemical company to merge with ENI – became a show-trial for the regime. Di Pietro conducted humiliating cross-examinations of the politicians involved, notably Forlani whose career ended with a sentence to perform community service. 'Thanks Di Pietro' was scrawled on walls throughout Italy, as the public prosecutor became the most popular man in the country.

*Tangentopoli* escalated so rapidly because in the political insecurity following the election results, parties were no longer able to provide protection, and hence exercise control, through their agents within the state. While this phenomenon was primarily seen in the plethora of politicians who found themselves under investigation for the illicit financing of political parties through corruption, it also extended to the criminal world. Although the Mafia killed Falcone and Borsellino in an attempt to warn the state to back off, Toto Riina, the notorious head of the Mafia, who had been living under the noses of the police in Palermo for years, was arrested in January 1993. In March, Andreotti, who had been Prime Minister in seven administrations, was charged with membership of the Mafia. Thirty-four previous investigations into Andreotti had been dropped, but this time a trial was held, with much of the case centring on an alleged kiss given by Andreotti to Riina.[2] Whatever the truth of the allegations, the decision to prosecute demonstrated the extent to which the climate had changed.

Public contempt for politicians, and the system they had created, pushed the purge onwards. Italians sat glued to their television sets as each evening brought news of further arrests while the regime's failings were dissected by a new style of highly critical political discussion programmes with titles such as 'Milan, Italy' and 'Deepest North'. Satirical programmes exposed politicians to far worse mockery than that which cost Beppe Grillo his career. The Italian version of the British 'Spitting Image' satirical puppet show portrayed Andreotti as Pinocchio, his nose growing each time he spoke. When Amato proposed a decree law that effectively offered an amnesty to politicians involved in the illegal financing of their parties, a flood of outraged faxes from the public to Scalfaro's office led the President to refuse to sign it, forcing Amato to step down.

Amato was succeeded by an entire 'government of technicians' led by Carlo Ciampi, the governor of the Bank of Italy. It drew up a new electoral law, whereby 75 per cent of seats in parliament would be elected on a first-past-the-post system, while the remaining 25 per cent were to be distributed on the basis of proportional representation. This would force parties to contest the election in large blocs from which a clear winner would emerge. The hope was that this would lead to stable government, enabling Italy to begin the transition to a 'Second Republic'.

As the parties in the *pentapartito* were thoroughly discredited (all five were wound up in 1994), there was a huge political vacuum on the right. Gianfranco Fini, the svelte leader of the neo-Fascist MSI, took this opportunity to move his party back into respectable mainstream politics. Although insisting that Mussolini was 'the greatest statesman of the century', he broke with the legacy of the Salò Republic through gestures such as the laying of a wreath at the Ardeatine caves, scene of one of the worst Nazi massacres in Italy. He set up the National Alliance (AN) as a 'post-Fascist party' which found its constituency amongst those who were most directly threatened by the attacks on the Italian state – the pension holders and public-sector employees of the south. AN, then, was the antithesis of the League. It was only through the mediation of a third moderate force on the Right that the two could contribute to a coherent challenge to the Left.

In November 1993, the business tycoon Silvio Berlusconi

announced his intention of forming a new political movement, *Forza Italia*, to fill precisely this space. He presented himself as the saviour of the country, although many thought his primary motive was the preservation of Fininvest, his media holding company containing three private national TV networks, which the Left wished to break up. These channels were modelled on American television, combining high production values with an acute sense of the audience's preference for undemanding entertainment. Berlusconi also owned the football club AC Milan, which he had turned into the leading soccer power in Italy.

Berlusconi's political style drew heavily on this background. The name Forza Italia was taken from the shouts of 'Come on Italy' at football matches – and the movement was organised as a set of so-called supporters' clubs. Executives were brought in from Fininvest to promote the party as if it were a new brand. They used focus groups to identify a programme of popular policies even though these appeared to contradict each other – such as pledges to create a million new jobs while simultaneously cutting taxes.

Forza Italia allied itself with both AN and the League to form a Pole of Liberty to contest the elections against a Progressive Alliance of parties of the centre-left. An immaculately groomed and beaming Berlusconi fought the election on television in the American style. The Left had expected to benefit from their lack of involvement in *Tangentopoli* but Berlusconi branded the PDS as Communist relics from the 'First Republic', claiming that only the new parties in the Pole offered a fresh start. This was reiterated by the pre-pubescent dancing girls, stars of Fininvest's more questionable programmes, who interrupted their gyrations to warn viewers that the PDS were representatives of Satan. In March 1994, the Pole won 43 per cent of the votes and 58 per cent of the seats in parliament. Four months after entering politics, Berlusconi became Prime Minister.

Once in government, the incompatible outlooks of AN and the League, the conflicts of interest involving Berlusconi's business and political positions, and the lack of a fundamental guiding philosophy behind Forza Italia, led to a policy stalemate in the Pole. Berlusconi began campaigning against the magistrates conducting the *tangentopoli* inquiry, claiming that by continuing their investigations they were preventing the country from getting back to work, because so many public contracts had been frozen. The magistrates responded by serving a writ on Berlusconi as he chaired an international conference on crime in Naples. This concerned *tangenti* paid by Fininvest that the company claimed had been handed over by Berlusconi's brother, without his knowledge.[3] The League, having already refused Berlusconi's proposal for an amnesty, now withdrew their support from the government altogether. In December 1994 Berlusconi resigned, to be replaced by another technical government whose majority was provided by a combination of the opposition votes with those of the League.

The parties on the centre-left put together a more convincing platform for the next election. A so-called Olive Tree alliance was formed around a designated candidate for the job of Prime Minister – Romano Prodi, a technocrat from a social Catholic background. As the League refused to ally with the other parties of the right, the Olive Tree emerged victorious at the polls and the first Left government in the history of the Italian Republic took up office in April 1996. Italy had finally experienced *alternanza* – the replacement of one colour of government by another as a consequence of a democratic election.

The Olive Tree Alliance committed itself to 'normalising' Italy – turning it into an efficient state with a stable administration that had a strong focus on policy. Its principal success was ensuring that Italy qualified to take part in the European Union's introduction of a single currency. Here it was able to build on the work of the various technical governments which, unhindered by party ties, had begun restructuring the pensions system and reforming the conditions of state employment: even post offices now opened in the afternoons!

However the alliance was unable to maintain its promise of stable government. The Prodi administration fell in 1998 when the Communist Refoundation party refused to support its budget proposals. Massimo D'Alema, the leader of the PDS, formed a new administration. This was seen as the final crossing of the Rubicon from the First Republic – Italy now had a Prime Minister who, for most of his political life, had been a member of the Communist party. Yet D'Alema was also forced to resign in April 2000, having lost the confidence of his allies in the small centre parties who were suspicious of his attempts to reduce further the role of proportional representation in the electoral system, a proposal later defeated in a national referendum. He was replaced by Amato who remained in office until the general election of May 2001.

By then Berlusconi had reconstituted the centre-right bloc into a so-called 'House of Liberty', in a manner reminiscent of a business deal where one dominant party takes a stake in another. The League, for example, was reincorporated into the alliance, after Forza Italia became the guarantor for its bank loans. The contrast between a disciplined centre-right and a disunited centre-left – whose candidate for Prime Minister had not been a member of any of its administrations – gave Berlusconi a strong lead going into the election. He sought to build on this through a combination of slick electioneering (sending a 130-page colour magazine, detailing his life story, to every household in Italy) and a programme promising action on the voters' key concerns: crime, immigration and public administration. His support fell substantially, however, as doubts about his business dealings resurfaced, leading *The Economist* to publish an article entitled 'Why Silvio Berlusconi is unfit to govern Italy'.[4] Ironically it was probably the 4% share of the vote taken from the centre-left by a party founded by the 'Clean Hands' magistrate, Di Pietro, that eventually handed a narrow victory to the House of Liberty.

Italy has become a more 'normal' democracy in the positive sense that voters can now use elections to change their governments, passing judgement on politicians rather than simply restating sub-cultural or clientelist loyalties. Many problems remain unresolved, but the public's involvement in the transition from the First to the Second Republic still makes it possible to share Harry Hearder's optimism about Italy's role in the 21st century:

With her inheritance of the sublime culture of Dante and Michelangelo, it is unlikely that she will fail to contribute greatly to a Europe that may well be on the threshold of a brilliant new era.[5]

## NOTES

[1] Paul Ginsborg, *L'Italia del tempo presente* (Turin, 1998), p.525.

[2] In 2000, Andreotti was found not guilty of these charges, although an appeal was immediately launched by the public prosecutor.

[3] Although Berlusconi was found not guilty on these charges in 2000, the decision was based on a technicality, with the court describing this defence as not credible.

[4] *The Economist*, 28 April 2001

[5] Harry Hearder, *Italy. A Short History* (1st ed. Cambridge, 1990) p.267.

# A brief guide to further reading

All books were published in London unless otherwise stated.

### General

Christopher Duggan, *A Concise History of Italy* (1994)
George Holmes, ed., *The Oxford Illustrated History of Italy* (1997)

### 1. Italy in the classical world

Massimo Pallottino, *The History of Earliest Italy* (1989)
Graeme Barker and Tom Rasmussen, *The Etruscans* (1998)
Michael Crawford, *The Roman Republic* (1992)
Peter Garnsey and Richard Saller, *The Roman Empire* (1987)

### 2. The early Middle Ages

Christopher Wickham, *Early Medieval Italy 400–1000* (1980)
Jeffrey Richards, *The Popes and the Papacy in the Early Middle Ages 476–752* (1979)

### 3. The high Middle Ages

John Hyde, *Society and Politics in Medieval Italy, 1000–1350* (1975)
Phillip Jones, *The Italian City State: From Comune to Signoria* (1997)
Daniel Whaley, *The Italian City Republics* (1988)
John Larner, *Italy in the Age of Dante and Petrach* (1983)

# A brief guide to further reading

## 4. The Renaissance

Denis Hay and John Law, *Italy in the Age of the Renaissance 1380–1530* (1989)

George Holmes, *Florence, Rome and the Origins of the Renaissance* (1986)

Sir John Hale, *The Civilisation of Europe in the Renaissance* (1994)

## 5. The political and cultural eclipse of Italy

Eric Cochrane, *Italy 1530–1630*, edited by Julius Kirchner (1988)

Peter Burke, *The Historical Anthropology of Early Modern Italy* (1987)

Dino Carpanetto and Giuseppe Ricuperati, *Italy in the Age of Reason 1685–1789* (1987)

## 6. The Risorgimento, 1790–1861

Stuart Woolf, *A History of Italy 1700–1860* (1979)

Harry Hearder, *Italy in the Age of the Risorgimento, 1790–1870* (1983)

Denis Mack Smith, *Mazzini* (1994)

## 7. From Unification to Fascism

Martin Clark, *Modern Italy 1871–1995* (1996)

Denis Mack Smith, *Modern Italy* (1997)

Robert Lumley and Jonathan Morris, eds., *The New History of the Italian South* (1997)

## 8. The Fascist Disaster 1922–1945

Philip Morgan, *Italian Fascism 1919–1945* (1995)

Denis Mack Smith, *Mussolini* (1981)

David Forgacs, ed., *Rethinking Italian Fascism* (1986)

## 9. Italy since the Second World War

Paul Ginsborg, *A History of Contemporary Italy* (1990)

Christopher Duggan and Christopher Wagstaffe, eds., *Italy in the Cold War* (1995)

Patrick McCarthy, ed., *Italy since 1945* (2000)

# A brief guide to further reading

*Epilogue: From the First to the Second Republic*

Stephen Gundle and Simon Parker, eds., *The New Italian Republic: From the Fall of the Berlin Wall to Berlusconi* (1996)

Patrick McCarthy, *The Crisis of the Italian State* (1995)

Paul Ginsborg, *Italy and its Discontents* (2001)

# Index

# Index

# Index

# Index

# Index

# Index

# Index

# Index

Julius II, Pope, 120–1, 129
July Monarchy in France, 167
Justinian, Emperor, 43

Khruschev, Nikita, 257, 258
Kesselring, Field-Marshal, 246
Kublai Khan, 65

Labriola, Antonio, 219
La Farina, Giuseppe, 192
La Guérronnière, 188
Laibach, Congress of, 163
Landino, Cristoforo, 116
Lanzillo, Agostino, 233
Lateran Council of 1139, 57
Lateran Pact (1929), 230, 257
League of Nations, 234, 236
*Le Figaro*, 211
Lega Nord *see* Northern League,
Legnano, battle of (1176), 59
Leipzig, battle of, 160
Lenin, 222, 225, 231
Leo III, Byzantine Emperor, 59, 60
Leo I, Pope, 39, 40
Leo III, Pope, 49
Leo VIII, Pope, 54
Leo X, Pope, 55, 92
Leo XIII, Pope, 207
Leonardo da Vinci, 119, 122
Leopardi, Giacomo, 178
Leopold II, Grand Duke of Tuscany:
  in 1848, 176; leaves for Vienna in
  1859, 186
Leto Pomponio, 107
Levi, Primo, 240, 241
Liberal Party, 253, 255
Libya, 244; under the Normans, 67;
  Italian acquisition of (1911), 210
Lido at Venice, 60
Liri, River, 246
Lissa: taken by the Venetians, 62;
  battle of (1866), 202
Liverpool–Manchester Railway, 179
Livorno, 138
Livy, 11–12
Lloyd George, David, 212
Loches, castle of, 122
Lombard League, 58, 79
Lombards, 44, 45–7

Lombardy, 265
London, Treaty of, 215, 217
Longo, Luigi, 236, 260
Lorenzetti, Ambrogio, 100
Loreto, piazza in Milan, 248
*lottizazione*, 267
Louis II, Emperor, 51, 52
Louis VII, King of France, 62
Louis IX, King of France and Saint, 73
Louis XII, King of France, 128
Louis XIV, King of France, 139, 140
Louis XVI, King of France, 154
Louis XVIII, King of France,
  formerly Comte de Provence, a
  refugee in Venice, 155
Loyola, Ignatius, 133, 135
Lucretius, 27
Ludovico, King of Savoy, 148
*L'Unità*, 259

MacDonald, Ramsay, 231
Machiavelli, Niccolò, 126, 128; *The
  Prince*, 126, 127; *The Discourses on
  Livy*, 127; and mercenaries, 131
Mafia, 252, 267, 271
Magenta, battle of, 185
Magyar invasion of Italy, 54
Majorca, 235, 236
Malamocco, 60
Malatesta, the, of Rimini, 85,
  125
Malatesta, Enrico, 220
Malatesta, Sigismondo, 125
Malmesbury, Lord, 185
Malta, 67
Manfred, 72, 73
Manfredi, the, 85
Manin, Daniele, 174, 175, 189
Manuel, Byzantine Emperor, 63
Mantua; member of League of
  Cambrai, 129; siege of, 140;
  acquired by Austria (1713)), 140
Manuzio, Aldo (Aldus Manutius),
  110, 111
Manzoni, Alessandro, *I Promessi
  Sposi*, 138, 177
Marco Polo, 65
Marcus Aurelius, 33, 34
Marengo, battle of, 157

# Index

Maria Carolina, Queen of Naples, 143, 157
Maria Theresa, Empress of Austria, 143, 145
Marinetti, Filippo, 211, 223
Marius, Gaius, 24
Mark, Saint: Venetian claims to possess his remains, 61; church of, in Venice, 62
Mark Antony, 24–6, 34
Marne, battle of the, 214
Marsala, 191
Marseilles, 169
Marshall Aid, 252, 257
Martin IV, Pope, 75
Marx, Karl, 219
Marzabotto, 9
Masaccio, 113, 114
Masaniello (Tommaso Aniello), 137
Massawa, 206
Mattei, Enrico, 256
Matteotti, Giacomo, 228
Maximilian, Emperor, 128
Mazarin, Cardinal, 139
Mazzini, Giuseppe, 51, 165, 167, 169, 170, 175–6, 178, 188, 198, 249, 262; foundation of 'Young Italy', 169; attempts at insurrection in Piedmont in 1833 and 1834, 169–70; exile to London, 170; in Milan in 1848, 174; and the Roman Republic of 1849, 176; and the attempted rising of 1857, 182; death of, 205
Medici, the family and banking house, 102, 113, 16, 126, 128
Medici, Cosimo de', 109, 112, 113, 115, 121
Medici, Giovanni de', 113
Medici, Lorenzo de', 'Il Magnifico', 108, 112, 113, 116–18
Menotti, Ciro, 166
Mentana, battle of, 203
Merano, 213
Mercurius, 18
Messina, 7; arrival of the plague of 1347/8, 97; earthquake of 1908, 210
Metternich, Prince Clement, 163–5; resignation of, 173

Michael VIII Palaeologus, Byzantine Emperor, 64
Michael the Scot, 69
Michelangelo Buonarroti, 114; discovered by Lorenzo de' Medici, 116; architect of the dome of St Peter's, 117; and the Republic of Florence, 118–19; the Pietà in St Peter's, 120; and the Sistine Chapel, 121; and the Farnese Palace, 133
Milan: under Diocletian, 36; besieged by Alaric, 38; destroyed by Frederick Barbarossa (1162), 58; its commune in the twelfth and thirteenth centuries, 76, 78; population 76; the plague of 1348, 98; under the Visconti, 80, 121; passes under Spanish rule, 138; acquired by Austria at the Peace of Utrecht (1713), 140; and the Enlightenment, 146; occupied by Napoleon Bonaparte (1796), 154; revolution of 1848, 173, 174; *I Fatti di Maggio* (1898), 173, 174; industry in, 221; strikes in 1943, 241; liberated by the partisans (1945), 247; and *tangentopoli* scandal (1992), 270
Mithraism, 34
Mitterrand, François, President of France, 261
Modena: the thirteenth century commune, 76; and the 1815 settlement, 161; and the revolution of 1831, 166
Mondovi, 208
Monreale, 67
Monte Cassino, 246
Montedison, 271
Montefeltro, Federigo da, of Urbino, 125
Montelfeltro, Guido da, 125
Montesquieu, 144
Monza, 209
Moriale d'Albano, 96
Moro, Aldo, 259–61; his murder, 262
Morocco, 211, 241
*Movimento Sociale Italiano* (MSI or 'Missini'), 255, 258, 272

288

# Index

Mundy, Admiral, 192
Munich crisis (1938), 237–8
Murat, Joachim, King of Naples, 160; his campaign of 1815 and declaration of a united Italy, 161
Musolino, Benedetto, 149
Mussolini, Benito, 207–10, 218, 224; breaks tradition of friendship with Britain, 150; editor of *Avanti!*, 215–16; background, 223; policy in 1922, 226; becomes prime minister, 227; and the Matteotti crisis (1924), 228; and the Corporate State, 229; recognizes Soviet Russia (1924), 231; and the Dollfuss crisis (1934), 232; his African policy, 232–4; and the Spanish Civil War, 235–7; and the anti-semitic laws, 237; and the Munich crisis (1938), 237, 238; and disaster in the Second World War, 241–3; dismissal of, 244; President of the Republic of Salò, 244–5, death of, 248
Mussolini, Edda, 235, 246
Musurus, Marcus, 110

Naples: in the seventh and eighth centuries, 48; in the ninth and tenth centuries, 54; founding of the University, 70; and its commune, 72, 73; capital of Charles of Anjou's kingdom, 74; and Boccaccio, 95; in the fifteenth century, 101, 124; attracted emigration in the sixteenth century, 131; great rise in population since the sixteenth century, 136; Spanish conquest of, 136; acquired by Austria (1713), 140, 141; plague of 1656, 140; famine of 1764, 142; University of, 142, 143, 199; and the French Revolution, 156, 157; assumes the title of the 'Kingdom of the Two Sicilies' (1816), 161; revolution of 1820, 163; revolution of 1848, 172, 173; war with Austria in 1848, 175; and the arrival of Garibaldi in 1860, 193; plebiscites of 1860, 195,

196; Mussolini in (1922), 226; anti-Fascist insurrection (1943), 246
Napoleon Bonaparte (Napoleon I, Emperor of the French), 199; invades Italy (1796), 154; his Italian origins, 154; his creation of Italian republics, 154, 155; First Consul and the 1800 Italian campaign, 157; President of the Italian Republic, 157; King of the 'Kingdom of Italy', 157, 158; the Code Napoléon adopted in Italy, 160; on Elba and the Hundred Days, 160, 161
Napoleon III, Emperor of the French, formerly Prince Louis-Napoleon, 158; destruction of the Roman Republic (1849), 176; at the Congress of Paris (1856), 181; Orsini's attempt on his life, 183; at Plombières, 183–4; and the war of 1859, 184–5; signs armistice of Villafranca, 186–7; plans for a congress on Italy, 188–9; annexes Savoy and Nice (1860), 190; and the Thousand, 193; and the September Convention (1864), 201; his diplomacy in 1866, 202; defeat in 1870 and abdication, 203
Narses, 43, 59
National Alliance (AN), 273, 274, 275
National Society, 189, 192
NATO, 254, 260, 261
Nazism, 211, 223, 232, 245, 247
Nelson, Horatio, 156, 193
Nenni, Pietro, 229, 236, 254, 256, 260, 261
Nero, Emperor, 30
Neurath, Konstantin von, 235
Nice, 187
Nicephorus, Byzantine Emperor, 60
Nicholas V, Pope (Aeneas Sylvius), 119, 120, 148
Nievo, Ippolito, 177–8
Nigra, Costantino, 182, 183, 193
Nitti, Francesco, 221, 226
*Non expedit*, 203, 204; lifted by Pius X, 209
Normans, 55, 56, 66

# Index

# Index

# Index

# Index

Suetonius, 26, 34
Sulla, Cornelius, 24
Syracuse: in classical times, 7, 18;
  conquered by the Arabs (878), 51

Tacitus, 34
Tagliacozzo, battle of, 73
Talamone, 19
Tambroni, Fernando, 258
Tancred, 67
*tangenti* (bribes), 268, 269, 270
*tangentopoli*, 270–1, 273, 274
Tanucci, Bernardo, 142
Tarquin, 12
Tarquinia, 9
Tarquinius Superbus, 12, 13
Terence, 26
Thatcher, Margaret, 265
Theodora, 43
Theodoric, 41, 42, 51
Theodosius, 37, 38
Thomas, Aquinas, Saint, 92
Tiberius, Emperor, 28, 29
Titian (Tiziano Vecellio), 123
Titus, 31, 34
Togliatti, Palmiro, 229, 236, 254,
  256–60
Tornabuoni, Lucrezia, 115
Trajan, Emperor, 33, 34
Transpadane Republic, 154
Trastevere, 172
Trento, 213
Trieste, 215, 217, 218, 245, 248, 255,
  257
Triple Alliance (1882), 205, 210, 212,
  214, 215
Tripoli, 210, 211
Troppau, Congress of, 163
Tunis, 205, 206
Turati, Filippo, 218, 219, 226
Turin, 201, 202; incorporated in the
  Duchy of Savoy in the fourteenth
  century, 148; population growth in
  the eighteenth century, 149;
  Mazzinian attempt of 1833, 169;
  Carlo Alberto's reforms of
  1847/48, 173; first Italian
  parliament meets (1861), 196;
  capital of Italy, 200; industry in,
221; occupation of the factories
  (1920), 222; strikes in 1943, 241;
  emigration from the South to, 252
Tuscany, Grand Duchy of, 146;
  abolition of death sentence in (1786),
  146; restoration of 1815 in, 161;
  industry in, 265 *see also* Florence
Tyre, captured by the Venetians, 63
Ual Ual, 233
Uccello, Paolo, 96
Umberto I, King of Italy, 209, 220
Umberto II, King of Italy, 249
Umbrians, 15
United Nations, 259
*Uomoqualunque*, 253
Urban II, Pope, 62, 63
Urban IV, Pope, 73
Urban VI, Pope, 88
Urban VIII, Pope, 140
Urbino, 120
Uruguay, 176
Utrecht, Peace of (1713), 140, 150

Valla, Lorenzo, 40, 107, 108, 119;
  protected by Alfonso the
  Magnanimous, 124
Vandals, 38, 40
Vatican Council of 1869–70, 204
Veii, 12, 13
Veneto, 265
Venezuela, 103
Venice, 39, 59–65; allied to the
  Lombard League, 58; building of,
  60–1; population, 76; the Great
  Council, 78; plague of 1348, 97, 98;
  and printing, 108–10; in the
  fourteenth century, 122; wars with
  Genoa, 122; constitution in the
  fifteenth century, 123; alliance with
  Carlo Gonzaga, 140; in the
  eighteenth century, 145;
  destruction of the Republic by
  Napoleon, 155; becomes part of
  Napoleon's Kingdom of Italy, 158;
  becomes part of the Habsburg
  Monarchy (1815), 161; revolution
  of 1848, 174; resistance to the
  Austrians in 1849, 177; ceded to
  Italy (1866), 202

# Index